Another book by the bestselling authors of AS
FOR THE IBM® PC & XT and BLUEBOOK (
THE IBM® PC & XT. . . . And rave reviews ~~~~~ ~~~~p:

"One of the best books on Macintosh programming I have seen . . . every
Macintosh assembly programmer should own [it]."
                    —David Smith, reviewing *Assembly Language Primer*
                    for the Macintosh, in *MacTutor*

"Anyone who is new to assembly language programming on the IBM PC and
feels completely at sea will find a welcome port in Robert Lafore's *Assembly
Language Primer for the IBM PC & XT."*
                    —John Figueras, reviewing *Assembly Language Primer*
                    for the IBM PC & XT, in *Byte*

"[Chris Morgan] has succeeded in producing a volume that no assembly
language programmer can do without."
                    —*Bluebook of Assembly Language Subroutines,* reviewed
                    in *The Reader's Guide to Microcomputer Books*

"An outstanding example of how to write a technical book for the beginner
. . . refreshingly enjoyable . . . accurate, readable, understandable, and
indispensible. Don't stay home without it."
                    —Ken Barber, reviewing *CP/M Primer,* in *Microcomputing*

". . . does an excellent job of demystifying the whole study of computer
programming in BASIC."
                    —Annie Fox, reviewing *BASIC Primer,* in *Creative Computing*

Kevin Rardin is the owner of Electric Stylus, a technical communications and publishing firm in the San Francisco Bay Area. For over nine years Mr. Rardin has worked in the computer industry as a writer and consultant for such companies as Atari, Bank of America, Lucasfilm and Pacific Bell. Since acquiring his first Macintosh computer early in 1984 he has worked with and developed desktop publishing tools and techniques. When not writing or publishing, Kevin enjoys mountain biking, listening to compact discs, and enjoying the redwoods near his home in La Honda, California.

Desktop Publishing On The Mac

A Step-By-Step Guide to the New Technology

Kevin Rardin

A Plume/Waite Book
New American Library
New York and Scarborough, Ontario

Library of Congress Cataloging-in-Publication Data

Rardin, Kevin.
  Desktop publishing on the Mac.

  1. Electronic publishing. 2. Macintosh (Computer)—
Programming. 3. LaserWriter (Printer) 4. Self-
publishing—Data processing. 5. Business—Data proc-
essing. I. Title.
Z286.E43R37 1986   070.5′02855365   86-18090
ISBN 0-452-25902-9

 PLUME TRADEMARK REG. U.S. PAT. OFF. AND FOREIGN COUNTRIES
REGISTERED TRADEMARK — MARCA REGISTRADA
HECHO EN WESTFORD, MASS., U.S.A.

SIGNET, SIGNET CLASSIC, MENTOR, ONYX, PLUME, MERIDIAN and NAL BOOKS are
published *in the United States* by NAL PENGUIN INC., 1633 Broadway, New York, New York
10019, *in Canada* by The New American Library of Canada Limited, 81 Mack Avenue,
Scarborough, Ontario M1L 1M8

First Printing, November, 1986

3 4 5 6 7 8 9 10

PRINTED IN THE UNITED STATES OF AMERICA

Acknowledgements

Naturally, there is much more to getting a book off the ground than any one author can accomplish alone. I would like to thank Mitchell Waite for giving me the chance to achieve this work. I am much indebted to my editor, Robert Lafore, for his endless dedication, his caring advice and for his contribution of Chapter 7 when we were running up against a tight deadline. My appreciation extends to Jim Stockford, Editorial Director of The Waite Group, who shared his publishing know-how, enthusiasm and spent long hours carefully reviewing the manuscript in various stages of development. Jana Janus, the designer of this book, took desktop publishing to the limit in creating the pages you see here—a phenomenal effort and she deserves every bit of my gratitude. Jill Grossman of New American Library is entitled to our collective appreciation for her patience, responsiveness, support and encouragement throughout the project.

I'd like to thank John Relph for his help in the creation of *Audio Image*. Deanna Trimble, Design Director of LaserWrite, deserves much of the credit for the final design of *Audio Image*. John McWade of PageLab was extremely helpful in several discussions about design and typography for desktop publishing. I've received a generous amount of support from the developer community and I express my gratitude to Colin Stanton-Wyman and Coleen Byrum of Aldus Corporation, Liz Bond and Yvonne Perry of Adobe Systems, Brian Smith of Thunderware, Martha Steffen of Apple Computer, and I'd especially like to thank Andy Hertzfeld for getting me the latest versions of Switcher so I could simulate the actions I describe in the book at the same time I was writing them.

To Lyn and Lynn,
who know who they are
and why they deserve this
…thanks and love.

Table of Contents

Desktop
Publishing
On The Mac

Introduction

1

In this chapter you will discover:

- What desktop publishing is all about
- Some examples of desktop publishing
- Who can profit from desktop publishing
- Why we chose the Apple Macintosh

A revolution is taking place in the publishing business that may rival in importance Gutenberg's invention of movable type almost 500 years ago. This revolution is called *desktop publishing.* It refers to the use of a personal computer to perform all the steps necessary to create a finished, typeset-quality publication, ready for the printer.

Traditionally, publishing involved a number of complex operations, each carried out by a specialist. A graphics designer designed the publication, a typesetter set the type, a camera operator created halftone screens of photographs, and a pasteup artist assembled all the different elements. Now, desktop publishing enables us to set type, create images, and combine these elements into a finished original—all electronically. There is no longer any need for expensive typesetting machinery or for the hot wax and razor blades of traditional pasteup. And, because electronic layout is so fast and easy, it's possible to experiment with different designs until we achieve the effect we like, thus reducing or eliminating the need for an outside designer.

With desktop publishing we can create almost any kind of printed material, from newsletters and advertising brochures to complex reports and entire books. Large corporations, small companies, and even individuals can make use of the new technology to speed up the publishing process, reduce its cost, and permit a greater degree of control over the final product.

This book shows you how to get started in desktop publishing. This is very much a "hands-on" book. This means that you will follow the detailed steps necessary to create a typical publication. You are shown how to perform a particular operation as well as the results of that operation, so you can verify that you're on the right track at each point in the process.

If you want to get started in desktop publishing and aren't sure how to go about it, this book will explain how. If you're only curious about the field and want to know what's involved, this book will give you a detailed insight into the process.

This chapter starts by exploring the advantages of desktop publishing and showing you examples of things you can do with desktop publishing techniques. Then you will learn how desktop publishing can be used by a variety of organizations. Finally, the reasons are explained for choosing the particular equipment we used throughout the book: the Apple Macintosh computer, the LaserWriter printer, and the PageMaker layout program.

The next chapter explores some of the fundamentals of desktop publishing. The balance of the book will lead you step-by-step through the publishing process.

Why Typeset Your Publication?

Why should you go to the trouble of typesetting a publication in the first place? There is a big difference between something printed on a typewriter or a letter-quality printer and something typeset and printed on today's modern laser printer. You can tell the difference right away. The first figure shows an excerpt from a proposal that was printed using a letter-quality printer. The second example shows the same excerpt typeset with an Apple Macintosh and LaserWriter.

Typeset words and sentences speak with greater authority. The crisp, well-designed letters command your attention. Typesetting automatically implies that a certain amount of time and care was put into the publication. It is doubtful whether *Time* magazine or *Newsweek* would continue to command respect if one day they started printing their articles using a letter-quality printer.

Much thought and artistic planning has gone into typeset letters and numbers to make them instantly accessible and easy to read. Since typeset alphabetic characters are often reproduced photographically, the type designer can concentrate on the elegance and readability of the type. Type made to be pounded onto a page with key hammers or printwheels must be designed more with the limitations of the typewriter or printer machinery in mind than with how well it reads.

Typewriters and letter-quality printers use a ratchet mechanism to control spacing; the spacing between letters and words is a result of the limitations of the machinery rather than the tastes of an individual writer or designer. The letters and words in a typeset sentence, however, are each proportionally spaced one from another, giving a more polished look to the page and making typeset text more compact. You can put much more information onto a page and make better use of paper. You can exercise a greater degree of control over where and how the words appear on the page to achieve a number of different effects.

Desktop publishing enables you to bring the clarity and authority of typeset text to any printed material whether it is a management report, a prospectus, a balance sheet, or a thank-you note to someone special.

Words and Pictures

Nearly any publication benefits from the combination of typeset text and artwork presented on the same page. But how do you combine them? Traditionally, you would have to prepare the type in galleys—photographic sheets of typeset text—and prepare your art separately. Then you would painstakingly combine the type and the art on a page by cutting them up and fixing them into place with glue or wax. Unless you are a pasteup artist by trade, you probably don't have the skill to do this without paid professional help.

You certainly wouldn't go to all this trouble and expense to write a letter to a close friend. And if you wanted to quickly prepare a report that commands the attention of the board of directors, you'd be hard pressed to complete all this activity successfully in a few days. However, with an Apple Macintosh and LaserWriter you can easily assemble typeset text on a page, combine it with graphics, and print several copies directly.

Once you master desktop publishing skills, you'll be able to create anything from greeting cards to winning proposals. And this book will help you learn those skills quickly and easily. Let's take a quick look at what you can do with desktop publishing using a Macintosh and the LaserWriter.

```
                         USER COMMUNITIES

        Potential user groups were identified as early in the
   research as possible.   From these potentials an iterative
   process began which further narrowed the groups into five
   user communities listed and described below.  The "user" can
   be defined as an individual or group who either has a need
   for or can benefit from the information made available
   through the information system.

   User Community A: Education

        The educational community would, by far, be the largest
   single group served by the information system.   There are
   over 5 million students attending schools in this state.  The
   levels of formal education range from pre-school to
   university.  Within this are elementary and secondary
   schools, high schools, community colleges, state colleges,
   and universities.  The needs of users in education will vary
   greatly and it is within this field that both contributions
   to the system and interaction amongst users may be the
   greatest.

   User Community B: Industry

        All branches of business, trade and manufacturing
   regardless of size comprise the category of industrial users.
   Their needs not only center around maintaining safe working
   conditions for their employees and the safety of industrial
   property and premises; they are also concerned with the
   protection of their customers.  Their needs from a fire
   education information system would vary greatly from
   situation to situation.  A grocery store would have different
   needs than an oil refinery or chemical laboratory.  Some
   industrial users would want information about materials
   relating to a specific fire problem indigenous to their
   trades.  The ready availability of information regarding
   industrial problems would be encouraging.

   User Community C: Civic Organizations

        There are non-profit organizations located throughout
   the state and in nearly all communities which could benefit
   from a fire education information system.  Such groups
   include service clubs, fraternal organizations, state and
   local agencies and departments, charities, and churches.
   Examples of these groups would be the Kiwanis, Rotary, the
   Red Cross, B.P.O.E., departments of health and welfare,
   United Way agencies, hot lines, youth groups, senior citizen
   groups, Sunday schools and church groups.  The members of
   this user community reach a broad cross-section of society
   and their influence is great.
```

Figure 1-1. Typed Proposal Excerpt.

USER COMMUNITIES

Potential user groups were identified as early in the research as possible. From these potentials an iterative process began which further narrowed the groups into five user communities listed and described below. The **user** can be defined as an individual or group who either has a need for or can benefit from the information made available through the information system.

User Community A: Education

The educational community would, by far, be the largest single group served by the information system. There are over 5 million students attending schools in this state. The levels of formal education range from pre-school to university. Within this are elementary and secondary schools, high schools, community colleges, state colleges, and universities. The needs of users in education will vary greatly and it is within this field that both contributions to the system and interaction amongst users may be the greatest.

User Community B: Industry

All branches of business, trade and manufacturing regardless of size comprise the category of industrial users. Their needs not only center around maintaining safe working conditions for their employees and the safety of industrial property and premises; they are also concerned with the protection of their customers. Their needs from a fire education information system would vary greatly from situation to situation. A grocery store would have different needs than an oil refinery or chemical laboratory. Some industrial users would want information about materials relating to a specific fire problem indigenous to their trades. The ready availability of information regarding industrial problems would be encouraging.

User Community C: Civic Organizations

There are non-profit organizations located throughout the state and in nearly all communities which could benefit from a fire education information system. Such groups include service clubs, fraternal organizations, state and local agencies and departments, charities, and churches. Examples of these groups would be the Kiwanis, Rotary, the Red Cross, B.P.O.E., departments of health and welfare, United Way agencies, hot lines, youth groups, senior citizen groups, Sunday schools and church groups. The members of this user community reach a broad cross-section of society and their influence is great.

Figure 1-2. Typeset Proposal Excerpt.

Some Examples of Desktop Publishing

There is practically nothing you would care to put into print that can't be handled using a Macintosh and LaserWriter. From audiovisual (AV) transparencies to data sheets, annual reports to office forms—if it goes into print, you can achieve the results you want with desktop publishing.

Let's take a look at what people have done using desktop publishing. Except where noted, all the materials shown were developed using an Apple Macintosh 512K or Macintosh Plus, and a LaserWriter or Laser-Writer Plus.

An Annual Report

The annual report shown in Figure 1-3 was developed by John McWade for the California Indian Manpower Consortium, Inc. John, a former art director for *Sacramento Magazine*, owns and operates PageLab, a design firm in Sacramento, California. PageLab designs and prepares camera-ready art for a variety of clients, including Apple and Aldus, and uses desktop publishing tools exclusively, primarily a Macintosh Plus and LaserWriter Plus.

The annual report was created with PageMaker using a letter size page format oriented horizontally. The illustration of an eagle on the cover was digitized with ThunderScan and touched up in MacPaint.

Seminar Materials

Skunk Camp is an intensive workshop for executives conducted by Tom Peters' A Center for Management Excellence in Palo Alto, California. It is based on the principles contained in his books, *In Search of Excellence* and *A Passion for Excellence*. The seminar materials for Skunk Camp were developed by Judith Maurier of du Maurier Associates in Menlo Park, California. The sample shown in Figure 1-4 is from a 30-Day Action Agenda intended for post-workshop use by executives and corporate leaders when they return to their homes and offices from Skunk Camp.

Seminar materials of this type are one of the most practical uses of desktop publishing. They can be easily updated when changes occur in the seminar curriculum and are inexpensive to produce. The typesetting and clean lines give them a very professional look and feel.

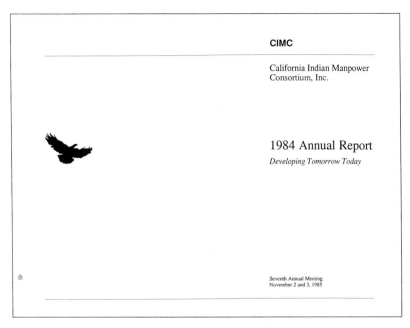

Figure 1-3. Cover and Page from the CIMC Annual Report.

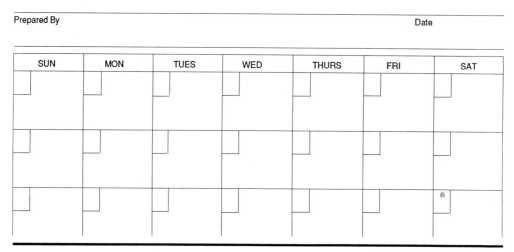

Figure 1-4. 30-Day Action Agenda from Skunk Camp Seminar Materials.

A Specialized Newsletter

José Ramos began publishing the *WYSIWYG* (What You See Is What You Get) newsletter in March of 1985 using a proprietary publishing program for the IBM PC. He converted to desktop publishing with a Macintosh and LaserWriter later that same year. José uses a number of programs on the Macintosh and IBM PC to typeset and lay out different issues of *WYSIWYG*. Since his publication deals exclusively with tools of this type, he varies his experience by using many different systems. The issue shown in Figure 1-5 was created using a Mac and LaserWriter.

    WYSIWYG is a specialized monthly newsletter which surveys marketing trends in the WYSIWYG style computer-aided publishing and desktop publishing field. With an annual subscription rate of $195 for twelve issues and a circulation of over 3,000, the newsletter is very successful. Using desktop publishing, José is able to keep all of the production in-house, and keep costs to a minimum. The logo was designed separately using conventional typesetting and artwork.

Business Forms

The invoice, purchase order, and letterhead for the fictional jeweler, Cameo and Locket, shown in Figure 1-6 was created by John McWade as a part of Apple's desktop publishing advertising campaign. The materials were conceptualized, designed, and produced in the course of a single workday. The image of a woman was digitized with ThunderScan, touched up in MacPaint, and all three business forms finalized with PageMaker.

Personal Correspondence

Once you know how desktop publishing works, you'll find uses for it you never would have imagined. The thank-you note shown in Figure 1-7 was created in roughly fifteen minutes using PageMaker, was printed on a LaserWriter and mailed. The note was assembled by combining electronic clip-art with previously written text.

|W|Y|S|I|W|Y|G|

The FIRST NEWSLETTER ON ELECTRONIC PUBLISHING

Vol. 2, No. 2   February 17, 1986

INSIDE THE MARKET

FROM DEDICATED SYSTEM VENDORS

IBM TO MARKET INTERLEAF SOFTWARE ON THE NEW RT-PC - Interleaf's Workstation Publishing Software (WPS) will run on IBM's new *RT Personal Computer*.

Significantly, all IBM branches and selected authorized personal computer dealers will sell WPS at a per-copy price of just *$1,995*. That's $6,000 *less* than its price on most other computer platforms, including Sun, Apollo and DEC. Availability is in 60 days.

The deal represents still another coup for Interleaf, which also won a major contract with the Army just last month. The company, with IBM's support, should easily double sales in fiscal 1986 to $40 million. (617) 494-4826.

600S AWARD DISPUTED - Electronic Data Systems (EDS), teamed with IBM, TPC Logistics Services, Interleaf and Custom Printing Company, have run into a snag as they attempt to cash in on the Army's 5-year contract to establish 200 integrated publishing centers worldwide. Just about everyone has complained, and Xerox has taken the issue to the Government Service Administration's Board of Contract Appeals (Xerox's dispute has no relation to AT&T's protest last month). The dispute appears to center around pages 57 and 59 of the RFP issued for project 600S by the Government Printing Office. According to Texet president, Al Ireton, "Interleaf's software does not possess the capability to handle the more complex tasks specified as standard operating features in the RFP."

Richard E. Lee, superintendent of terms contracts at the Government Printing Office, has informed us that the appeal will be settled in 45 days. "Normally these things are handled by the General Accounting Office, but Xerox chose to go the route of GSA. If they (Xerox) are not satisfied with the appellate decision they have the option to bring the matter to court." (202) 275-2225

SUN INTRODUCES $7,900 DISKLESS WORKSTATION - Sun was ready with an announcement of its own on January 21st, the day IBM introduced its much-anticipated RT-PC. Sun's double-barreled announcement shocked competitors by setting the lowest prices for 68020 performance workstations in the industry. The first product is intended as a diskless node on an Ethernet network. This is the *Sun 3/50M*, a complete workstation (save a disk drive) including a 10-inch high resolution display, a 15-Mhz 68020 microprocessor, 4 MBytes of RAM, Ethernet and bundled software. The other model, *Sun-3/52M*, listing for $13,900, is a full-function standalone system packaged with disk and tape. Both systems are fully software compatible with the rest of the Sun-3 workstation family. In addition to product announcements, Sun also dropped prices for add-on memory boards a full 40% to $833 per MByte. That move alone most surely hurt competitors; memory boards had become one of the most profitable products offered in their catalogs.

According to Carol Bartz, vice president of marketing at Sun, "The new systems are aimed at three specific applications: artificial intelligence, computer-assisted engineering, and *computer-aided publishing*." (415) 960-7533

(see photos on page 6)

IN DESKTOP PUBLISHING

DESKTOP PUBLISHING MAGAZINE BOUGHT BY PC WORLD COMMUNICATIONS- Just two issues old, *Desktop Publishing* is joining PC World Communications, publishers of *Macworld* and *PC World* magazines.

"Desktop Publishing is personal computing's next major growth area," said David Bunnell, Chairman of PCWCI. "Publishing words and graphics with IBM-type PCs and Apple Computers is a technological breakthrough that will have far more impact than spreadsheet programs. People in the PC industry have been looking for the next VisiCalc and this is it."

The new version of *Desktop Publishing* will be inserted in the July issues of both *PC World* and *Macworld*. Tony Bove and Cheryl Rhodes, founders of *Desktop Publishing* will join PCWCI as editors of the magazine. Subsequent to the July insert, *Desktop Publishing* will appear bi-monthly.

PC World Communications, Inc. is a subsidiary of Computerworld Communications, Inc., the publisher of *Computerworld*, *Infoworld* and over

(continued on next page)

In this Issue

Inside the Market:
          IBM TO SALE INTERLEAF
In Depth:
          WHEN PCs AND
          WORKSTATIONS MERGE

Company Profile: XYVISION

People & Places: AUTOLOGIC'S
          NEW GENERAL MANAGER FOR
          ELECTRONIC PUBLISHING

José Ramos, Publisher   © Ramos Publishing, Inc.

Figure 1-5. The *WYSIWYG* Newsletter.

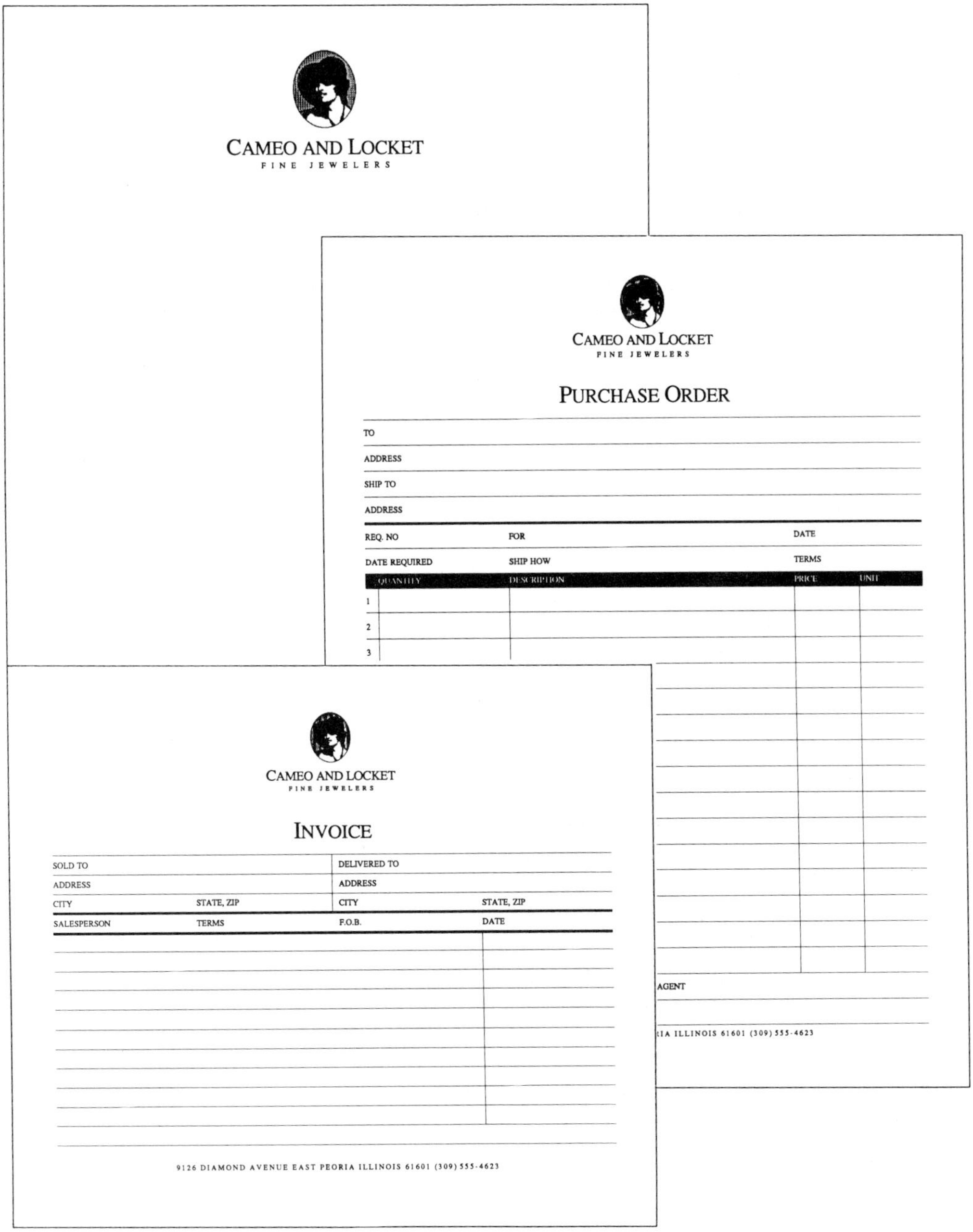
CAMEO AND LOCKET
FINE JEWELERS

CAMEO AND LOCKET
FINE JEWELERS

PURCHASE ORDER

TO
ADDRESS
SHIP TO
ADDRESS

REQ. NO	FOR	DATE
DATE REQUIRED	SHIP HOW	TERMS

	QUANTITY	DESCRIPTION	PRICE	UNIT
1				
2				
3				

AGENT

IA ILLINOIS 61601 (309) 555-4623

CAMEO AND LOCKET
FINE JEWELERS

INVOICE

SOLD TO		DELIVERED TO	
ADDRESS		ADDRESS	
CITY	STATE, ZIP	CITY	STATE, ZIP
SALESPERSON	TERMS	F.O.B.	DATE

9126 DIAMOND AVENUE EAST PEORIA ILLINOIS 61601 (309) 555-4623

Figure 1-6. Cameo and Locket Business Forms.

Thank You

Dear Susie,

I wanted to send you a special thank you note. You are a most gracious host and I enjoyed my week with you in Hawaii immensely. I wanted to thank you specifically for taking time out of your busy schedule to show me a good time, for sharing your friends with me, your hot shopping spots, your delicious eateries, your orange Bug (making it possible for Mother and I to investigate the island properly) and last but not least, for sharing yourself.

I've thought an awful lot about all the wonderful people I met. I'm sure in another week my vacation will seem even more like a dream than it did at the time. I love all the things I brought back with me and they will hold a special place in my heart as the years go by. All of this was possible because you extended to me an invitation and a place to stay. Thank you again so much.

Figure 1-7. Thank-You Note to a Friend.

Your Own Publication

There are hundreds of publications we could show you if space permitted, but these examples give you an idea of what you can do with desktop publishing and how you can improve the quality of communication in your office or home. With desktop publishing tools you can typeset and electronically pasteup any kind of printed material imaginable.

Who Can Profit from This Book

Just about anyone who works with the written word or publications of any kind can profit from an exploration of desktop publishing techniques. If you do not own a computer but are considering desktop publishing as a cost-effective and time-saving alternative, this book is for you. If you already own a Macintosh and a LaserWriter, or own the Mac but don't know whether the LaserWriter is worth the investment, read on—you may be surprised.

The desktop publishing methods used in this book can be applied to any combination of words and pictures you'd like to see typeset and combined on the same page. Whether it's a café menu or a complex report, a viewgraph for overhead projection, a formal proposal or your personal memoirs, this book will teach you what you need to know to use an Apple Macintosh and a laser printer to put that material into print. The following types of organizations are obvious candidates to profit from desktop publishing, but of course there are many others as well. If it goes into print, it can be desktop published and this book will show you how.

Corporations

You can apply desktop publishing skills to develop newsletters, reports, and office forms in-house to increase both employee and customer confidence. Your managers can learn to create winning presentations with a professional touch. Clerical staff will be able to turn memos and letters into typeset correspondence that gets noticed. In-house graphics and publishing staff will appreciate the addition of desktop publishing equipment that will decrease their dependence on outside typesetters and will allow them to turn around material faster and give it an added professional touch.

Ad Agencies and Graphic Designers

With desktop publishing you can bring in more projects and increase productivity. You can offer design, consulting, and layout services to those just starting out in desktop publishing. For your existing work, you can use desktop publishing tools to clarify client projects with near-camera-ready composites. Also, you can increase your customer base by satisfying the needs of low-budget clients.

Nonprofit Organizations

Nonprofit organizations can use desktop publishing to produce newsletters in-house, cutting costs and turnaround time. The documents you produce will get the attention they deserve because, with desktop publishing, anything from the simplest report to the most complex funding proposal can be typeset and illustrated. You'll be able to let the community know what you are doing with information-packed brochures and let them know your services and hours of availability with clever handbills.

Restaurants and Cafés

Menus are a natural for desktop publishing. What about those specials? Wouldn't it be nice to have a typeset specials menu for each day of the week? And if you decide to change your prices or update your wine list, you'll already have the basic layout stored on a diskette. All you need do is type in the new or altered information and print out a complete new menu. Take it directly to the printer or, if you use only a few dozen or so menus, print them straight from the laser printer.

Schools and Universities

With desktop publishing, you'll be able to design and print many educational publications in-house, professionally and at reduced cost. Forms, applications, certificates, newsletters, curriculum vitae, and syllabi can be designed and later updated easily to reflect changes or new information. Students at all levels can learn to use desktop publishing equipment and acquire valuable skills. Course catalogs can be written once and updated each quarter or semester to reflect changes in personnel or scheduling—the entire catalog need not be rewritten or retypeset. These and other scholarly papers can be given a professional look.

Copy and Print Shops

You can offer your customers value-added services. As desktop publishing grows in popularity, you'll want an understanding of how your customers developed material in a desktop publishing environment and how your business can supplement their efforts. Add to that all the capabilities of having this equipment available in-house for your own use and expand your customer service capabilities.

Businesses and Professions

Anyone in business or a profession can benefit from using desktop publishing methods to produce letterhead stationery and invoices; perhaps even to design and prepare camera-ready art for your own business cards. Correspondence, estimates, and accounting reports all look more professional when typeset and illustrated. You can create price lists, catalogs, and data sheets once, and thereafter simply enter or adjust changed information and print it over again. You don't have to go back and have each section or product specification retypeset once it's been developed.

Individuals

Maybe you have a Macintosh at home already or one you can use at the office. If you are having a party, throwing a shower for someone or maybe have something to sell, you can design a clever invitation or handbill with desktop publishing tools and, for less than a dollar, print it out on a service bureau laser printer. Go to the nearest copy center, choose your paper and the results are professional and command attention. The same is true of resumés, newsletters, and booklets. You can even go into business as a desktop publisher, work at home, and set a course for total independence.

Or, perhaps you've written the Great American Novel and would like to publish it yourself at a fraction of the traditional cost. With desktop publishing the only limit is your own creativity.

What This Book Does

In a simple and straightforward manner, this book shows you how we produced a four-page newsletter using an Apple Macintosh and Laser-Writer with specific desktop publishing software. These skills are taught in a "hands-on" manner. Looking over our shoulder, so to speak, you can duplicate our efforts nearly every step of the way. Once you've learned the basics, you can transfer what you learn here to publications of your own design. This approach seems the quickest and most direct way of helping you become productive in desktop publishing.

The Macintosh is one of the easiest computers to use, and in some ways this is deceptive. Although anyone, having never used a computer before, can sit down with a Mac and, in a matter of minutes, learn to compose a letter, this does not mean that all the arts of publishing can be picked up so quickly. Computer consultants have rescued people who have gone out one day and, having bought all the requisite software, thought they would turn out their newsletter by the next afternoon. It's not quite as easy as that; some study is required.

Be assured, however, that if you follow through to the end of the book, you will learn everything necessary to use desktop publishing tools and to create your own publication. Some of the techniques used in this book are advanced. If you plan to follow along and duplicate our efforts, you should already be familiar with the Macintosh, the programs it uses, and have worked through the tutorials accompanying each. If you encounter an unfamiliar term, a complete glossary is in the back of the book.

Audio Image: A Model

This book follows the development of the premier issue of *Audio Image: The Modern Music Review of Digital Audio,* a newsletter that focuses on recorded music in the compact disc format. Since the most practical way to learn things is "on the job," a genuine, live subject was chosen—a real newsletter with real subscribers. The four-page spread developed throughout the following chapters serves as a prototype for the actual published version.

A newsletter was selected because newsletters are one of the most popular uses of desktop publishing and because the newsletter format manages to incorporate nearly every technique you would ever need to use in any other type of publication. So, from initial concept all the way through production, you will witness how the premier issue of *Audio Image* came to be.

As with any publication, *Audio Image* had to be planned, designed, written, edited, laid out, and printed. A logo and nameplate were designed, and a chart with Microsoft Excel was created for use with the lead article. A diagram was fashioned with MacDraw for another article. Artwork from compact disc booklets was captured using a digitizer and doctored in Mac-Paint. Finally, all the pieces were assembled and laid out on the page using PageMaker. When satisfaction with the results was finally achieved, the pages were taken to a print shop for final printing.

How to Use
This Book

For beginners in desktop publishing there are really two phases in achieving a finished publication: learning how to do it and doing it. Correspondingly, you may find it convenient to read this book twice (or at least once and refer to it later). The first time through you should follow along with our newsletter example, creating enough of the text and illustrations so that you can duplicate the effects shown in the book. This way you'll learn how things are done, even though the publication you create will not be one of your own.

The second time through you'll be working on your *own* publication. You will probably need to refer to specific places in the book where you forgot about a particular procedure. You will also need to start making contacts with outside vendors. Specifically, you'll need to find a printshop and discuss your publication with them, as described in Chapter Seven. You may also need to to make arrangements with other professionals you might need, such as a graphic designer (discussed in Chapters Three and Six) or possibly a pasteup artist.

So work through the book once, using your Macintosh to learn about the process, then use it again when you are ready to put together your own publication.

A Specific Set
of Tools

In order to achieve exactly the same results in desktop publishing that we demonstrate in this book, you should use the same equipment that we have chosen, namely the Apple Macintosh, the Apple LaserWriter, and Aldus' PageMaker. We will explain our reasons for these choices.

Criteria for Equipment Selection

Desktop publishers are not likely to be computer professionals to start with, so the first criteria for choosing equipment is whether the system is easy to learn and use. If you have invested in a desktop publishing system, you probably want to publish professional-quality work as fast as possible. So, if you have to spend weeks just learning how to operate the computer—the first step in this process—you have wasted a lot of time and made the learning curve that much steeper.

Do you have to learn arcane commands or filename conventions before you can get to work? Is there only one way of entering information into the computer (the keyboard) or is there also a mouse or stylus pointing device? In other words, does the computer meet you halfway or do you have to spend hours reading through manuals to find out how to get your work done?

The second criteria is system integration. Appropriate system integration is a demanding prerequisite for any desktop publishing hardware and software combination. Personal computers are general-purpose machines. You can buy a word processor from one manufacturer, a drawing program from another, and a laser printer from yet a third, but will they all work together when you set them up and learn how to use them? If you write wondrous prose in the word processor, can you combine it with the graphics from the drawing program? If they can be combined, will they print together on the same laser printer? The desktop publishing system recommended in this book is an integrated system; all components—hardware and software alike—work in harmony.

The third criteria is expense. The Macintosh is somewhat less expensive than a similarly configured IBM PC (with a graphics card and monitor) but the LaserWriter is more expensive than laser printers from other manufacturers. However, it does more: it prints in a variety of typefaces, styles, and sizes and it can accept downloadable fonts. Most importantly, it can print full-page graphics alongside typeset text, an essential characteristic if you are to realize the full potential of desktop publishing. When we added up the cost of making an IBM PC compatible with graphics-intensive desktop publishing, plus the LaserWriter (which we would need anyway), the Macintosh-LaserWriter combination quickly fell in line with our budgetary considerations.

The hardware and software recommended in this book is used daily to do desktop publishing on a professional basis. The process of learning how to use this equipment is not difficult. An inordinate amount of time does not need to be spent away from your work reading through manuals to figure things out. You can turn out satisfactory work within a few days of acquiring this equipment.

Why Apple's Macintosh?

The Apple Macintosh provides a rich graphics environment that was designed into the machine from the start. All material—text and graphics—are represented in the computer in the same fashion, as graphic images. You do not have to buy an expensive graphics adapter card to plug into the computer to enable you to draw with it. All programs used on the Macintosh share a common command structure, so moving from program to program, as you do with any desktop publishing system, is easy and virtually transparent—the commands in one program generally work the same way in another.

Ask yourself this: would you rather drag a line representing the edge of a column to a certain place on the screen with a mouse, as you can on a Mac, or would you like to guess how wide to make the column, type in the number of inches, print the document to see what really happens, and then repeat the whole process over and over until you get it right? That is roughly the difference between using a Macintosh and any other machine, such as an IBM PC. We are beginning to see improvements in the IBM environment, but for now, practically speaking, the Mac is the only way to go.

Apple certainly has the leap on other manufacturers when it comes to desktop publishing, especially in this equipment price range. The Macintosh and LaserWriter make a perfect marriage between words and pictures, typesetting and graphics—for several reasons.

First and foremost, the Macintosh is a graphics-oriented computer, while most others are word-oriented and have to be modified in some way to handle graphics. Second, since Apple was first to introduce such a desktop publishing system, it has the software support of dozens of companies who want to capitalize on this burgeoning market. New and more powerful developments will continue to be seen in both hardware and software for desktop publishing for some time to come.

Finally, Apple continues to show a strong commitment to desktop publishers and promises to continue developing products that can only enhance its position in the market and make your job easier.

Why PageMaker?

Aldus' PageMaker is, in our opinion, the premier page composition and layout program available for the Macintosh. There are less expensive page layout programs on the market, but here, as elsewhere, it is a matter of "you get what you pay for."

We tried all the page layout programs available for the Macintosh at this writing and evaluated them on how easy they were to use and whether we could achieve the design results we wanted. For example, working with a small nine-inch screen, it is important to have multiple views of the page at various reductions and enlargements. All the programs offer this capability to some degree. But we want to be able to pick up and move our text or graphics at these various views in order to make refined adjustments, and neither Manhattan Graphics' ReadySetGo or Boston Software Publishers' MacPublisher I or II permit this.

And when we move text or graphics on the page, we want to control the shape it takes. In both of the other programs, the text or graphic image takes the shape of a box or rectangle, so we can't clearly see what dimensions we're dealing with. In PageMaker, when we positioned a picture of a rose on a page and then decided to move it elsewhere, we moved a picture of a rose, not a box representing it. It is attention to details like this that convinced us that PageMaker was the layout package to invest in.

PageMaker gives the most accurate image of what we're going to print before we print it. It is the most realistic WYSIWYG page layout program available for the Macintosh.

Getting Started

2

In this chapter you will learn about:

- The desktop publishing process (an overview)
- What hardware and software you need
- The LaserWriter and PostScript
- The AppleTalk Personal Network

In Chapter One we told you of all the things you could do with desktop publishing. This chapter tells you what you need to know in order to actually get started using a desktop publishing system. It begins with an overview of the desktop publishing process to give a clear idea of what it takes to carry out a project from start to finish. Next, we will tell you what kind of hardware and software you need and why these specific items are likely to do the job best.

In the following section we are going to pay particular attention to how the LaserWriter printer works. We will describe PostScript and how it works and discuss the AppleTalk Personal Network. If you are contemplating the purchase of a Macintosh-based desktop publishing system or if you already own one, you'll want to know how AppleTalk is used to connect the Macintosh to the LaserWriter and how you can go on from there to create a fully integrated office system. All in all, you'll find everything you need to know about getting started with desktop publishing using an Apple Macintosh.

Of course, if you've already made a commitment to the specific system recommended here and are currently using this equipment, you can skim through the chapter. In any case, you'll want to read through the overview of the desktop publishing process; it contains many helpful pointers on the best way to organize your work and make the most of the equipment you have.

21

The Desktop Publishing Process:
An Overview

Publishing has many common elements, whether for a small business, a corporation, a newsletter, or a newspaper. You start with an idea and transform it into a printed product. Desktop publishing shares much in common with the larger publishing systems that have been operating for many years. No matter what you want to put into print or how you do it, the essential tasks remain the same—writing, editing, typesetting, illustration, photography, design, layout, and pasteup. These are all a part of the publishing process.

The central difference between conventional publishing and desktop publishing is that with desktop publishing you can carry out all of these activities in the space of a small office or in your home, whereas at a newspaper or book publisher these tasks are divided into specialized departments that involve many people. Desktop publishing puts all of this capability in a single office, often in the hands of one person. Of course, you don't need to do it all yourself. You can solicit articles or, borrowing a term from conventional publishing, solicit *copy* from several writers if you don't want to write everything yourself. The initial design of the publication can be handled by a graphic designer or, if you have some experience with this, you can do it yourself. You can also do the copyediting, the artwork, and the page layout, or you can farm these tasks out to others more familiar with how it's done using desktop publishing tools. Even if you use a lot of outside help, however, you can exercise a previously unattainable degree of control over every step in the process, from concept to camera-ready art. The only outside services you will almost certainly need are those of a printer.

The sequence in the remaining chapters involves the following activities: the initial design of a publication, preparing copy, preparing artwork, doing page composition and layout, and finally, printing (see Figure 2-1). Each activity is covered by a separate chapter as we go about preparing our four-page issue of *Audio Image* for publication.

However you choose to carry out the desktop publishing process, this distinct sequence of steps is recommended. Experience has shown that any wide deviation from these steps can lead to a marked decrease in efficiency.

It would be nice to be able to do things on the fly, but in most cases this does not work out. If you end up trying to do the final layout before all the writing or artwork is complete, you'll find yourself spending hours doing it all over again once the materials are finished. If you don't have a clear visual image or a template of what the publication will look like or how many pages it will contain, you won't be able to assign the copy or develop the art to fit well within the page boundaries or columns of your publication. All of these tasks interact from one level to the next and you may find that strict adherence to the sequence shown assures a smooth and trouble-free desktop publishing experience.

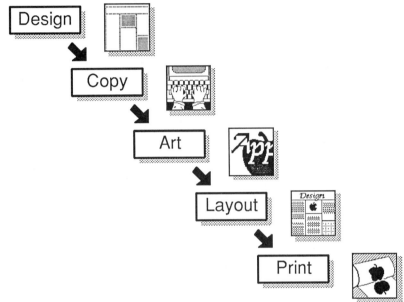

Figure 2-1. The Desktop Publishing Process.

Planning and Design

Planning is the most important first step towards a successful publication of any kind. Having a well-thought-out design goes hand in hand with planning. The kind of planning and design discussed here is simply that of having a good visual image of your publication and the elements it contains.

We will cover this step much more thoroughly in Chapter Three, but you should know as you get started in desktop publishing what it takes to pull all the pieces together and to assemble them painlessly. A few quick rules of thumb will help you get this in perspective.

KNOW YOUR AUDIENCE

Whether you are publishing a periodical for the general public or a brochure promoting a single product, understand thoroughly who your publication is going to address and at what level of expertise you intend to address them. Target your audience as narrowly as possible. Are they old or young? Are they self-employed or employees? Are they conservative or liberal? What is their average annual income? Use available market research statistics if available or conduct your own research. Examine similar publications that already exist in the same field.

SET GUIDELINES FOR EDITORIAL CONTENT AND ART DIRECTION

Establish guidelines and priorities for the editorial content and art direction of your publication and stick to them. This will simplify decisions about what kind of material to include and what to reject. Based on your audience assessment, decide what topics you'll cover, what topics you don't want to cover, and what ideas will remain consistent over the lifespan of your publication. If you choose to cover medical issues, will you limit your editorial content to physicians only or will you include nurses as well?

Art direction guidelines apply to the artwork used in your publication as well as the design. You want to present both copy and art in a consistent manner. If you choose to use a particular style of chart or line art in the publication, continue to use the same style of art throughout each issue. You may need to consult a professional graphics designer in order to establish art direction guidelines.

KNOW EXACTLY WHAT THE CLIENT WANTS

If you are creating a publication for an outside client or your boss in an organization, make sure you know exactly what is expected. It's far easier to discuss the design before you produce the material than afterwards. Make sure you thoroughly understand the client's expectations before you start out.

DETERMINE THE SIZE OF YOUR PUBLICATION

Will the publication measure 8.5 by 11 inches or 7.5 by 9.25 inches? If you're doing a brochure, will it be three-fold or four? You should decide early on what the physical dimensions of the publication are, how many columns it will have and how many pages it will have. Having a clear image of the publication size helps when you talk to designers and printers and even when you begin designing a template in PageMaker. You should also have a good idea of how many copies of the publication you want to have printed.

DESIGN A TEMPLATE IN PAGEMAKER

This is where you really start to design the overall look of your publication. If you've never designed a publication before or have limited experience doing so, you may wish to consult a professional graphics designer at this point. Make sure the designer understands desktop publishing with a Macintosh and uses the same tools you do. Be prepared to provide a sample of the editorial content and any artwork you plan to use.

Before you go on to giving out copy and art assignments or begin developing them yourself, you want to design a template in PageMaker. A template is a dummy page layout that brings together such consistent items as the publication logo or nameplate, the way columns are laid out, and headers and footers. If it's a catalog, you can probably enter in the various categories you plan to use. Since you know how many pages are in the publication, you can set this up as well. Essentially, you want to create a shell into which you can later pour your text and position your art.

TALK TO THE PRINTER

When you are ready to create your own publication you should select a printing firm that specializes in your type of publication, set up an appointment and visit the print shop. Have a printed version of your template available and talk to the sales representative about how best to plan the publication for printing. Make sure you familiarize yourself with the material in Chapter Seven of this book first.

Preparing Copy

Once you've planned your publication and have solid design goals in mind, you can go about preparing written material, usually called *text* or *copy*. In most cases, you'll want to do this before you develop art for the publication. Artwork usually supports the text in a publication. However, in some types of publications like greeting cards, brochures and handbills, the art and copy go hand in hand and you should feel free to develop them simultaneously.

The important thing here is to have both copy and art prepared and finalized before you go into PageMaker to do your final layout. As far as copy is concerned, although PageMaker's text editor is powerful, it is not meant to be used as a word processor. So you want to make sure your copy is fully edited and proofread before you do your layout. It is often much easier to plan artwork if your copy is complete.

It is appropriate at this stage in the desktop publishing process to copy-edit all written material whether it's solicited from outside authors or written by you. You will want to convert into Macintosh formats any copy originally developed on another computer's word processor. Spell-checking is a good thing to do here. You want to select the typeface for the body type. Using Microsoft Word, you can even set the leading and establish line lengths for column placement.

Ultimately, you want to end up with perfect copy that is as completely prepared for layout as it would be if you were using conventional publishing methods and were ready to take it to the pasteup artist. You make much less work for yourself by thoroughly finalizing your copy at this step in the process. When you get to the layout phase, you'll have much more freedom to play with things until you get them just right. We cover the preparation of copy in Chapter Four.

Preparing Artwork

Just as you prepared and finalized your copy, you want to prepare and finalize any artwork that you plan to use in your publication. Chapter Five shows in detail how to do this and gives you plenty of examples of how we prepared art for *Audio Image*.

Using the Macintosh, you can create a chart in Microsoft Excel or Chart, easily copy it and paste it into a funding proposal you might develop to obtain a foundation grant. You can also create a diagram or line art using MacDraw or MacPaint, save the document to disk and place it directly into PageMaker when you do your page composition and layout. You can use digitizing equipment to capture existing art, such as an already established company logo, save it to disk and later use it wherever you like on letterheads, invoices, or purchase orders.

The main thing is to develop and finalize your art at this time and place, before you begin the page layout process. You want it all signed off and ready to insert as you move on to the next phase.

Page Composition and Layout

Now that everything is ready—template, copy, and art—you are prepared to embark on page composition and layout. This is the key process in the creation of your publication. As closely as possible, you will be finalizing your entire publication at this time. You will create what are called *camera-ready mechanicals* that you will take to the printer.

PageMaker is what we have chosen to do this. As easy as it is to learn to operate, there is nothing at all easy about coming up with an elegant page layout unless you already have a strong background in pasteup or graphic design. You may wish to consult with a graphics designer regarding page layout or consult again with the designer who helped you with your template. We provide guidelines for developing simple page layouts in Chapter Six.

Printing

Once you have completed your page composition and layout and have your camera-ready mechanicals prepared, you are ready to return to the printer. Chapter Seven tells you what you need to know about preparing your laser-printed mechanicals for printing.

Printing is the stage where your idea for a publication is finally mass-produced and readied for delivery to your anticipated audience. You want to make sure you have everything ready: mechanicals, drop-in photos and any preprinted matter. You should already know from your previous visit what kind of paper and ink the printer will use.

Of course, if this is a limited circulation publication, you can probably photocopy it in small quantities or simply print several directly from the laser printer. At any rate, printing is the final step in the desktop publishing process.

What Hardware You Need

Now that you have some understanding of how desktop publishing works, this section tells you what equipment you need. If you are already using the Macintosh as part of a desktop publishing system, you can skip this part of the chapter. However, if you are considering the purchase of a computer for desktop publishing and haven't made up your mind, read on. We will try to make your decision easier.

We wrote and developed this book using our ideal desktop publishing system: a Macintosh Plus, Apple's Hard Disk 20 and a LaserWriter Plus.

Apple Macintosh 512K or Macintosh Plus

As mentioned in Chapter One, the Macintosh is a visual computer. It works well with pictures and data, graphics and words. It is an easy computer to learn how to operate. For us, it is the core of desktop publishing.

CLIPBOARD AND SCRAPBOOK

In addition to being a visual computer, the Macintosh employs a method whereby we can easily copy text and graphics from one program to the next. The device used to do this is called a *clipboard*. The clipboard is a temporary storage area, predefined in the Macintosh's memory, which allows you to copy text or graphics from one program, quit the program, start up another and paste the information in the new program's document. In this way, you can create a drawing in MacPaint, copy it to the clipboard and paste it into a letter or report in Microsoft Word or MacWrite. No other micro-computer has this capability.

For longer-term storage of text and graphics, you can use the *scrapbook*. The scrapbook can hold many different pieces of text and graphics and keep them available for copying and pasting. The clipboard is short-term; it can only hold one piece at a time. If you copy something else, the first thing you copied gets erased and is no longer available; while the scrapbook retains the image or text you copied there indefinitely in serial order so you can simply access the scrapbook and scroll from one item to the next until you find the one you want to use over again.

Both the clipboard and the scrapbook make the Macintosh a perfect system for desktop publishing in that you can easily move text and graphics from program to program as you do your work. This is only one of many major features that make the Mac a powerful tool for desktop publishing.

THE MOUSE POINTING DEVICE

The mouse is a pointing device originally developed in 1964 by Douglas Englebart at Stanford Research Institute (now SRI International). With the mouse you can move a pointer on the Macintosh screen by moving the device along your desk surface. Push the mouse to the right, the pointer on the screen moves right; push up, the pointer moves up. The Macintosh mouse lets you draw with a drawing program much like you would with a pencil. You can point at text in a page layout program, pick it up and move it or select text in a word processor and make corrections by simply typing in the new information. These and many other complex activities can be carried out by simply pointing and clicking.

CONSISTENT USER INTERFACE

All Macintosh programs share a consistent user interface. The way in which you use one program is much the same when you use another completely different program. All share common features like pull-down (window-shade style) menus.

All have access to the same memory-resident desk accessories from a pull-down menu that permit you to do things like quickly look up a client's phone number, jot a quick reminder, or even check the time.

Most programs share a common keyboard command structure so the command for copying something in one program is the same in all programs. This consistency permits you to quickly learn how to use Macintosh programs and get right to work.

FONTS AND TYPESTYLES

Macintosh was the first computer to offer a variable selection of fonts and typestyles. You can simply select a section of text and then, without resorting to arcane commands, tell the program you want the words in boldface, italics or underlined by choosing items from a menu. In this way, if your Macintosh is connected to a LaserWriter, any document, even a spreadsheet, can be automatically typeset in Times, Helvetica, Palatino or Garamond, to name a few.

DIFFERENT MODELS

You should be aware, however, that Apple has introduced, over the past three years, several different models of Macintosh computer and discontinued some of the earlier ones.

We do not recommend doing any kind of desktop publishing with the original 128K Macintosh; there simply is not enough memory.

There are two versions of the Macintosh 512K and you should seek out the newer of the two, called the Macintosh 512K Enhanced (the earlier one has a 400K internal disk drive and the newer one has an 800K drive).

The older Macintosh 512K with 400K internal and external floppy drives is a passable desktop publishing system. With proper disk management (see Appendix C) you can do desktop publishing with two 400K drives but it's preferable to have either a hard disk or at least an 800K external floppy drive.

And finally, there's the Macintosh Plus, sporting a full megabyte of memory—plenty to handle any desktop publishing task—and highly recommended. Combine the Macintosh Plus with either a hard drive or an 800K external floppy drive and you have what is, in the author's opinion, the best desktop publishing system currently available.

SWITCHER AND MEMORY

If you plan to use Switcher (see Appendix A), the Macintosh Plus offers distinct advantages. Switcher is a program, available from Apple, which permits you to load several programs into memory at once and to switch rapidly between them. You can carry the contents of the clipboard from one program to another and access the scrapbook from them as well. However, since when you use Switcher, each program is loaded into the Macintosh's memory, the number of programs you can have in Switcher at any time depends on how much memory you have available. You can use Switcher with a Macintosh 512K but it becomes a really powerful tool using the full megabyte of memory available with the Macintosh Plus.

Hard Drive or External Floppy Drive

In the course of doing desktop publishing with a Macintosh, you will inevitably begin to accrue a large amount of text and graphic documents, all of which take up space and must be stored somewhere. The Macintosh comes with one internal floppy drive, either a 400K drive on the earlier models or an 800K drive on current models. A 400K disk has just enough room for a program and little if any left over for storage of your text or graphics. The 800K drive will provide much more space for a single program and more space for your text and graphics documents. Graphics documents nearly always take up more space than text documents, so, depending on how many graphics are used in the publication you may have very little room left at all on a 400K disk.

For this reason we highly recommend you invest in a hard disk drive of at least 10 megabytes (Mb) capacity. As a matter of fact, these days, you can probably afford to get a 20 Mb hard drive for only a little more than a 10 Mb drive. If you plan to do desktop publishing professionally, the convenience of a large capacity hard drive will be well worth the investment over the long run.

The minimum configuration useful for desktop publishing requires either a 400K external floppy drive or preferably one of the newer 800K external floppy drives. Without a doubt you need at least one external storage device; either a hard drive or an external floppy drive (see Appendix C for more on how to manage disk space in any configuration).

LaserWriter or LaserWriter Plus

If you can fit it into your desktop publishing budget, either the original LaserWriter or the newer LaserWriter Plus gives you a definite advantage. These are expensive laser printers, but reasonably so. They are fully programmable, have their own built-in computer and memory, and deliver the typeset copy and crisp graphics desktop publishing prides itself on. The LaserWriter is the workhorse printer of desktop publishing. Its groundbreaking technology has, in fact, enabled the desktop publishing revolution.

You can also make use of LaserWriters at copy shops, service bureaus and print shops that rent time on them. These establishments charge anywhere from ten cents to two dollars per printed page and may also charge an hourly rate for using the Macintosh connected to the printer. Shop around; prices are competitive.

You will find much more detail on the LaserWriter's technology later in this chapter.

We don't recommend that you use the dot matrix Imagewriter or Imagewriter II printer commonly sold with the Macintosh. While it can give you a good rough draft of what your publication may look like, the print quality is simply not up to the standards of serious work.

AppleTalk Connectors and Cables

If you plan to purchase a LaserWriter, you'll also need AppleTalk connectors for both the Macintosh side and the LaserWriter side. The connector kits come with enough cable to link the two machines in a single office. If you plan to implement an AppleTalk Personal Network, as described later in this chapter, you'll need additional AppleTalk connectors and cable. Your Apple dealer can help you determine how much you need.

LaserWriter Cartridges

A LaserWriter toner cartridge should also be on your list if you plan to purchase a LaserWriter. You will need to replace these periodically (each is good for about 3,000 full-page images). The toner cartridge contains the imaging toner and those moving parts that are likely to wear out quickly. This looks basically the same as the cartridge replacement for a Canon personal copier. Don't be confused by appearances however. The two may look alike, but the LaserWriter toner cartridge is different from the Canon cartridge and the two are not interchangeable. Make sure you get the LaserWriter cartridge.

Digitizers

A useful (though in many cases not essential) addition to any desktop publishing system is some kind of digitizer. A digitizer lets you transform ordinary photographs, company logos, existing line art or just about any visual image into a form that can be used and manipulated on the Macintosh. Once the image is digitized, you can refine it further in MacPaint or place it directly into your document. Digitizers let you capture and use artwork even though you may not be a skilled illustrator or line artist.

Digitizers come in two varieties. There are optical digitizers and video digitizers. Both are described in the following sections. The two we use are ThunderScan (optical) and MacVision (video). Manufacturers are introducing new models all the time. Some are extremely sophisticated and expensive. Others are targeted at the low-budget market. Digitized images require a phenomenal amount of disk storage space, so make sure you have at least an 800K external floppy drive or a hard disk before you invest in one.

OPTICAL DIGITIZERS

Optical digitizers, like Thunderware's ThunderScan unit, scan your image by reflecting light off of the surface of the original art and recording the levels of grey in the original image. This information is stored on disk and remains accessible using the program that accompanies the digitizing unit. This program can automatically create MacPaint documents or, if the image is larger than a MacPaint-sized page, you can copy the image to the clipboard (on a Macintosh Plus) and paste it directly into your publication.

Optical digitizers employ a feed mechanism much like a typewriter's platen to move your image through the device. ThunderScan, in fact, uses the Imagewriter printer to scan images. Therefore, your images must be available on a flat, two-dimensional surface—paper or photographic sheets—which can be fed into the device.

VIDEO DIGITIZERS

Video digitizers, on the other hand, use a video camera to capture the original grey levels of a three-dimensional object to disk. Most video digitizers, like Koala Technologies' MacVision, let you adjust the brightness and contrast before you start the scan using either an external device connected to the Macintosh or using software control.

Video digitizers, like photographic equipment, are sensitive to lighting conditions and, in some situations, you may find this a drawback. Unfortunately, you can't just set these devices up and scan images in any situation. They are particularly sensitive to low light and reflected light situations. You may find yourself having to invest in and learn about lighting equipment, in addition to the digitizer and video camera, in order to obtain satisfactory results. Then again, the initial cost of the digitizer is relatively small and you can rent the video camera and lighting equipment.

In general, video digitizers are the only way to capture three-dimensional objects or images and transfer them into a form the Macintosh can use. They are excellent for making portraits and digitizing large objects such as buildings and heavy equipment.

ThunderScan and MacVision are both covered in more depth in Chapter Five, "Preparing Artwork."

As you move along into the recommended software you will begin to see how a low-cost, sophisticated desktop publishing system comes together.

What Software
You Need

Now that you know your hardware options, you will want to know about specific recommendations for software. Essentially, you'll need a word processor, some drawing tools and a page-layout program. Keep in mind that all this software will function on any Macintosh-based desktop publishing system regardless of the configuration you choose to install.

Word Processing

There are only two major word processing programs for the Macintosh as of this writing: Microsoft Word and MacWrite. We constantly hear rumblings from various corners of the software development community about new and forthcoming word processing choices for the Macintosh. With the desktop publishing market heating up and growing more competitive all the time, this is likely to be true. By the time you read this, there may in fact be more choices. Examine them carefully. Most of all, you want to make sure the disk-based documents produced by these new word processors are compatible with and can be placed directly into PageMaker. Secondly, you want to make sure they include the same features we talk about in Chapter Four, "Preparing Copy," and that, if anything, they exceed the claims of other word processing manufacturers. Any word processor you use must work well, as Microsoft Word does, in the desktop publishing environment.

MICROSOFT WORD

The true workhorse of Macintosh word processing is Microsoft Word. It gives you the most control over the preparation of your copy for use in a desktop-published publication. You can specify any combination of type-face, style and even type sizes between 4 points and 127 points. You can, likewise, control the leading (line spacing) in half-point increments. You can also adjust column widths or line length and do multi-column documents. And Microsoft Word provides a points and picas ruler so you can set all your dimensions using true typesetting measurements.

In fact, if it isn't critical that you have artwork placed side-by-side with the text, you can use Microsoft Word as the final layout tool for a desktop-published document. For office memoranda, correspondence or reports, Microsoft Word works well as the final copy preparation tool.

But anything you prepare in Microsoft Word, including tabs, line length and leading, can be transparently placed in PageMaker and, in fact, we advise that you do this. PageMaker is not a word processor, per se, and all copy should be preprocessed as thoroughly as possible before you use it in PageMaker. Microsoft Word functions best this way right down to the last point or pica.

MACWRITE

You can use MacWrite as a word processor for desktop publishing with the Macintosh but you may find it a limited tool. You cannot set the leading in MacWrite and it provides no alternate typesetting rulers like Word does. It works fine with short articles and may be a good place to develop headlines and such.

The best way to use MacWrite is simply as a fast and efficient bare-bones word processor. That is, use it just to get the text written. Then save the document as *text-only*. When you get to PageMaker, you can spec the typeface, style and size as well as set up the tabs and column width. Then, when you place the MacWrite document, it will flow into PageMaker using those specs.

MOCKWRITE

Another useful word processor—more to the point, a *text processor*—is a shareware desk accessory called MockWrite by CE Software (you can get it free but are asked to send to the author an amount specified in the program). It is a convenient place to create headlines, captions, and short pieces of text. All writing done with MockWrite is saved text-only but since you can easily spec the type in PageMaker, this poses no major problem. Since it is available as a desk accessory, you can use it in any program at any time. Surprisingly, you can set up tabs and perform searches as well as create text. It includes word-wrap and, of course, you can use the mouse to select and change text as you go along. All in all it can be quite useful.

MockWrite is part of the MockPackage desk accessories available from CE Software of Des Moines, Iowa. It is available to subscribers of public information utilities like CompuServe and GEnie and is also offered through Macintosh user groups and Macintosh bulletin board services.

SPELL-CHECKING

You should also seek out and purchase a good spell-checking program. It is a useful accessory for catching misspelled words, typos, and performing hyphenation. There are several commercially available, but the one used in Chapter Four is MacSpell+ from Creighton Development of Irvine, California.

Drawing

If you want to use figures or illustrations in your publication you will probably need to use special Macintosh drawing programs (although this isn't always true—see Chapter Seven on printing for another way to incorporate art into your publication). If you don't need any art or illustrations (a pity) then you can skip this section and probably Chapter Five as well.

In order to create illustrations and artwork and to use clip art you will need to use Macintosh drawing tools. For our purposes, MacDraw and MacPaint suffice and work well in a desktop publishing environment. There are many others available. Some drafting tools allow you to create three dimensional drawings, others permit more complicated technical illustrations. Make sure that any program you buy can save the document in either a PICT format (see Appendix B) or as a MacPaint image. These are the only types of drawing accepted by PageMaker as of this writing.

Use of MacDraw and MacPaint in desktop publishing is covered in Chapter Five, "Preparing Artwork."

MACDRAW

Apple's own MacDraw is a facile drawing tool that lets you create structured graphics using lines and circles, rectangles, ovals, and other graphic objects. It is an excellent stand-alone, electronic drafting table with which you can create flow charts, forms, viewgraphs, floorplans, and such. You can add text labels in any font, style or size. You can paste these drawings into other word processing or layout programs or you can use MacDraw as a layout tool by itself—it is especially good for doing menus and handbills. Anything created in MacDraw can be printed directly with the LaserWriter; it will be typeset and ready to go.

MACPAINT

Apple's MacPaint was shipped with the Macintosh when it was first introduced and helped make the Macintosh an overnight success. Almost every drawing program developed since then is, in some way, modeled after MacPaint. It has become a de facto standard for excellence in electronic drawing tools.

MacPaint lends itself to freehand artistic creations. Some people object to the jagged edges on artwork created with MacPaint but if you draw the image large and shrink it down in PageMaker or reduce it in Microsoft

Word, you can all but eliminate this effect. The LaserWriter's smoothing routines also help.

Depending on your artistic ability, you should be able to come up with just about any piece of art you like using MacPaint. Practice makes perfect. The program is intuitive; all you need do to learn it is to experiment.

ELECTRONIC CLIP ART

There are many commercial sources for electronic clip art. Electronic clip art is essentially canned art that you can work with in MacPaint. You can select part of an image or all of it and use it anywhere else in the Macintosh environment using the clipboard or scrapbook. Clip art generally includes such images as borders, landscapes, trees, flowers, human figures in various poses, machinery, and typesetting dingbats, to name a few.

Some of the most popular packages are from Miles Computing of Van Nuys, California, makers of the Mac The Knife series (Volumes, I, II and III) and T/Maker of Mountain View, California, makers of the Click-Art series (Click-Art, Click-Art Letters, and Click-Art Publications). Another fine collection called The Card Shoppe comes from Axlon of Sunnyvale, California. Originally conceived as a kit for assembling greeting cards —another creative use of desktop publishing—the clip art in this package is useful in many other ways as well.

Perhaps the most ambitious collection of clip art to date is contained in the MacMemories Series from ImageWorld of Eugene, Oregon. Most of these images are captured from turn-of-the-century catalogs, book illustrations and advertisements. The older, antique style of art and the many art nouveau styles are particularly well suited to reproduction on the LaserWriter. All of the images are quite large, some taking up a full page in MacPaint. This makes them infinitely reducible to eliminate MacPaint jagged edges while retaining much of their original detail. The entire set includes thirteen disks and an excellent Image Index that makes it easy to locate and use the images.

To summarize, we use both MacDraw and MacPaint—MacDraw for structured images like diagrams, MacPaint for more artistic work and to operate on clip art.

PageMaker

As we said in Chapter One, Aldus' PageMaker is in our opinion the premier page layout tool for the Macintosh. It is the only one we recommend. PageMaker is a sophisticated electronic layout board bringing many of the features common to expensive computer-aided publishing systems to the desktop publishing arena. It is easy enough for someone with no prior pasteup experience to learn and use, yet powerful enough for skilled designers to use for complex and creative page layouts.

Copy can be created in any of the current Macintosh word processors and placed directly into a PageMaker layout. Likewise, artwork created in MacPaint or MacDraw can be placed in the layout and then proportionately resized or cropped to the dimensions you've established for the publication. Once the material is positioned on the page, it can be repositioned by simply picking it up with the mouse cursor and laying it down somewhere else.

In order to suit all measurement tastes, PageMaker supports rulers in three different scales: inches, metric, and picas. You can choose to view your page in any of five sizes and make changes to any part of it in any of these views. You can see the entire page layout by viewing a mini-page that fits in the center of the PageMaker window or you can zoom in closer on areas of the page in increments of 50 percent and 70 percent of actual size. You can also view portions of the page in its actual size or even zoom in to a 200 percent enlargement of the page to make minute adjustments to suit your tastes. PageMaker's rulers automatically scale themselves to accurately represent page dimensions at any of these views.

We will show you further uses of PageMaker in Chapters Three and Six.

The LaserWriter and PostScript

The Apple LaserWriter has been called Apple's "most powerful computer." It can be thought of either as a computer or as a sophisticated and highly programmable copy machine. It uses the same internal parts as the Canon Personal Copier series. However, Apple added both a computer and memory to this laser copier technology and modified it in many ways.

When you tell Microsoft Word or PageMaker to print your document, the document is translated into a *page description* programming language called PostScript. The computer built into the LaserWriter understands this language and uses it to create the page image that is printed. This all happens without your needing to know a word of the programming language or how to program—it is automatic.

If you wish to program in PostScript, you can, and we talk about that shortly. First, however, you need to know more fundamental aspects of the LaserWriter, such as the differences between the LaserWriter and the LaserWriter Plus and what you need to have on your disk if you plan to use someone else's LaserWriter.

The LaserWriter and LaserWriter Plus

The differences between these two machines are largely a matter of the number of fonts each has built into the machine's read-only memory (ROM). You should realize that, for the purposes of laser printing from either a LaserWriter or a LaserWriter Plus, each type style is considered a separate font. That is, Times is one font, Times Italic is a different font; Times Bold and Times Bold Italic are also different fonts. Considered this way, there are thirteen fonts built into the LaserWriter and thirty-five built into the LaserWriter Plus (see Figures 2-2 and 2-3).

Courier
Courier Oblique
Courier Bold
Courier Bold Oblique

Helvetica
Helvetica Oblique
Helvetica Bold
Helvetica Bold Oblique

Times Roman
Times Italic
Times Bold
Times Bold Italic

Symbol: ∩ ⊇ ♠ ℘ ↔
♥ ⌐ ℜ √ Φ Π ∃ Σ ◊ ↓
© ∅ © ⌋ ® ⌊ ® ™ ™ ℵ

Figure 2-2. Fonts Built into the LaserWriter.

Both printers have 1.5 megabytes of memory and both accept from two to six downloadable fonts, available from a number of companies. The most refined fonts are from Adobe Systems of Palo Alto, the creators of both PostScript and the ROM-resident fonts in the LaserWriter and Laser-Writer Plus. The fonts Adobe builds and markets are licensed versions of the same fonts available to conventional typesetters from the type libraries of companies like Mergenthaler, International Typeface Corporation (ITC) and Letraset. Adobe plans to release twenty-five new downloadable type-faces each quarter.

ITC Avant Garde Book
ITC Avant Garde Book Oblique
ITC Avant Garde Demi
ITC Avant Garde Demi Oblique

Helvetica Narrow
Helvetica Narrow Oblique
Helvetica Narrow Bold
Helvetica Narrow Bold Oblique

New Century Schoolbook Roman
New Century Schoolbook Italic
New Century Schoolbook Bold
New Century Schoolbook Bold Italic

Palatino Roman
Palatino Italic
Palatino Bold
Palatino Bold Italic

ITC Bookman Light
ITC Bookman Light Italic
ITC Bookman Demi
ITC Bookman Demi Italic

ITC Zapf Chancery Medium Italic
ITC Zapf Dingbats: ✗ ➡ ✎ ☿
❋ ☙ ✍ ➏ → ✒ ➥ ➦ ✆ ✃
❝ ❞ ✳ □ ○ ⟶ ✂ ✈ ✉ ✔

Figure 2-3. Additional Fonts Built into the LaserWriter Plus.

USING SOMEONE ELSE'S LASER WRITER

If you plan to use a LaserWriter but don't own one, you will need to "laserize" your System disk. You must do this to prepare documents for printing on the LaserWriter whether you're working from home or in an office near the LaserWriter you will use to print.

First off, the Chooser desk accessory must be installed in the System file so it is available from the menu. Chooser enables you to select a LaserWriter already connected to the Macintosh via AppleTalk (which is discussed later in this chapter). If you are still using the earlier Choose Printer desk accessory from Apple, make sure you get the newer Chooser from your Apple dealer.

The LaserWriter and LaserPrep print drivers—and, if you're using PageMaker, Aldus Prep—must be in the System Folder of the disk (see Figure 2-4). These files load the LaserWriter with special PostScript commands that Apple and Aldus have put together specifically to enable printing of Macintosh documents on the LaserWriter.

Using Font/DA Mover, you must install the Macintosh screen fonts for the equivalent LaserWriter fonts you'll use. If you are going to prepare publications for printing on the LaserWriter you will need to specify from Character Formats (in Microsoft Word) or the Fonts menu (in MacWrite) which laser fonts you wish to use. To do this, these fonts must be installed in the System file of the disk you plan to develop documents on or print from.

You can acquire these print drivers, the Chooser desk accessory, Font/DA Mover, and laser fonts from several sources: friends with a LaserWriter, your nearest Apple dealer, or the business whose LaserWriter you plan to use.

You should also prepare a set of traveling diskettes to take with you to an offsite LaserWriter; one diskette containing a small system file and the program (like Word or PageMaker) you're using to print from and another diskette with your document files.

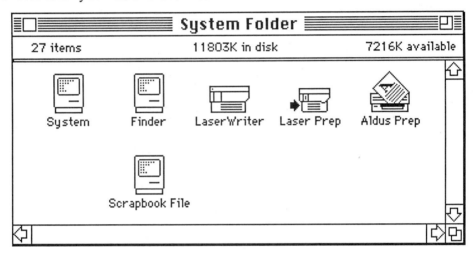

Figure 2-4. Files Required to Print with a LaserWriter.

PostScript

You don't really need to know very much about PostScript to do desktop publishing. However, a little background information may prove interesting.

PostScript is Adobe Systems' powerful, device-independent, page description language. It is used by Macintosh desktop publishing programs to describe each page to the LaserWriter so it can be printed. By *device independent* we mean that any printer—and there are several besides the Laser-Writer—which uses PostScript can print your document. This includes the high-resolution image setters from Allied Linotype Corporation—the

Linotronic 100 and Linotronic 300—which print with resolutions of 1,200 lines per inch and 2,400 lines per inch, respectively.

Instead of using optics to create a duplicate image of an original as you would with a copier, PostScript and the LaserWriter's electronics replace the copier's optics to create the image from scratch. Every black dot that goes onto the page is told how to get there by PostScript. Every curve in every letter "S," every crossed "t" and dotted "i" is described in PostScript. PostScript, as a programming language, passes instructions to the computer in the LaserWriter, which, in turn, creates an image of your page in memory. This image is then transferred electronically onto paper by the laser copying mechanism.

This is what happens when you send a document to be printed on the LaserWriter: the program you're using—Microsoft Word, for example —invokes the LaserWriter print driver that takes each line of type from your page and automatically writes a program in PostScript to describe the exact location on the page where the text is to be printed as well as its typeface, type size and style. If your publication contains illustrations from MacDraw or MacPaint, these too are described in terms PostScript can manipulate.

If you should ever want to see what a PostScript file looks like, simply press [Command] [F] immediately after you press "OK" in the Print Dialog Box of any Macintosh program (providing the Macintosh you are using is connected and ready to print on the LaserWriter). This will cause the PostScript file to be written on your disk. PostScript files created this way are stored with the filename PostScript or, when doing this from PageMaker, as PostScript1, PostScript2, and so on. You can open these files from MacWrite and take a look.

PROGRAMMING IN POSTSCRIPT

Programming in PostScript is fairly easy to learn and gives you the power to create your own special effects or complete page images. As in the Forth programming language, PostScript statements are assembled on a stack with the last item placed on the stack processed first. PostScript statements can be grouped into procedures and later called as part of the PostScript program. As a programming language it can handle anything most programming languages can, such as arrays, strings, Booleans, and variables. In addition to this, however, it is a graphics programming language so whatever you tell it to do will end up being drawn on the page, whether it is a simple shaded box, a line of text or a complete new typeface of your own design.

A SIMPLE POSTSCRIPT PROGRAM

You will find below an extremely simple program that, when dumped to the LaserWriter, will take the word "typography" and print it at a 45° angle across the page. You can type this into any word processing program on the Macintosh, save it as text-only and download it to the LaserWriter using Adobe's Font Downloader (available free from any authorized Apple dealer). The results of this program are shown in Figure 2-5.

/Times findfont 12 scalefont setfont	Selects 12 point Times as the font.
/inch {72 mul} def	Defines "inch" as a procedure.
gsave	Saves the current graphics state on the stack.
3.75 inch 7.25 inch moveto	Sets the location on the page to print using "inch."
45 rotate	Sets the angle of rotation.
(typography) show	Defines the word to be printed.
grestore	Restores the current graphics state.
showpage	Directs the LaserWriter to print.

Figure 2-5. "Typography" at a 45° Angle Printed with PostScript.

If you wish to know more about the LaserWriter and PostScript, see the Recommended Reading section at the end of this book.

The AppleTalk Personal Network

AppleTalk is what connects a Macintosh to a LaserWriter. Although it may look like a simple cable connecting computer and printer, it is the gateway through which a complete desktop publishing communication network may be developed. Writers, editors, and graphic designers can all be hooked up on the same network, and share copy and artwork. This can lead to a very creative and efficient desktop publishing environment.

The AppleTalk Personal Network may connect as few as two devices or as many as thirty-two, including computers, file servers, and printers.

Over a distance of up to 300 meters (approximately 1,000 feet), AppleTalk enables these devices to communicate with one another at a much greater speed than normal telecommunications. Hooking it up simply involves connecting the devices together with AppleTalk connection boxes. Apple-Talk is also one of the most inexpensive ways to connect personal computers in a local area network (LAN). Each device to be connected costs only about fifty dollars, compared with hundreds or even thousands of dollars for other LANs.

Let's take a closer look at how AppleTalk is installed.

Installing AppleTalk

First, you should understand that AppleTalk cables and connectors connect your Macintosh to a LaserWriter (see Figure 2-6). They are simple enough to connect. However, you should make sure you have the proper connectors. The connector for a Macintosh 512K is different from the one used for a Macintosh Plus. Your Apple dealer will help you in choosing the correct set-up.

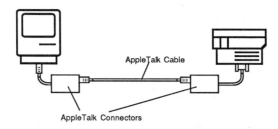

Figure 2-6. Macintosh Connected to a LaserWriter via AppleTalk.

When you first install the connectors and cabling between your Macintosh and LaserWriter, you'll notice that you use only one of the slots on the connection box. The remaining slot is available for expansion and, as we've said, you can connect up to thirty-one Macintoshes (or other computers) on the same AppleTalk network accessing a single LaserWriter. Your investment in the LaserWriter can quickly pay for itself as you add more users in an office environment.

You continue to add Macintoshes or file servers (you'll learn more about those shortly) and LaserWriters as needed. Simply connect a cable to the remaining end of a connection box and connect the other end to the Macintosh or LaserWriter. Continue this way until all devices are connected to the network. Just make sure the network is linear and not circular; that is, the network should be assembled as if it were in a straight line and should not come together in a loop. The cable with an X in Figure 2-7 would have made the network circular. Apple provides plenty of detailed information along with the cables and connectors to set it all up. In our experience, AppleTalk is about the easiest network there is to install.

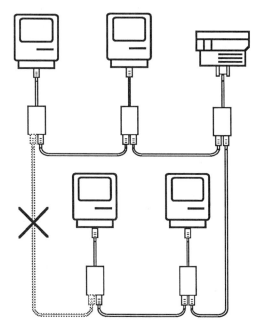

Figure 2-7. Linear AppleTalk Network.

Possible Network Configurations

Now let's look at some ways you could configure an AppleTalk Personal Network for desktop publishing. Let's say you've teamed up with another writer and have just decided to put out a newsletter using two Macintosh computers and a LaserWriter. This is perhaps the simplest of all possible configurations. You simply connect both Macintoshes with AppleTalk connectors to the LaserWriter (see Figure 2-8). You can be busy at work with your Mac in your office and your partner can be busily writing away in his or hers. When you want to print something, you simply pull down the File menu on the program you're using and select print. Later, when your partner wants to print something, he or she can do the same. Neither of you has to leave your office. If the printer's tied up it will tell you so and you can print later.

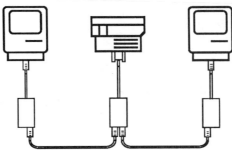

Figure 2-8. Two Macs and a LaserWriter on AppleTalk.

Another situation might be this: suppose you're an art director who is just getting an ad agency off the ground and you've decided to do most of your development using the desktop publishing system recommended in this book. You've hired a copywriter, a graphics designer and an account representative. You've decided to invest in a Macintosh Plus for everyone and a LaserWriter Plus and two 20 Mb hard drives—one for your Mac and another for the account representative's. You start off without AppleTalk but soon enough the writer and the graphic designer get tired of flipping floppies from one drive to another and you get tired of having everyone come in to your office to use your Mac to print things on the LaserWriter.

So you decide to connect everyone up to the LaserWriter with Apple-Talk—easy enough (see Figure 2-9). With the use of a file server, all users on the network can share that forty megabytes of hard drive storage and peace will finally reign in your budding ad agency once again.

Network File Servers

With a network file server you can share storage resources and, in some cases, even programs, among Macintoshes on the same AppleTalk Personal Network. If you want to use a file on someone else's hard drive, that disk appears on your Macintosh as a separate icon. You double-click the icon with the mouse pointer and you can use the storage device as if it were directly connected to your Macintosh even though it may be two offices away.

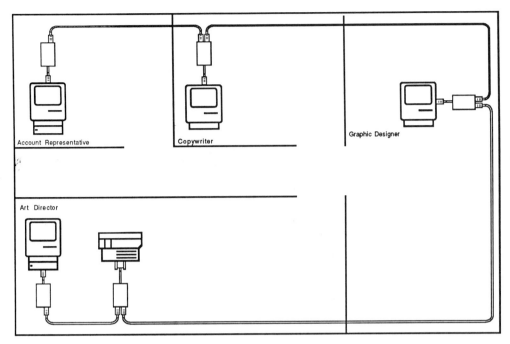

Figure 2-9. A More Complex Appletalk Network.

Some file servers are hardware based, like the 3Server from 3Com Corporation, and are connected to AppleTalk as a separate device. Others, like MacServe from Infosphere and HyperNet from General Computer Company, are software packages that are installed on individual Macintoshes and operate in the background, leaving you free to do more important work in the foreground. While you exercise your artistic freedom with MacPaint, the file server hums along minding its own business. When you decide to save your work on someone else's hard drive or fetch another document, the file server comes into action and enables you to do this.

The performance of a file server is completely transparent to you; storage space on a remote hard drive looks to you like just another disk icon on your Macintosh desktop or another file in the directory.

What's Next

You are ready now to learn the details of the desktop publishing process. You should have a computer system at your disposal in one of the configurations discussed in this chapter, and you should also have the software tools you need available; at the least you'll need Microsoft Word and PageMaker.

As mentioned in Chapter One, it is not the purpose of this book to provide a complete tutorial on how to use these individual software products. By now you should have looked over the instruction manuals for these products, tried them out, and completed the tutorials that accompany them.

The first time through the book you don't need to be thinking about your own publication; just follow along with our example. Once you've mastered the fundamentals, you can turn your hand to whatever you want, from an invoice to the Great American Novel, using this book as a guide.

Designing Your Publication

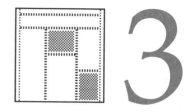

3

In this chapter you will learn about:

- How to develop a concept for your publication
- How to assess and understand your audience
- How to use PageMaker and MacDraw as creative tools
- How to put together a publication template

In publishing, as in other fields, thorough planning and good design is crucial to a successful product. You can't build an efficient and pleasing house without a good architect, no matter how good the carpenters are. In the same way, no matter how hard you work on the details of a publication, if the overall design is not right, your publication will not successfully project your message.

What constitutes good design and how do you go about achieving it? There are many aspects to the problem and there is no universally accepted right way to do things. Design is an art, not a science. Nevertheless, a step-by-step approach and some general guidelines will go a long way in ensuring a good design.

In this chapter we begin the adventure of developing the design for our newsletter. As you follow along, you will learn about the importance of early development of the overall concept for a newsletter: issues of audience, editorial content, art direction and publication size. We will show you how to create the initial master page layout (the template), how to design a logo and nameplate for this layout, and finally how to add those design elements to the master that will remain constant from page to page. You will also see how to use PageMaker and MacDraw together to achieve the design. By following the steps of the process, you'll come to understand the general outlines of the design process and will be able to modify them to fit your particular circumstances.

Developing the Concept

Before you can sit down to the nuts and bolts of design—selecting fonts, deciding on the column widths, and so forth—you must develop the overall concept of your publication. Start out by trying to define for yourself exactly what purpose your publication is to serve. Our newsletter, *Audio Image,* was born out of a need for reviews of compact discs from a specific point of view: that of the audiophile seeking a dramatic listening experience. The available literature did not address this point of view and so we began developing the concept for a quarterly newsletter. We took the idea to several high-end stereo stores, talking to both customers and salespeople. Nearly everyone gave us positive feedback; the idea for such a newsletter was well received.

Of course, you may not need to worry about the issues of audience. If your boss gives you a handwritten report and tells you he needs a desktop published version by three that afternoon, you don't need to worry about market research. However, if you follow through the conceptual development for *Audio Image,* you'll be able to appreciate the importance of global planning in any publication.

Since we already owned the requisite desktop publishing tools—an Apple Macintosh Plus, a LaserWriter, a 20 Mb hard disk drive, PageMaker, Microsoft Word, MacDraw and MacPaint—we decided to put them to the test and develop a premier issue. Could the Macintosh-based desktop publishing system enable us to create a stylish and well-informed newsletter for our specific market? We decided to go ahead with our idea and test-market the first issue through a number of stereo shops and record stores specializing in compact discs. Our first idea was to offer the newsletter by subscription only, but we wanted some idea of how it was received locally before investing in the advertising budget necessary to generate subscription sales.

Once we decided to go ahead with the newsletter concept, we had a number of preliminary decisions to make. We had to deepen the focus on who our audience was, determine the page size, decide how many pages our first issue would hold, and create a template for the newsletter into which we would later place articles and illustrations. Based on the needs of our intended audience, we had to formulate guidelines for editorial content. These are tough decisions, sometimes requiring intensive research and speculation.

You need to make the same decisions whether you are producing a brochure, newsletter, technical manual, or sales flyer.

Issues of Audience

For any publication you need a clear perception of who your audience is and how your publication meets its needs. You can access available market research or conduct your own in order to define your audience as accurately as possible. Often, personal interviews with a sample of the people you plan to reach will suffice. And you need to take a look at other publications in the same field. All this is part of careful planning. The more advance work you do, the easier other steps in the desktop publishing process will be.

CLARIFYING THE SUBJECT MATTER

The initial market research for *Audio Image* showed that our audience would have to be the owners of high-end audiophile-class (expensive) stereo equipment. Their audio system would of course include a compact disc player. More than that, though, they would be seeking from that system an audio experience of dramatic proportions.

As with vinyl records, some discs are better prepared than others. Even all-digital discs have flaws in the recording, and some are more spectacular than others. At anywhere from $12 to $20 a disc, anyone on a budget can only afford to make a few mistakes. Collections can quickly become littered with inferior material. Our audience would be concerned with all of these issues, and there was no publication on the market that addressed them in as much depth as we would.

In developing a concept for your publication, you should carefully examine the subject matter. Do whatever you need to understand it as fully as possible. Conduct research, interview experts, and make lists of what you plan to communicate. From this, narrow down the focus of your subject so that you have a manageable publication concept that you know well enough to communicate to others.

MARKET RESEARCH

After careful analysis of the subject matter we conducted market research into who was buying compact discs and what kind of equipment they were using. We found that this was an extremely wide market. Most buyers were between twenty-five and forty years of age with an annual income of between $30,000 and $60,000. The equipment they used was of many types, both low end and high end, with a noticeable trend towards the high end. This group also tended to upgrade its equipment beginning approximately six months after the initial investment in compact disc technology. A number of personal interviews convinced us that the audience was, in fact, interested in disc quality and the re-creation of a spectacular psychoacoustic event in their own listening rooms.

LOOKING AT OTHER PUBLICATIONS

The last phase of audience assessment involved taking a look at the publications to which our imagined audience currently subscribed. These included *Stereo Review, Digital Audio, Audio, Opus, Gramophone, Stevenson Compact Disc Review Guide,* and a few others. Although the competition was tough in spots, we remained convinced that none of these publications addressed the same issues we would deal with, and that there was indeed a niche to be filled. We also took a careful look at the style and format of these publications so that the design we eventually came up with would fit within the perceived norms of our potential audience.

Editorial Content

Now that our audience was clearly defined, we could go on to develop guidelines for editorial content. What we have to say largely determines not only how we say it but how we present it visually on the page. As we said in Chapter Two, establishing guidelines for editorial content and art direction simplifies decisions about what kind of material to solicit and what to reject.

From the audience analysis, we determined that the typical *Audio Image* reader would be interested in technical criticism of compact discs. The reviews should stress how the original recording was mixed at the recording studio, how it imaged on a high-end stereo system, and—if it was originally an analog recording—how successfully it made the transfer to the digital format. The reader would also be interested in particular disc manufacturers that demonstrated a continuing level of excellence. Finally, the reader would want to know more about how specific recordings were made and how recording studios achieve certain special effects. The reader would not be interested in performance reviews or specific artist interviews (which abound in many other popular publications), nor in ways to make equipment purchase decisions.

Based on our analysis of the research, *Audio Image's* editorial content consists of technical critiques of only the best compact discs, interviews with recording engineers, in-depth coverage of disc manufacturers and studios, and some filler items addressing psychoacoustics and ancillary news items related to compact disc technology. By clearly defining our editorial content and narrowing our focus in this way, we are in a much better position to make editorial and design decisions about layout and about how to select illustrations and material submitted to the newsletter.

Art Direction

Art direction goes hand in hand with editorial content. Setting guidelines for art direction is also much easier with a clear concept of our audience. In large-circulation publications, evaluating editorial content and guiding art direction are in fact two separate jobs handled by different people. In desktop publishing, this may still be the case but more often you'll handle both jobs yourself.

The general design of *Audio Image* continues to evolve throughout this chapter and the rest of the book. Artwork will include simple charts that show an evaluation of compact discs, art captured from liner notes and compact disc covers, and small pieces of clip art we feel are appropriate to supporting our editorial content.

In designing *Audio Image* we decide on a nameplate that spreads across the top of the first page and a three-column layout for most pages of the publication. Once these are established we'll use them from issue to issue.

We have definite experience in art direction and publication design; you may not. If you are in the least bit concerned about how professional your publication will look, or how you go about setting guidelines for art direction, you may want to enlist the help of a professional graphics designer who knows desktop publishing and how to get the most out of these tools. When you've read through the rest of the book you'll have a better sense of what kind of help to seek and where you need it most.

Publication Size

Once you have a clear concept of your audience, editorial content, and art direction, you are able to choose the physical size of your publication. Publications are printed in many shapes and sizes. Certainly the most common is 8.5 by 11 inches but many books and technical manuals use smaller page dimensions. Paperback books most often measure 4.25 by 7 inches, trade paperbacks are commonly 5.25 by 8 inches and the page size for most Macintosh manuals (a typical size for today's microcomputer manuals) measure 7.5 by 9 inches. All of these publication sizes are easily accommodated by the desktop publishing system used in this book.

Working in the Macintosh environment with a LaserWriter, the most common page sizes are letter size (8.5 by 11 inches) and legal size (8.5 by 14 inches). The LaserWriter cannot, however, print all the way out to the edges of these pages. In fact, for letter size, the LaserWriter can image a space measuring 8 by 10.92 inches, centered on the page and for legal size, the *imageable* area is 6.75 by 13 inches, centered on the page.

Knowing these maximum image sizes, we decided to play it safe and keep our image sizes within the limits of the LaserWriter's page size.

Given our market research and knowing how we plan to distribute this first issue, we've estimated an initial press run of two thousand. This doesn't have much to do with how we go about designing *Audio Image,* but it helps to know as much as we can in advance. If we decide to seek outside help from designers, or when we go to talk to the printer, we have a ballpark figure everyone can use as a point of reference.

Your publication may have different requirements. Look around and see what common sizes there are for other publications of the type you're doing. If it's a brochure, collect sample brochures. If it's a paperback novel, look at other paperbacks. Also, if you stick to a common page size, you can ensure that when you go to the printer, he or she won't have to make any special (and perhaps costly) effort to accommodate your job.

Creating the Initial
Page Layout

We are now able to begin creating our initial page layout. We may make other design decisions later but before we go on to anything else, we want to determine how large an area we have in which to place our text and graphics. We need to design a logo for *Audio Image* and establish our column widths. Typefaces need to be selected for both headlines and text. If we make these basic design decisions before we go on to creating copy or art for the newsletter, these other tasks are easier to plan for.

An overriding design principle guiding our design decisions is to keep it simple. Nothing looks more amateurish than a complex design executed by the inexperienced. Only the most advanced designers can create a successful complex design. By keeping our layout simple we can deliver a product to our readers that is easy on the eye and keeps the information instantly accessible.

The Hands-On Experience

This is the first time in the book where you actually follow along and do what we do. So let's take a moment to tell you how this works.

If you have a Macintosh desktop publishing system similar to what is recommended in Chapter Two, you should easily be able to duplicate what we will demonstrate in this chapter. We assume you've spent some time learning how the Macintosh works, how to load disks, start up programs, and such. If you haven't, please do so before you go on.

This chapter provides detailed hands-on experience using PageMaker and MacDraw to design and develop the initial page layout for *Audio Image*. We assume you've read through the manuals and have worked through the tutorials accompanying each.

We don't use numbered steps or anything like that. We simply describe actions directly in the text. You'll find the narrative contains both instructional and commentary material.

Determining the Image Area

Knowing that we want to use an 8.5 by 11-inch letter-sized page, we can easily calculate the maximum image area within which the text and graphics will appear. *Audio Image* is a four-page, double-sided publication— a front, back, and two inside pages. Working with PageMaker, we can set up page margins that provide an image area well within these boundaries.

STARTING PAGEMAKER

If you decide to duplicate our process, you should make sure the PageMaker icon is represented among the programs shown on your Macintosh desktop. If you're using a system with two floppy drives, the PageMaker program disk must be in one of the drives. If you're using a hard disk drive, make sure you have the folder or drawer open that contains PageMaker. Double-click the PageMaker icon. When it completes loading into memory and presents the menu bar, select "New..." from the File menu. PageMaker displays the "Page Setup" dialog box (see Figure 3-1).

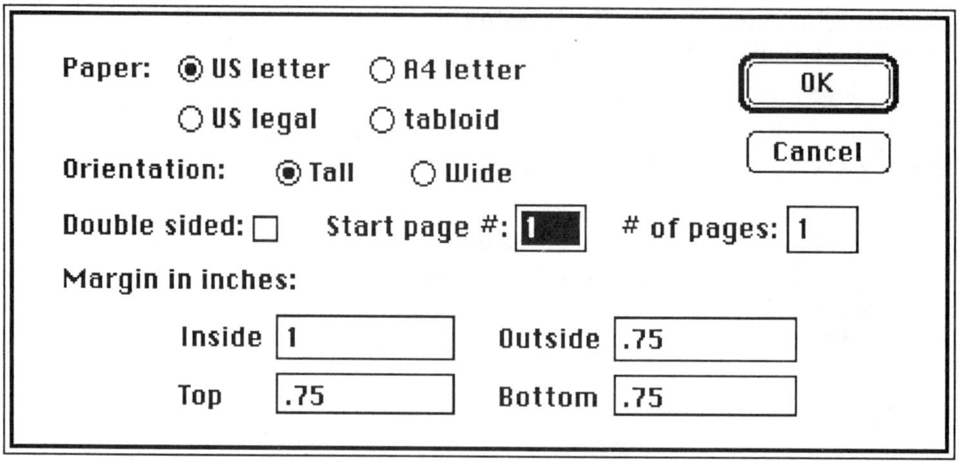

Figure 3-1. "Page Setup" Dialog Box in PageMaker.

SETTING PAGE MARGINS FOR *AUDIO IMAGE*

The first job we face is to establish our page size. PageMaker supplies preset values for each of the selectable items. Some of these we'll leave alone, others we'll change to suit our requirements.

The "Paper:" buttons give us four choices with "US letter" already selected. The other choices include standard "US legal-size" paper, "A4 letter"(a European paper size slightly larger than our own letter size), and "tabloid," which measures 11 by 17 inches. We'll accept the preset selection since that is the size we plan to use.

Likewise, we'll use the "Tall" orientation rather than "Wide." Choosing a wide page orientation in PageMaker turns a tall page on its side and is useful for producing brochures or sideways-formatted publications like the annual report shown in Chapter One.

Audio Image is a double-sided publication so, taking mouse in hand, we position the pointer on top of the "Double sided:" box and click once. This puts an "X" in the box to show our choice. This permits us to see the two inside pages facing each other anytime we wish to use PageMaker's "Show facing pages" feature.

"Start page #:" tells PageMaker which page number we would like it to start counting from when it automatically paginates the publication. If we had a separate title page we might type in "3" so our first page would be page three. *Audio Image* starts on page one so we'll leave the preset number alone.

However, we do plan more than one page, so we press [Tab] to move to the "# of pages:" box and type in "4."

The next move sets our page margins and thereby defines the space on the page within which we'll position our text and graphics. For *Audio Image* we decided on a page spread measuring 7.5 by 10 inches. This was an arbitrary decision based on examinations of several other newsletters we felt were typical of the type we wished to produce.

We [Tab] to the "Inside" box and type ".5" (point five). This inside margin corresponds to what is known as a gutter along the inside fold in a two-or-more page spread. With another publication we might add some space to the inside margin to create a gutter, but with *Audio Image* we only have a single fold so we're going to leave it at .5 and use the same half-inch measure for all our remaining margins as well.

We use the [Tab] key to move to the "Top" margin and again fill in ".5" to set the Top-of-page margin. We [Tab] to "Outside" and do the same for the outside margin. [Tab] again and we repeat this for the Bottom-of-page margin. This completes our page setup and functionally defines the page margins for our premier issue of *Audio Image*.

We click "OK" button (or press [Enter]) and PageMaker displays a blank mini-page that fits in the PageMaker window (see Figure 3-2). We'll use this page to do the initial design of *Audio Image's* template in PageMaker.

The dotted-line borders around the page represent the page margins we'll use throughout our development of *Audio Image*.

Take a careful look at this page, either in Figure 3-2 or on your screen if you're following along with the Mac. This is where all the elements of the page layout are assembled and where the publication begins to take shape. When we finish Chapter Six you will see that this now-empty page will be full of text and graphics ready to take to the printer.

Zooming In on the Page

We often use techniques that call for zooming in on the page to an "actual size" or a "200 percent view" of the page. Here is a quick way to do this.

What you see in Figure 3-2 is a representation of the page called "fit-in-window." To view the page at actual size (the best representation of what actually gets printed on the LaserWriter) you can choose "Actual size" from the Page menu or press [Command] [A] but this method is somewhat generic in its operation. It simply zooms into the center of the page at actual size from whatever view you've selected. If you want to look at a specific part of the page. [Command] [A] will not always show you that specific part.

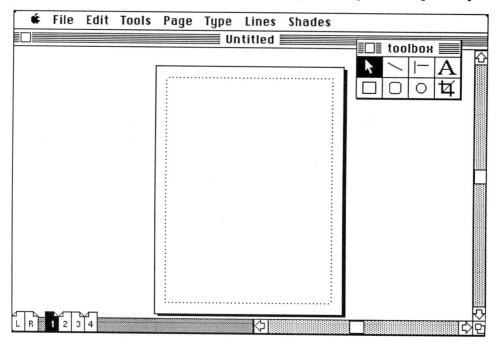

Figure 3-2. Fit-in-window Page (a Clean Slate).

Try this: draw a small box on the page and then zoom in to look at it in each of these views using the shortcut.

With the page still on your screen, expose the rulers by choosing "Show rulers" from the Tools menu. Now click on the square-corner tool in the Toolbox, position the crossbar so it lines up with the three-inch mark on the horizontal ruler and the one-inch marker on the vertical ruler and draw out a small box. Choose "Black" from the Shades menu and you have a small black box on your screen (see Figure 3-3).

Now press [Command] [A] to view the page in actual size. This will take you to an empty part of the page. Where's the box? Who knows? It could be anywhere. From this point you'd have to scroll up and down and sideways before you found the actual-size representation of the box you were looking for on the page. Press [Command] [F] to fit the page back in the window and get ready to learn a better way.

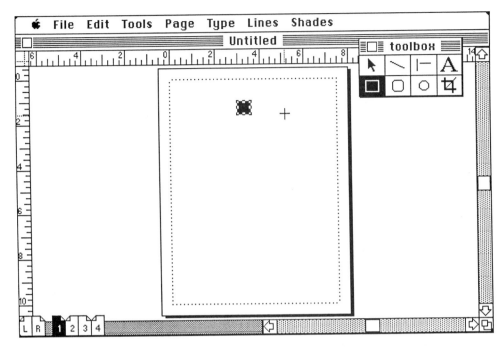

Figure 3-3. Small Black Box on the Page.

Click on the pointer in the Toolbox and position the pointer on top of the box. Hold down the [Command] key and click once. This takes you directly to an actual-size view of the box (see Figure 3-4). While you're here let's go one step further.

You will often make use of the 200 percent view of the page to make minute adjustments and refine your page layout. You could select "200 percent size" from the Page menu but why not try a short cut? Position the pointer on top of the box again and this time hold down both the [Option] and the [Command] keys at the same time and click. This shows you the box at twice its actual size (see Figure 3-5). Anytime you want to view the page in 200 percent size (from any other view) you can point at that part of the page, press [Option] [Command] and click to take you to that view.

To back out of these views simply press [Command] and click once—this takes you to actual size. Press [Command], click again—this takes you to Fit-in-window.

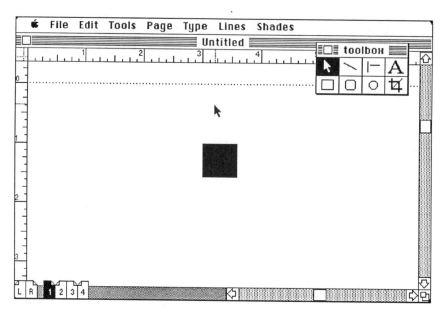

Figure 3-4. Not-so-small Box on the Page.

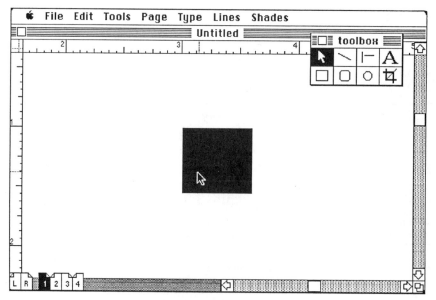

Figure 3-5. Black Box at 200 percent of Actual Size.

Removing Unwanted Page Elements

Whenever you have an element you don't want on the page (and this black box has nothing to do with *Audio Image*), simply position the pointer on top of the element—the black box in this case—click on it and press [Backspace] once. This is the best way to remove anything from the page that you don't want. If you've made a mistake or you've placed the wrong text on the page, simply select it by clicking on it and backspace to get rid of it. This is the way Aldus recommends you remove unwanted page elements.

Save as You Go

It's always a good practice to save our documents to disk as we go along. Now is a good time to save our document, to disk, with the name "Audio Image Layout" by choosing "Save As..." from the File menu. When the dialog box appears on the screen, we type in "Audio Image Layout" and click "OK" to save it. From then on, every ten minutes or so we choose "Save" from the File menu or, more conveniently, simply press [Command] [S] whenever we've achieved some effect we wouldn't want to repeat.

Now that we've learned a few tricks with PageMaker we're ready to design a logo and nameplate, set up columns, establish page numbers and otherwise flesh out the publication's template.

Designing a Logo and Nameplate

The name of the newsletter, *Audio Image*, needs to be shaped into what is known as a *logo*, short for *logotype*. The logo fits inside what is known as a nameplate, which may contain other enhancing art, the date of issue, a subtitle and edition number. Almost all publications use a logo or nameplate, whether they are plain or decorative; the name of any publication is presented as a logo on the cover or at least on the first page. The characters that form the name of the magazine are often boldfaced, oversized, hand-drawn in calligraphy, or given some sort of special effect that makes the name stand out from the body of the publication. The words *National Geographic* or *Time* are positioned on the covers and given the necessary emphasis to be used as the magazine's logo. With a magazine such as *Omni,* special typefaces were created to represent not only the logo but also the headers for various continuing columns throughout the publication.

The logo we had in mind for *Audio Image* is not as special as these, but we would still like it to stand out from the body of the text and create a memorable image in the reader's mind.

Using PageMaker as a Creative Tool

When we began the logo design process we knew we would want to try many different solutions to our design problem. As noted earlier, there is no one right solution to a graphic design problem. The designer, amateur or professional, tries to find the best solution among several alternatives. We wanted to look at several different variations of our potential logo.

You don't need to attempt each of these but we'll tell you exactly how we created our final choice so you can follow along.

DEVELOPING COMPS OF OUR LOGO

Comp is an abbreviated form of the word *composite,* used in graphic design circles to refer to sketches and preliminary pasteups developed to work out a creative design solution. They are not the final product but composite representations of the final art that show all the elements on a page but do not yet have the actual art or typesetting pasted onto them. However, with desktop publishing, your comps can look more like finals than they would using any other publishing method. In fact, more often than not, your comp ends up being your final art, since the typesetting and art are already in place the way you want them.

We saved our original Audio Image Layout document as another file called "logo comps," thus keeping our original for more formal use later and retaining the correct page dimensions for use in our comps document.

Then we selected "Page Setup" from the File menu and clicked the double-sided option off, which gave us four single-sided right-hand pages. We knew we would need more than four to play with so we chose "Insert page..." from the Page menu and clicked on "After current page" and repeated this three more times so we had a total of eight pages to work with.

We used these pages to mock up several different versions of our logo using both Helvetica and Times Roman typefaces, trying each in various combinations of upper and lower case as well as italic (see Figure 3-6).

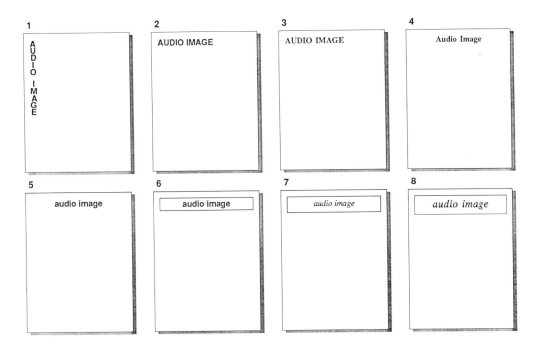

Figure 3-6. Logo Comps.

You can see how our ideas evolved. The first formulation was too ambitious and difficult to read. We tried two left-aligned examples, but became more satisfied with a centered logo. Nearly a dozen logo ideas were developed using various typefaces, sizes, and effects. Figure 3-6 shows the best of these.

PageMaker allows us to play with a number of solutions at once. Incorporating a sense of play and a certain amount of detachment into our work enables us to create enough ideas to have something worthwhile to choose from without losing the freedom to throw away what is useless. By using PageMaker as a tool for creativity, we can test any solution as many times and in as many ways as we like. We are not restricted by physically having to pasteup every idea that comes along.

We took a good look at our all-lowercase samples and felt this was a unique direction to pursue. We added a box, starting at an inch deep and continued adding a quarter inch at a time until we ended up with one measuring 1.5 inches. On a whim, we increased the type size of our last rendition from 48 points to 60 points and, with the type selected, chose Shadow from the Type menu. All along, we had printed out samples of each variation we tried. When we felt satisfied enough to look at the best of our ideas, we had PageMaker print all eight pages with the "Thumbnails" option selected in the "Print..." dialog box. PageMaker's thumbnails give us an instant platform from which we can choose any of several different ideas.

We had used these pages only to develop ideas. Finally satisifed with the results, we wanted to duplicate these efforts in the original document. We closed (and saved) the Logo Comps document, opened our original Audio Image Layout document, and returned there to finalize the logo.

Creating Our Preferred Logo

Once the Audio Image Layout document opens, we expose PageMaker's rulers by pressing [Command] [R]. If we work in PageMaker with the rulers exposed, we can use consistent measures and have a constant point of reference. Whenever we move the pointer (or any object) on the page, grey lines appear on the rulers to show the coordinates of our current position.

With our blank page on the screen (as originally shown in Figure 3-2), we can zoom in to actual size along the upper left part of the page near the inside margin.

CHOOSING TYPE SPECS

Choosing type is an important design decision. A general rule of thumb states that there should never be more than one or two different typefaces in a publication. Much can be done with a single typeface. We can achieve a consistent yet interesting look by simply mixing italic, boldface, and outlined characters within the same font. You should keep in mind that underlining is rarely used in a typeset publication—underlining is a characteristic of typing and not typesetting. After extensive experimenting we chose 60 point Times italic for our logo.

We want to set *Audio Image's* logo in 60 point Times, italicized and shadowed. To choose a typeface, we select the text tool from the Toolbox. Before we position the I-beam pointer on the page, we want to choose "Type Specs..." from the Type menu. We'll use a combination of pointing, scrolling, and clicking in the dialog box. Since the Times font is preselected, we'll keep that choice. We position the pointer on the bottom arrow of the size window, hold the mouse button down, and scroll until we see "60." We click on that number which enters it into the "Points" box. If we like, we can accomplish the same results by typing the number "60" into the box.

We italicize the font by positioning the pointer on top of the "Italic" box and clicking the mouse which shows our selection by putting an X in the box. We choose shadowing in the same way, by moving the pointer on top of the "Shadow" box and clicking the mouse to make the selection. The resulting type specs are shown in Figure 3-7.

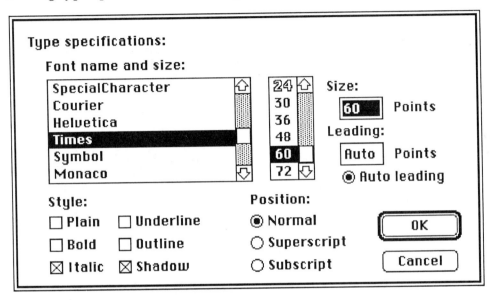

Figure 3-7. Type Specs for *Audio Image*.

The next thing is to choose "Align center" from the Type menu. Now our type is set up and ready to go.

To save time, we do this anytime we want to use a specific typeface, size and style. We set the type specs first, then position the I-beam pointer on the page and start typing.

There's one final detail before we start typing. When we place the I-beam pointer down on the page we want it to use the inside and outside margins in order to perfectly center align the text on the page. We choose "Column guides..." from the Tools menu. When the dialog box appears, we type "1" and press [Enter]. This sets up a single column within which all text can be positioned, using the complete width of the page. Had we not done this, our text would be placed arbitrarily on the page wherever we placed the I-beam pointer.

Recall from reading the PageMaker manual that all text flows between column guides. Without at least one column set up, PageMaker does not know what dimensions to use for placing text.

TYPING THE TEXT

Now we position the I-beam pointer next to the left margin, click once to position it on the page and type "audio image." The window automatically scrolls to the right as we type into the outer edge. The screen representation of the words "audio image" may look rough-hewn to you (see Figure 3-8). That's because there is no screen font available for 60 point Times and the Macintosh has to analytically scale the font to show it on the screen. There is no cause for concern; when it prints on the LaserWriter, it looks fine.

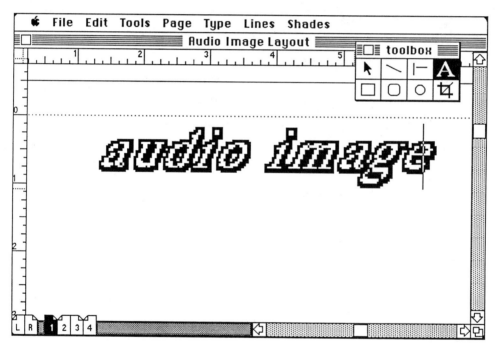

Figure 3-8. Typing "Audio Image" in Actual Size.

DRAWING THE NAMEPLATE BORDER

Now that we have the type on the page, we need to draw the 7.5 by 1.5-inch border. We scroll the window back to the left to see the corner where the inside and top margins come together.

We select the square-corner tool from the Toolbox and position the crossbar to align with the 0 (zero), 0 (zero) point on the horizontal ruler. We press the mouse button, drag down to the 1.5 mark on the vertical ruler, and continue drawing across to fill the page (see Figure 3-9). We continue drawing out to the right until the border aligns with the outside margin. When it's lined up with the 7.5 and 1.5 marks on the horizontal and vertical rulers respectively, we release the mouse button.

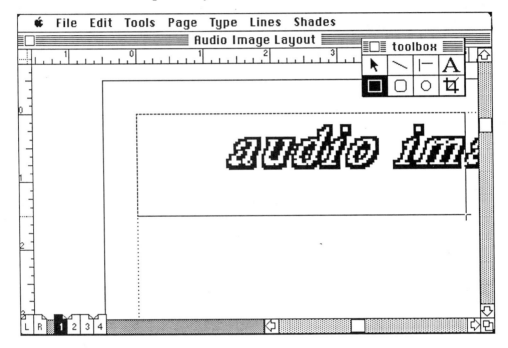

Figure 3-9. Dragging a Rectangle to Form a Border.

CENTERING THE LOGO WITHIN THE BORDER

Now we scroll the window back towards the middle of the screen so the words "audio image" are centered in view. We click on the pointer in the Toolbox to get the arrow pointer back and position the pointer on top of the words. We press the mouse button and, looking at the grey lines in the vertical ruler that show the top and bottom text dimensions, drag the text until it is centered vertically within the border (see Figure 3-10). This completes the creation of our preferred *Audio Image* logo, a printed version of which is shown in Figure 3-11.

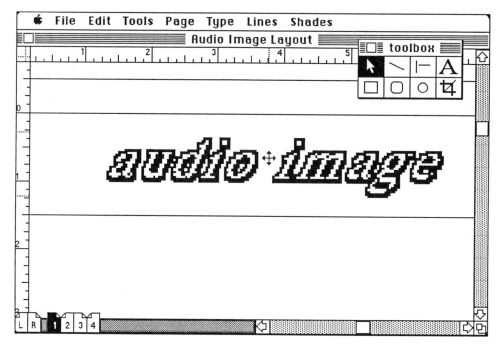

Figure 3-10. Text Centered within Border.

audio image

Figure 3-11. Our Logo and Nameplate Thus Far.

We were happy with the typestyle, size and shadowing of our image and its border but, after looking at the sample from the LaserWriter, we felt it was somewhat plain. Wanting to add something to our nameplate that would make it more visually interesting, we went into MacDraw to create some enhancing line art.

Feel Free to Abandon an Unworkable Solution

Just as with our logo comps, we were not satisfied with our first attempt at creating a backdrop for our logo and fleshing out our nameplate. We decided to try something else.

This is one of the true advantages to working with a desktop publishing system. Since everything occurs in an electronic environment and nothing ends up on paper (or has to be pasted down) until you print it on the LaserWriter, you're free to try as many solutions as possible. Using tools like MacDraw you can create an image in a few minutes, place it in PageMaker, print out a test sheet (or carefully examine it on the screen) and judge quickly whether the idea is taking the direction you want. If you don't like what's happening you can toss out that idea and try another approach. Nothing is written in stone (or even on paper); you should feel free to abandon an unworkable solution and try something else.

THE FIRST TRY

Knowing better than to make the nameplate very complex, we kept it simple and tried out a few uncomplicated shapes at first. The first idea we had was to make a simple representation of a compact disc, duplicate it several times, and create an image that made it appear as if several compact discs were rolling behind our logo. We'll describe this process briefly but don't try to duplicate our efforts, which were not the final image. We only want to show how one approach can evolve into another.

We opened MacDraw, our drafting tool of choice, and drew a circle. Within that circle we drew two smaller circles to complete our graphic representation of the compact disc, as if it were standing on edge. Then, with all the circle objects selected, we grouped the circles into a single object to easily manipulate the image in the MacDraw window. We made duplicates of the single compact disc image and, using the grid to keep them aligned, began placing them on top of one another, separating each object by one, then two, then three grid spaces until the final disc representation emerged as a whole (see Figure 3-12). The intention here was to show a single disc emerging from a backdrop of many—much as our reviews would single out the best discs from many also-rans.

We quit MacDraw and launched PageMaker by opening our Audio Image Layout document. We then selected "Place..." from the File menu and picked up the art from MacDraw that we planned to drop in behind the words, "Audio Image." As directly imported from MacDraw, the drawing was too large to fit neatly within the border and settle comfortably behind the logo. PageMaker, however, makes very fine and proportionate reductions of any MacPaint or MacDraw image. By holding down the shift key and grabbing the lower right handle with the pointer, we were able to shrink the image down to fit snugly behind the words. After a few minor adjustments, made by zooming in to both actual size and 200 percent enlargement, we printed out the results (see Figure 3-13).

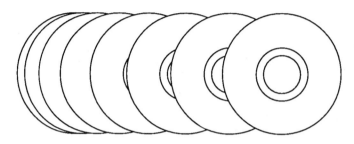

Figure 3-12. A Backdrop Image for the Nameplate Created with MacDraw.

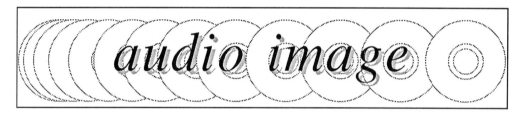

Figure 3-13. Backdrop Image Placed behind Logo in PageMaker.

Our design objectives were not achieved with this image. Where had we gone wrong? Why was the image not working? To us it seemed too large an image for the page; it dominated the nameplate and, in general, the eye had a difficult time scanning the image or taking it in as a whole.

We felt we had attempted to create a complex image in a situation where our experience was limited. There is nothing wrong with this. We often have to try out many different solutions before we get the right look—something that appeals to our eye. Taking into account, however, that this entire process, from start to finish, had taken less than half an hour, we abandoned the idea as unworkable and went on to try something else.

Achieving an Acceptable Image

Recalling that the first rule of thumb was to keep it simple, we rethought the idea we wanted to get across to our readers using this logo. We were talking about *audio imaging* and *sound space;* the publication had more to do with helping our audience re-create a spectacular sonic event in their listening rooms than simply playing a compact disc to achieve it. It had to do with recording techniques and how the record was mixed; engineering and room dimensions; psychoacoustics and the psychology of sound perception.

This was a broad and sweeping topic. How could we imply this in the logo? At this point, we actually went away from the Macintosh, took pencil and sketchpad in hand and drew out some simple lines, sketching the logotype for *Audio Image* over the lines and viewing this from different angles. We knew we had it this time. A few simple lines drawn in perspective from a vanishing point would imply the spaciousness we wanted. Not letting our excitement run away with us, we returned to MacDraw and sketched the image you see in Figure 3-14.

Figure 3-14. Vanishing Point Lines Drawn in MacDraw.

DRAWING THE VANISHING POINT LINES

This image is simple enough that we could have drawn the lines in black using PageMaker's diagonal lines tool. However, learning from our previous experience, we knew we wanted the lines grey so we could give the logo the best chance to emerge from the background. MacDraw allows us to make the pen color any shade, and MacDraw's snap grid allows us to give the lines uniform spacing.

We start up MacDraw from the Macintosh desktop. As soon as the window is displayed we choose "Show Rulers" from the Layout menu. (If you turn on "Show Size" from the Layout menu, you'll be able to follow along exactly as we draw the image.) The resulting vanishing point line is larger than the image area for a single page in MacDraw at 100 percent, so we need to reduce the page image slightly to get it to fit on the page. With the LaserWriter we can reduce the page to 95 percent by choosing "Page Setup..." from the File menu. (If you do not have a LaserWriter and haven't laserized your disk, as recommended in Chapter Two, you can simply double the page size by choosing "Drawing Size..." from the Layout menu.) We click in the square to the right of the current page representation to add another page. We can choose "Hide Page Breaks" from the Layout menu if we don't want the page boundary upsetting the continuity.

We choose the diagonal lines tool and position the crossbar pointer on the page at a point equivalent to the one-eighth-inch mark on the horizontal ruler and the seven-eighths-inch mark on the vertical ruler. Then we press the mouse button and drag out a 2.87-inch diagonal line so it rests at a position on the page where the rulers show grey at the 2.5-inch mark (horizontal and vertical) and release the mouse button (see Figure 3-15).

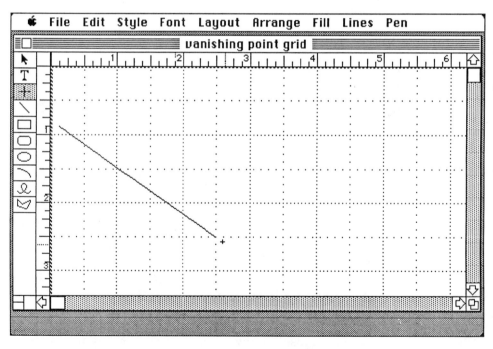

Figure 3-15. A 2.87-Inch Diagonal Line in MacDraw.

Each line in the image begins at the same point (the vanishing point). By pressing the [Command] key and clicking once we automatically reselect the diagonal lines tool. Positioning it again at the same point where the first line begins, we press the mouse button and drag a 4.10-inch diagonal line out so it aligns with the 3.875-inch mark on the horizontal ruler and the 2.5-inch mark on the vertical ruler (see Figure 3-16).

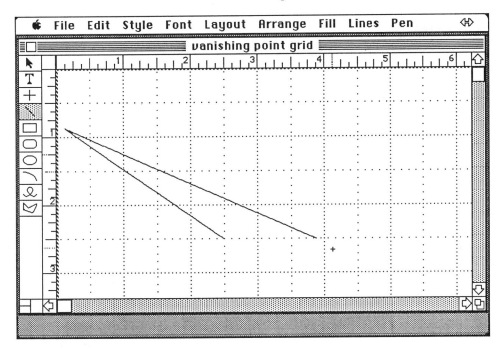

Figure 3-16. A 4.10-Inch Diagonal Line in MacDraw

We can repeat this procedure for each line, positioning the crossbar pointer at the same point each time and dragging the line out near the 2.5-inch line on the grid.

You don't need to do this but just to make sure we were getting it right, we saved our drawing, quit MacDraw for a minute, and dipped into PageMaker to make a copy of the frame we had drawn around our logo area. Then we returned to MacDraw and pasted the frame on top of our vanishing point lines, carefully positioning the border so it aligned with the origin of our vanishing point. Knowing we could crop the image to fit later using the cropping tool, in PageMaker, we quickly drew the lines out beyond the frame of the box just to make sure they would fit snug when we placed the image into our Audio Image Layout. We removed the border when we finished drawing the lines. The remaining grid points and lengths are shown in Figure 3-17.

As long as each line begins at the same point, you should be able to duplicate our efforts, using this illustration as a guide. Each line length is stated in inches as shown with MacDraw's "Show Size" feature turned on.

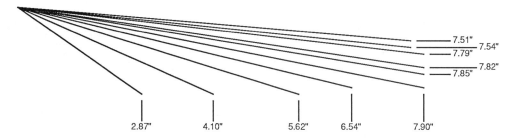

Figure 3-17. Vanishing Point Drawing with Line Lengths in Inches.

If you are doing this as we describe it, you should have noticed by now that each time you position the end of the line somewhere in the drawing space it tends to jump from point to point. This is MacDraw's invisible snap grid in action. The preset grid has snap points at every eighth-inch spot on the page. You can create a custom grid by accessing "Custom Rulers..." under the Layout menu or you can likewise turn it off by choosing "Turn Off Grid" in the same menu.

We find the grid handy whenever we want proportionate dimensions in our drawings.

TURNING THE LINES GREY

To change the lines into a grey shade instead of black, we choose "Select All" from the Edit menu and then access the Pen menu to choose an appropriate shade of grey (fifth from the top left of the menu selections). This changes the pen color to grey and turns any selected lines in the drawing grey. Take another look at Figure 3-14 to see how it turned out.

We save the drawing as "Vanishing Point Grid." The next, and last step prepares it for placement in PageMaker.

SAVING THE DRAWING AS A PICT IMAGE

There are a few ways we could move the image into PageMaker. We could copy it to the clipboard, quit MacDraw, launch PageMaker, and paste it into the document. Or we could paste it into the scrapbook and copy it from there when we go to PageMaker.

Another way is to copy the elements of the drawing, open a new MacDraw window, paste the image in the new window, and save it in the PICT format rather than the original MacDraw format. This allows us to use the "Place..." command when using PageMaker. PageMaker accepts line art in one of two ways—either in the PICT format or MacPaint format. Appendix B discusses using the PICT format in greater detail.

Any of these methods is acceptable but if you want to make changes to the drawing, use it over again, or use it in several places; saving it in the PICT format from MacDraw is the best of these methods. There are times when the drawing is too complex and has too many elements to fit on the clipboard (especially if you're using a Macintosh 512K) and the only alternative is to use the "Place..." command in PageMaker having already saved the document in the PICT format. If you are following along, we'll show you how to do that now.

Our last action selected all the elements. We press [Command] [C] to copy the image, press [Command] [N] for a new MacDraw document and press [Command] [V] to paste the copy in the new window. We then choose "Save As..." from the File menu and, when the dialog box appears, click the PICT button. We type in a new name, "Vanishing Point/PICT," and click "OK" to save it. We are now ready to quit MacDraw and go to PageMaker to complete the nameplate design.

Finalizing the Nameplate in PageMaker

We return to PageMaker by opening the Audio Image Layout document from the Macintosh desktop. When it is finished loading, we see the page as we left it in Figure 3-11. Press [Command] [F] to fit the page in the window and we're ready to place the vanishing point lines into the border.

PLACING THE MACDRAW ART

We choose "Place..." from the File menu, select the "Vanishing Point/PICT" document, and click on the word "Place" in the dialog box (see Figure 3-18). Immediately the PICT image icon appears (see Figure 3-19). We position it in the upper left corner of the logo and border (it snaps into place) and click the mouse button once. The image flows into the space.

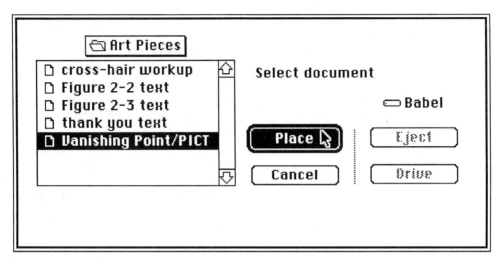

Figure 3-18. "Place..." Dialog Box in PageMaker.

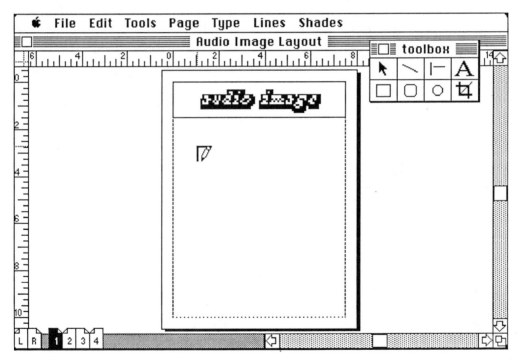

Figure 3-19. PageMaker's PICT Image Icon.

CROPPING THE IMAGE

We knew that the image in MacDraw would be larger than the nameplate border; this was intentional. Now we need to crop it to fit snug within the border.

To do this, we zoom in to the right edge of the nameplate border at actual size, select the cropping tool from the Toolbox, and click once on the vanishing point image to select it, thereby exposing the crop handles (see Figure 3-20). We position the cropping tool on top of the middle handle, press the mouse button, drag in until the cropped edge aligns with the edge of the border, and release the mouse button.

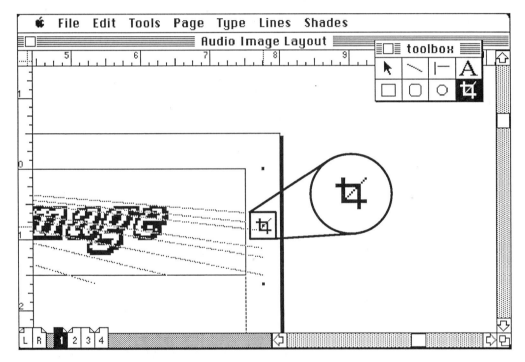

Figure 3-20. Cropping an Image in PageMaker.

We then scroll back to the left and do the same with the middle handle at the bottom of the image. We select "Send to back" from the Edit menu to push the image back behind the words "audio image."

Now, all that remains is to flesh out our nameplate with the subtitle, date, and issue information. We'll also add a ruled line to make it more visually interesting.

PREPARING THE SUBTITLE, DATE, AND ISSUE INFORMATION

Let's add the words "Premier Issue"; the subtitle: "the modern music review of digital audio"; and the date of issue, "Fall 1986" just underneath the nameplate border. To do so we scroll over to the pasteboard, left of the publication border, to type out the text we wish to position under the nameplate. Then we select the text tool and place the I-beam pointer anywhere on the pasteboard that will allow us space to type the phrases (see Figure 3-21).

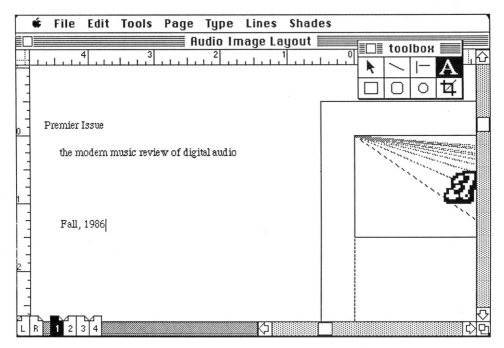

Figure 3-21. Subtitle Phrases Typed on PageMaker's Pasteboard.

Knowing that these phrases will overlap when placed on the page, we want to make sure they are exactly the way we want them before we reposition them. When we type "Premier Issue," we add one space before the letter "P" so it doesn't touch the left edge of the margin too closely. We type the remaining phrases separately, lifting the I-beam pointer when we finish the first phrase and repositioning it elsewhere on the pasteboard to type the next phrase.

Now let's make some specific changes to the subtitle and the date of issue. Positioning the I-beam pointer on top of the "modern music review" line, we triple-click to select the entire line. We want the subtitle slightly larger than the other two phrases, so we choose "Type specs..." from the Type menu, scroll to fourteen points, click on it and then, click on the "Outline" box to create outlined characters for the phrase. We click "OK" and then choose "Align center" from the type menu.

With "Fall 1986" all we need to do is add a space after "6," triple-click the words to select the line, and choose "Align right" from the Type menu.

PLACING THE TEXT UNDERNEATH THE BORDER

Whenever we work with text, which is measured in points and picas, we use PageMaker's picas and points ruler. Choose "Preferences..." from the Edit menu and, when the dialog box appears, click the "Picas and points" button to change our preference; then click "OK."

We'll show you more about picas and points later, but for now you should know that when the rulers are scaled to the fit-in-window dimensions, each minor tick mark represents one pica; each major tick occurs every six picas. In actual-size view, each minor tick represents one-half pica (or six points) and each major tick is set every three picas. At 200 percent size, each minor tick represents two-point increments and each major tick occurs at one-pica intervals.

Placing the text underneath the nameplate border is a bit tricky. First let's place the words "Premier Issue." Viewing the page at 200 percent size, we scroll over to see the words "Premier Issue." We then click on the text with the pointer, position the pointer on top of the # handle, press the mouse button, drag up until the bottom handle touches the top handle, and release the mouse button. Next we click the + handle and we see the text icon. When we scroll over and down we can see the left side of our border and logo and position the text icon inside the margin just underneath the border (so it aligns near the 9.5-pica mark—see Figure 3-22). We click the mouse button once and the text flows onto the page.

We repeat this for each of the remaining text blocks, positioning each at the same relative spot on the page and flowing the text underneath the border. When we place text on top of existing text, sometimes the text block doesn't show the text; instead we see two thin lines with the two text handles touching. All we need do is scroll the page over until we see the +

handle, position the pointer on top of the plus, press the mouse button, pull the + handle down, and let go. This exposes the text.

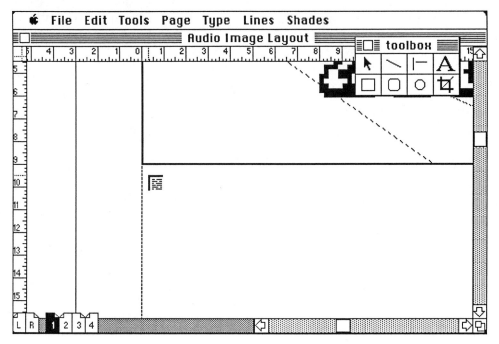

Figure 3-22. Text Icon Ready to Place Text under Nameplate.

We'll fine-tune text placement shortly but first, we need to refine the border to encompass all the text in the nameplate.

LENGTHENING THE BORDER

We want the border to surround not only the words "audio image" and the vanishing point grid but also the subtitle, date of issue, and edition information. To do this, we zoom in to 200 percent view (or scroll if you're still at that view) so we can see the left edge of the border. With the pointer, we click on the outer edge to show the handles, then grab the lower left handle and drag it down so it aligns with the 0 (zero) mark on the horizontal ruler and the 11-pica mark on the vertical ruler.

ADDING A RULE

The line widths shown under the Lines menu are known universally to typesetters and graphic designers as *rules*. You often see them in magazine articles or in brochures positioned at the end of columns or to separate one page element from another. In general, only one or two weights of rule are used per publication to set off one element from another and make the page visually interesting.

Now let's add a rule between the subtitle text and the vanishing point lines to keep them separate and add visual interest to the nameplate. Zoom back out to actual size so you can view most of the border in the screen, particularly the left side. Select the perpendicular tool from the Toolbox and choose the tenth rule from the top of the Lines menu. We position the crossbar on the left side of the border so it lines up with the 0 (zero) on the vertical ruler and the 9-pica point on the horizontal ruler, press the mouse button and drag the line across the page until it touches the right side of the border and then release the mouse button (see Figure 3-23). The page scrolls automatically.

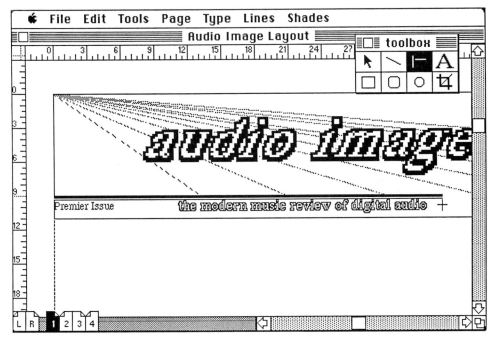

Figure 3-23. Drawing a Rule across the Page.

Whenever text or graphic elements are placed on top of one another, PageMaker arranges them in layers, one of which is in the foreground, the others in the background. When we go to center the subtitle text elements between the rule and the bottom line of the border, clicking on one of the text elements may not give us the specific line of text we want. In this case, we select "Send to back" from the Edit menu and try again.

This is a genuine instance of trial and error; you can experiment with it yourself.

We managed to carefully align the text and center it, top to bottom, between the rule and the bottom line of the border. We adjusted one line where we wanted it and then sent it to the background. Then we adjusted the next text layer and sent it back and so on. All the while we kept an eye on the vertical ruler so our alignments would remain consistent.

This completes the logo and nameplate. We are now prepared to finish the remaining tasks of setting up columns and establishing our page numbers.

Completing the Design

Before we can go on to preparing copy and art for *Audio Image*, we need to complete the design of the publication template by adding those elements that will remain constant throughout the publication. We can determine and set column widths, then set up page numbers. These are all small jobs but essential insofar as they complete the design and give a complete image of the page into which the copy and art will be placed. The work done here makes an easier task of the final layout process, covered in Chapter Six. When finished, we'll have created a template which can be used repeatedly for every issue of *Audio Image*.

Establishing Columns

Choosing the number of columns and column width is another important decision. Column placement and line length influences how readable the publication is and how easily the reader can find information on the page. PageMaker makes this task easier for people with little design background, however, by automatically calculating the appropriate column width within the stated margins, once we have decided how many columns to use.

For *Audio Image* we chose three columns. This decision was based primarily on the small size of both graphics and articles we planned to use. Were our articles lengthy we might have decided to use only two columns.

CHOOSING COLUMN WIDTHS FOR YOUR PUBLICATION

You should use at least two columns in any publication other than a book, formal report, scientific paper, technical manual, or flyer. Newsletters, annual reports, brochures, catalogs, directories and such require a multi-column layout. Even if text appears in only one of the columns and the remaining column is left as white space, this is still considered a multi-column layout. PageMaker supports up to ten columns. However, the number of columns for an 8.5 by 11-inch publication should never exceed four and should never exceed five in a tabloid-sized publication. Using PageMaker, it is wisest to use two or three columns in an 8.5 by 11-inch format and up to four columns in a tabloid.

True column width or line length is often determined on the basis of type size and style. A handy rule of thumb states that the optimum length of a line for maximum readability is one and a half times the length of the lowercase alphabet printed on the LaserWriter in the type style and size of choice. You can set the line length 25 percent narrower than this measure or 50 percent wider and still achieve an acceptable level of readability. Using PageMaker, this requires a number of iterative steps: physically measuring sample text with a pica ruler, and hand-setting the column guides to fit your custom measurements.

Given the fact that we can achieve a readable line either 25 percent narrower or 50 percent wider than the recommendations, we'll let PageMaker set the columns automatically for *Audio Image*.

USING PAGEMAKER'S MASTER PAGES

You'll notice two page icons at the bottom left of the PageMaker window marked L and R. These are PageMaker's master pages and anything you establish on them will reflect on all pages throughout the publication. They are an especially convenient way to set up and establish those page elements you wish to remain constant in a template of your publication. Having these items already set up greatly eases the remaining steps in laying out a publication. You only have to set them up once for all left pages and once for all right pages. Master pages are used to set columns and page numbers. You could also use them for a running header or footer or for establishing nonprinting horizontal or vertical ruler guides you want to appear on all left or right pages.

SETTING THE COLUMNS

Recall that several pages back we chose to use a single page-width column on page one of our layout to give our text some bounds within which to be placed. We will get rid of that column. We press [Command] [F] to shrink the page so it fits in the window, choose "Column guides…" from the Tools menu, type "0" in the dialog box, and click "OK."

To set up a three-column layout for all our pages, we'll use the column guides to set up the master pages so all the pages will have a consistent layout. We click the page icon marked L at the bottom left of the screen to choose the left-hand master page and then select "Column guides" from the Tools menu. The column guides dialog box offers a choice in number of columns and space between columns. We select three columns and accept the default value of .25 inch for the space between columns, then click the page icon marked R and repeat the column layout for the right-hand pages. We may alter the gutter measurement to suit the eye later, but for starters, let's accept the default value. When we decide what style and size of type to use, the column layout decisions may change.

Pagination

Pagination in PageMaker is completely automatic and transparent. Once we set up pagination on the left and right master pages, using [Option] [Shift] [3], the page numbers are inserted on each page, no matter how many pages we have. We can position the page number anywhere on the page that we want. PageMaker increments the pages based on the "Start page #" item in the Page Setup dialog box.

Let's position page numbers so they appear on the outside edge of the left and right pages. Returning to the left master page, we zoom in to the lower left corner at actual size, then select the text tool from the Toolbox and, with "Type Specs…" choose nine point Times italic (page numbers can be extremely small; no smaller than nine points, however). We position the I-beam pointer on the left of the page so it just touches the left margin at the bottom and then type the word "Page" followed by [Option] [Shift] [3]—PageMaker's special character for automatic page numbering.

We want to make sure that when we place text on the page (later in Chapter Six), it doesn't overrun the bottom of the page and cover up the page number. So we pull a horizontal ruler guide out of the ruler by positioning the pointer on top of the horizontal ruler, pressing the mouse button, dragging the dotted line down the page, and aligning it with the 9.75-inch mark near the bottom of the page.

Now just for the sake of consistency, press [Command] [F] to fit the master page in the window. This signals that the page is complete and requires no further modification. Repeat this entire procedure for the right master page and the initial page layout and the template is complete.

Clicking the page icon marked "1" flips us back to the cover page of *Audio Image* and provides a look at the emerging grid (see Figure 3-24). (You may have to select "Copy master guides" from the Tools menu to get the master items represented in Figure 3-24.) By clicking on the additional page icons (2, 3, and 4) we can see that the remaining pages are also set up. We will save the Audio Image Layout one final time before going on to other tasks (like quitting PageMaker and taking a short break). A printed version of the final cover page is shown in Figure 3-25.

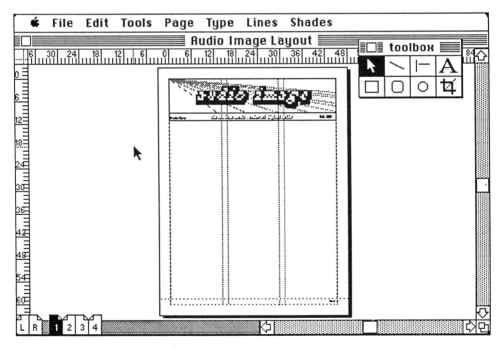

Figure 3-24. Cover Page of *Audio Image* Thus Far.

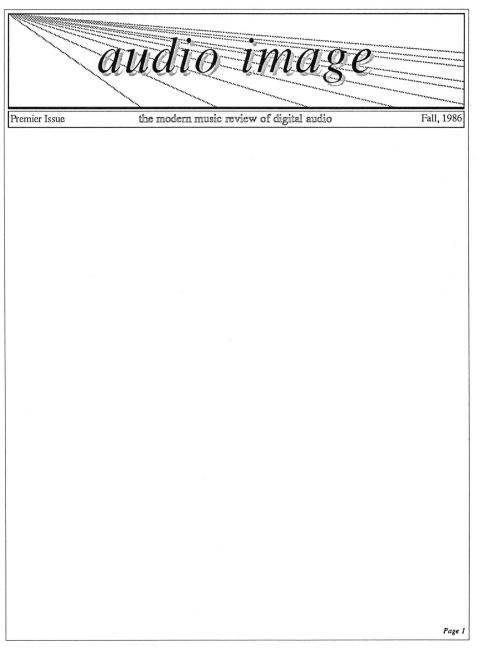

Figure 3-25. Cover Page as Printed on the LaserWriter.

Summary

This completes the initial planning and design preparation of a PageMaker template that we can use again in Chapter Six when we discuss the actual layout.

In this chapter, you have learned what it takes to develop a concept for your publication, assess your potential audience, establish editorial and art direction guidelines, and determine the page size. You witnessed (and hopefully tried out) ways to use PageMaker and MacDraw as tools to create solutions to design problems. And you've seen how these tools can be combined to create a publication template that establishes the design goals for *Audio Image* and gives a reusable shell into which text and graphics can be laid out for this and future issues.

When you set out to do your own publication, you may want to look this section over again. No matter what kind of publication you're trying to produce with desktop publishing—a brochure, a newsletter, a technical manual, or a funding proposal—planning it and designing it in much the same way we have is important. This will save you time and energy later. As previously mentioned, if you don't plan or design, you'll quickly increase the number of iterative tasks it takes to get useful results.

GO VISIT THE PRINTER

When developing your own publication, this is a good time to find a printer. You can make some preliminary decisions about such elements as paper stock, drop-in photos and art, and ink color in order to see how these requirements will impact the remaining steps in the desktop publishing process. Even though printing is discussed at the end of the book (where it logically occurs), you make contact with the printer as early in the publishing cycle as you can. With a well-designed template in hand, you are now in a position to do so. You might also familiarize yourself with the material covered in Chapter Seven before you select and visit a printer.

What's Next?

The next chapter details everything you need to know in order to prepare text and copy for a publication. You'll learn how to use Microsoft Word to its fullest, how to convert documents from other computers into text you can use on a Macintosh, and how to turn ordinary word processing into effective typesetting.

Preparing Copy

In this chapter you will learn:

- How to use word processors to develop copy
- Converting copy from non-Macintosh sources
- How to choose type and understand typography
- How to turn ordinary typing into typesetting

Now that you have the most complete view possible of the framework into which text and graphics will fit, you can go on to the detailed work of preparing copy—the words or text—for placement in your publication. You have already sampled PageMaker and felt some of its power as a layout tool. Keep in mind, though, that PageMaker is only a layout tool and not a word processor. Making major changes to the text of a publication while in PageMaker is similar to going into your mechanicals with an X-Acto® knife to cut and paste photocomposed type to make a revision. You can avoid the problems associated with major editorial changes by making sure your text is as complete as possible before you place it in PageMaker.

This chapter tells you how to use any of three word processing programs for the Macintosh. These include MacWrite, MockWrite, and Microsoft Word. Although you can use any of these to develop copy for desktop publishing, the major software tool we have chosen to prepare copy for *Audio Image* is Microsoft Word. We use Word as both a word processing program to create text and as a photocompositor to actually do typesetting. Since Microsoft Word lets you spec type and set column widths and line spacing (all of which carry over to PageMaker), this chapter tells you how to make the most of Word's strongest features.

The chapter also covers the conversion of text from non-Macintosh sources as well as copyediting, spell-checking and proofreading text. We will show you how to choose type for the publication and format the text for final layout in PageMaker. By the time we show you how to do page composition and layout in PageMaker in Chapter Six, the text will have been already typeset in section-length galleys that are easy to place into the template we designed in Chapter Three.

Word Processing For Desktop Publishing

Words are the basis of any publication. Moving those words from your mind (or the minds of your authors) onto paper in an elegant and readable arrangement is what desktop publishing is all about. It would be nice if you could simply talk to the computer and have it automatically typeset and lay out your publication, but the technology isn't yet that sophisticated. You have to move those words through any number of different processes to get them into print. Essentially, this is called *word* processing. With the Macintosh it's almost as simple as typing.

Words will come to you and your publication in several forms. Some of it may be handwritten, some typed and some (most we hope) on disk. You are encouraged to create or solicit your copy with a computerized word processor. We recommend that it be done on a Macintosh but that may not always be possible. All of your text for desktop publishing with a Macintosh must ultimately end up on the Mac in one form or another. This section shows you how to create it with the Mac; another section shows you how to convert text from outside authors' computers into Mac formats.

We will show you how we use Microsoft Word to create copy and we will take a brief look at the only other word processing programs currently available for the Macintosh—MacWrite and MockWrite. If you plan to use any of these, make sure you've read the manuals and worked through the tutorials accompanying each (MockWrite doesn't come with a manual but if you know how to operate MacWrite, you already know everything you need to about MockWrite).

Microsoft Word

Microsoft Word is as central to the development of our desktop-published publication as is PageMaker and the LaserWriter. We use it as a word processing program to create original copy for our publication. We use it to convert existing copy created in MacWrite or in other computers. We can use it as a photocompositor to do our typesetting. Microsoft Word can also be used as a stand-alone typesetter and page composition tool if the publication isn't too complicated and has no requirement for placing text and graphics side-by-side.

This chapter uses a review of Elton John's album titled *Elton John* to demonstrate how to use Microsoft Word. The review is just over a page long and you may wish to type a few of the paragraphs in yourself so you can follow along. We are assuming you have used Word before and know the fundamentals. We are primarily concerned with optimizing the use of it towards greater productivity, so we will cover those features that apply specifically to desktop publishing.

USING WORD

Starting from the Macintosh desktop, we double-click the Microsoft Word icon to start up the program. Within a few seconds the program displays an untitled window with the cursor flashing in the upper left corner of the screen. The first thing we do whenever we begin using Word is to change the font.

If you started typing right now, the font you would see on the screen would be 12 point New York, Microsoft Word's preset font selection. New York is an ImageWriter font and does not print well on the Laser-Writer. Since all of the LaserWriter fonts are mounted on our System File, before we type anything we will change this font into a readable 12 point LaserWriter font: we choose Times. We do this in one of two ways, either with the combination of the mouse and the menus or with the keyboard.

It's a real timesaver to learn Microsoft Word's many keyboard commands. We significantly increase our word processing productivity by leaving our hands on the keyboard as much as possible. Ninety percent of anything we want to do with a Word document can be done from the keyboard. To change from the New York font to Times, we press [Command] [Shift] [E] and then type the number from the top row of the Macintosh keyboard associated with the Times font, in this case, [4]. Any characters we type now are displayed in 12 point Times.

Font-number associations are dependent on the names and numbers of fonts in your Macintosh System File. If we type [Command] [D] to open the character "Formats..." dialog box, we will see the font currently selected. We can use the mouse to scroll up and down through the "Font Name:" box. Microsoft Word numbers the fonts from 0 to 9 starting with the topmost font (see Figure 4-1). This is entirely dependent on which fonts are in the System File and in what sequence they were installed (yours may differ from ours). If we count down from the top and assign each font a number from 0 to 9 we will know which font number to use with the [Command] [Shift] [E] sequence.

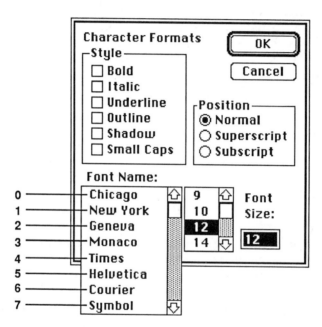

Figure 4-1. Font Name and Number Equivalents.

We now type in the title "Elton John-Elton John"—we may replace this title with art later but this is what we choose to use for now—and then save the document as "Elton John Review." (We always save our document right away and keep saving it every ten minutes or so as we go along to avoid losing too much of our work if there's a power or system failure.) Next, we press [Return] and move to the next line. A simple [Command] [Shift] [O] gives one line of open space above the paragraph (also accessible from the Paragraph menu). We use open space to save keystrokes, and to keep paragraphs separate and easy to read when copy-editing. Since typeset publications rarely have space between paragraphs, we will take it out when we do the final typeset version. If you don't want space between paragraphs when you create copy, there's no need to put it in.

⚡ [Command] [Shift] [F] indents the paragraph a half-inch (one default tab stop). Now that we have completed our set-up, our prose can stream out as fast as we can write. Each time we get to the end of a paragraph, the formats carry over when we press [Return]. Since we have included open space above each, this saves a keystroke between paragraphs.

Now we can type the first sentence of our review:

The piano emerged from a background of absolute silence and spread across the full breadth of an apparent 20-foot sound stage.

USING WORD'S GLOSSARY

The second sentence we type reveals one specific time and keystroke saving step you can use throughout the document: Microsoft Word's Glossary. Look at this sentence:

When Elton John's voice broke into "It's a little bit funny...," the opening verse of "Your Song," it was chills and goosebumps for me.

Between the title of the review and this sentence we have typed "Elton John" three times and can expect to type it several more times throughout the piece. To save keystrokes, we will highlight the name "Elton John" by darkening it in with the mouse (if you have a keypad you can select the word with cursor moves using [Shift] and the num-bers—see the documentation accompanying your version of Microsoft Word). After selecting the name with this highlighting technique, we copy it to the clipboard with [Command] [C], pull down the Edit menu and select "Show Glossary." When the Glossary dialog box is displayed, we type in "ej" and [Command] [V] to paste "Elton John" into the Glossary. At this point you can either save the glossary (a good idea) or click the close box and go on. Each time we want to use the word "Elton John," we simply type "ej," press [Command] [Backspace] and Microsoft Word supplies the whole name. Any word you plan to use often should be placed in the Glossary. The Glossary is quite literal, however, so be careful where you use spaces and tabs. We have included in our Glossary such repeated terms as *"Audio Image"* (with the italics already done), "compact disc," and "digital audio."

CONTINUING WITH WORD'S KEYBOARD COMMANDS

You want to learn as many keyboard-based commands in Microsoft Word as you can remember and incorporate those keystrokes into the normal flow of your typing. If you are word processing for desktop publishing, this is a must for increased productivity. It smooths out an otherwise cumbersome task of having to move between keyboard and mouse too often—and increases your chances of getting it right the first time through. All of these tips and techniques are fully documented in the materials accompanying your copy of Microsoft Word (the keyboard shortcuts are also available from Word's built-in help facility by pressing [Command] [?] and clicking anywhere in the active window).

Now we can continue typing in the remainder of the review. When we get to something that needs bolding, we press [Command] [Shift] [B], type the word or phrase, and, when finished, press [Command] [Shift] [Spacebar] to return to normal print. Likewise with italicizing—[Command] [Shift] [I] starts italic print and [Command] [Shift] [Spacebar] returns to normal. When we want to change a paragraph format to flush left, we press [Command] [Shift] [P] to make it plain first, then press [Command] [Shift] [O] to add open space.

Let's take a look at how the unedited review turned out:

Elton John-Elton John

The piano emerged from a background of absolute silence and spread across the full breadth of an apparent 20 foot sound stage. When Elton John's voice broke into "It's a little bit funny...," the opening verse of "Your Song," it was chills and goosebumps for me. The piano, guitar, drums, string quartet, Elton's rich voice—all were crisp and clear as the day they were recorded. I could tell immediately that I had purchased a compact disc of rare quality. The thrill of listening to this masterpiece wasn't going to evaporate soon as it had with so many other past favorites clumsily transfered from an analog source to digital audio. This was sheer brilliance.

When the next song, "I Need You To Turn To" began, I did a dumb thing. The harpsichord breaks gently into the room filling the left listening arena without a hint of sound from the right speaker. I thought there was something wrong with it. I rushed over and put my ear up to it and, you guessed it, about this time Elton John starts singing and I almost went deaf. But that's the startling thing about this disc—as little extraneous noise as I have heard on any compact disc to date (excluding most digital recordings). After he finishes singing the first verse, the guitar gently breaks into the right of the listening room. Another verse and the lush orchestration of Paul Buckmaster overwhelms you.

By the time "Take Me To The Pilot" finishes—with its slight echo on voice, swirling orchestra effect and Caleb Quaye's funky guitar riffs—you suddenly realize this is one of your favorite albums and how wonderful it is to be able to listen to it and really *hear* it, the way Gus Dudgeon, the producer, must have heard it the day they finished mixing.

"Sixty Years On" is a special case in point. From the first bee-buzzing of the cellos at the beginning to the sudden decay and introduction of the harp, you know you've wandered into a sonic wonderland of undeniable beauty. What dimension! The masterful arrangement of the strings by Paul Buckmaster—who graces all of Elton John's early albums —transforms this into a performance rivaling any of today's modern string quartets. This isn't one of those set pieces where the strings are brought in to bolster a poorly written pop melody. Here they shine through as an unmistakeable part of the music, not an afterthought. The strings are mixed tight and share equal footing with the other instruments—piano, guitar and drums alike.

But this is not meant to be a performance review. You already know if you like this album or not. If you do, you are in for one of the most pleasant surprises compact disc technology has to offer. With no informative code in evidence anywhere on the package, we can only assume the disc was digitally mastered (*Audio Image* is checking into this) and, most likely, mastered from the original mix down tape. There are obviously very few generations of oxide between the source and your ears. Speaking of oxide, for a tape made 17 years ago, this one must have been watched over with extreme care. Only the slightest hint of hiss—difficult to discern with even the most critical of ears—was evident in any of the songs (see Evaluation Chart).

This attests to the continuing high level of excellence and superior attention to detail evidenced throughout Nimbus Records' repertoire of analog to digital masterings (see **Industry In-Depth** column, this issue). We can only hope that with the opening of their second CD plant that they are able to maintain the same level of quality.

This, Elton John's second album, is available as an import on the DJM label (British). Don't get it confused with the domestic release. It can't be nearly as good. Compared with the rest of *Audio Image's* Elton John collection which includes *Tumbleweed Connection*, *Madman Across the Water*, and *Goodbye Yellow Brick Road*, all on MCA, this is by far the best. It is, for now, the benchmark against which all other digitally mastered analog recordings will live or die on our CD player. The accompanying booklet is complete with lyrics, accompanist credits and color photos—a thorough reconstruction of the album sleeve right down to the purple print on the names of the songs.

Fact Sheet:

Title: **Elton John**. Artist: Elton John, vocals and piano. Lyrics: Bernie Taupin. Arranger and Conductor: Paul Buck - master. Producer: Gus Dudgeon. Label: DJM. Disc mastering: Nimbus Records. Mastering Facility: Great Britain. Original album copyright, 1970.

This now becomes the source material for the lead review in *Audio Image*. In the remainder of this chapter, we will continue to alter it until it is set up the way we want for placement in PageMaker. You may want to type your own copy of this article exactly, misspellings and all, using

Microsoft Word and the techniques just described. That way, you'll be able to follow along more closely as we change the article throughout this chapter and when we use it in Chapter Six as part of the layout.

Now let's take a brief look at two other word processing programs available for the Macintosh.

MacWrite

Apple's MacWrite was the original word processor included with early Macintoshes. If you've never used a computer before and know how to type, MacWrite is the easiest word processing program you can learn. You can sit down and, within a matter of minutes, figure out how to type a letter to a friend.

However, as far as word processing for desktop publishing is concerned, it falls short of our expectations. Since as much of the text as possible should be prepared in advance to use in PageMaker, we'd like to be able to set the line spacing at something other than MacWrite's pre-determined setting or the only other option of six lines per inch.

Oftentimes, we wish to set the type at something other than 9, 10, 12, 18, or 24 point type, but there's no way to do this in MacWrite. If we wanted to use 30 point type, we will have to change our document once it is placed in PageMaker.

There is also an anomaly in MacWrite's rulers that can make life difficult if we want to use those measurements to prepare text for Page-Maker (the PageMaker manual goes into great detail about this). An inch on the MacWrite ruler ends up being 1.11 inches when we get to Page-Maker. Additionally, there is no preferential ruler that lets us use true typographic measurement (points and picas), yet those measurements are critical to typesetting.

If the work you plan to do doesn't require the fine tuning we like, you may find that MacWrite works fine for you. It produces solid near-typeset quality copy with acceptable letterspacing when printed on the LaserWriter, and if all you want to do is type a quick letter or typeset a résumé, MacWrite may be all you need. As long as the placement of graphics and text one on top of the other (and not side-by-side) is acceptable for your publication, MacWrite does a good job of reproducing anything you put into it.

USING MACWRITE FOR DESKTOP PUBLISHING (ANYWAY)

We don't want to totally reject MacWrite as a word processing program for desktop publishing. If it's all you have, use it. We'll show you how to get the most out of it.

Essentially, what you want to do with MacWrite is just get your copy into the computer. From there, most of the finer adjustments (which are described in more detail later in this chapter) can be handled in PageMaker. Most important to remember, though, is that when you save your document make sure you save it as text-only. This strips all of the character and paragraph formatting information from the document, leaving you free to establish the formats you want in PageMaker.

When you get to PageMaker and want to place your MacWrite document, you can use "Type specs..." from the Type menu to spec the type and line spacing (also known as *leading*). You can also set first line indents and tabs with the "Tabs..." choice in the Type menu, as well as the column width. The method here is to spec the type, tabs, and columns before you place the MacWrite document in PageMaker. Then, when it flows into your columns, it will possess those character and paragraph formats you specified.

MOCKWRITE: A DESK ACCESSORY TEXT PROCESSOR

MockWrite is a desk accessory that you install in your Macintosh System File using Font/DA Mover. It is part of the MockPackage desk accessory software available from CE Software in Des Moines, Iowa. Once you install MockWrite you can access it from any program using the ● pull-down menu. MockWrite is the simplest way you can create or capture text for later use in PageMaker. However, it has no facility for making font changes or altering any other format in a character or paragraph with the exception of tabs. All MockWrite documents are saved text-only.

MockWrite simply lets you type text into a generic document as quickly as you can. MockWrite provides word-wrap so you can continue typing as you would in any Macintosh word processing program without having to press [Return] at the end of each line. It has a "find" command to let you locate items quickly. You can set tabs to any number of spaces.

After you've written something with MockWrite, you can spec the type, line spacing and tabs in PageMaker before you place the document into your columns. You do this the same as you would for a text-only MacWrite document. We will detail this process more thoroughly in Chapter Six on page composition and layout.

Converting Copy from
Non-Macintosh Sources

The need will undoubtedly arise for us to acquire copy from different word processing programs other than those used on the Apple Macintosh. The problem then is to transform that copy into a form usable by Microsoft Word. For example, one of our columnists writes his column using a minicomputer. Since his copy was already on a computer and computers store alphabetic and numeric characters in common ways, there was no reason to retype the column into our Macintosh. He had his computer dial up our computer and we transferred the text over the phone.

However, all word processors that store copy to disk have their own specific ways of indicating where paragraphs end, what words are in boldface or italics, which are underlined, and which are super- or subscripted. These formats, unlike the characters themselves, rarely share anything in common. Depending on which computer is used and which word processing program is used, these formats may not be compatible with Microsoft Word on the Macintosh. The copy will have to be converted from its existing storage format into one that Microsoft Word understands and can use.

This is no problem with MacWrite documents, as Microsoft Word does its own conversion automatically. You simply open the MacWrite document from Microsoft Word and Word displays an alert box telling you the file is being converted. Some very complex MacWrite documents will require minor adjustments in Word thereafter but, for the most part, the conversion is smooth and transparent. Likewise, if you are acquiring documents developed using MS-Word in the MS-DOS or Windows operating environment, Microsoft provides a conversion utility, called Word Convert, to translate those documents into the Macintosh-based Word formats. In fact, the Word Convert utility also translates Word documents created on the Mac into MS-Word PC formats so you can go both ways.

Nonetheless, you may not be lucky enough to get your copy from MS-Word. More likely, the copy may have been developed using Wordstar, MultiMate, Perfect Writer or PFS:Write, just to mention a few. The copy may have been developed using an IBM PC or some other entirely different computer such as a Wang word processor or an Apple II. There are several software utilities available that are aimed at helping you solve the conversion problem, with more arriving on the scene all the time. These conversion utilities are too numerous to thoroughly cover here. Some of these are commercial products, others are in the public domain, obtainable from service bureaus or through information services such as the Source or Compuserve. Some are considered shareware—you acquire the product free via an information service and, if you end up using the product, you send a specified amount of money to the vendor, whose name is listed therein (MockWrite is an example of shareware).

Our solicited column was received as text-only—absolutely no formatting information was included in the document. This is a worst-case scenario. If you cannot convert the text in any other way, you can always get it text-only. This means that where the author originally had paragraphs set up, there are now simply lines ending with carriage returns, which, in Microsoft Word, means that each individual line is a single paragraph. Tabs become white space made up of individual spaces. Any of the author's boldface, italics or underlining also goes away. If you receive text-only files, do your best to get a printed copy of the author's work so you can see what was originally intended.

A text-only document is by no means the end of the world. You do not have to rekey the copy at all, and you can use a few global search-and-replaces in Microsoft Word to fix up the document to fit your requirements in almost no time at all.

Converting "Digital Edge"

Our first issue of *Audio Image* includes "Digital Edge," a regular column that reviews unusual, off-beat, and new wave music available on CD (compact disc). The text for the article was developed on a system completely different from ours for which no standard conversion to Macintosh format exists.

Once we had successfully captured the text-only document by modem, we used MockWrite to take a quick look at it and make sure we had, in fact, captured all the author's precious words. The first thing we noticed was that accompanying the normal characters were a number of miscellaneous control codes that appeared on our screen as little boxes (see Figure 4-2). Let's examine the conversion process.

We knew that the author had used a word processor that did formatting, bolding, underlining and so on. We determined that the author did not have a way to save the file as text-only, and so assumed there would be some control codes still in the file. This meant that once we captured the author's file we would most likely need to examine the file and to search for and eliminate the control codes.

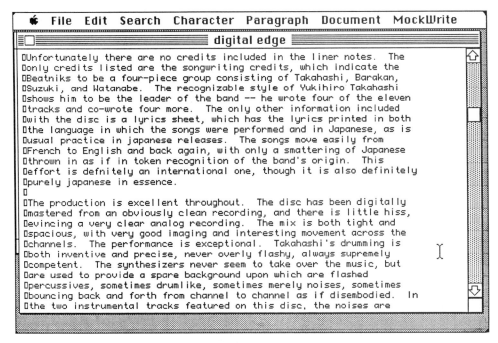

Figure 4-2. "Digital Edge" Copy as Transmitted to *Audio Image*.

USING MACWRITE FIRST

The first task is to remove these oddball characters. However, we don't know what the characters are or which keys will type their equivalents. Microsoft Word doesn't permit pasting into the search window from the clipboard, so we begin our conversion process with MacWrite, which does permit pasting into the search window.

Since text-only documents on a Macintosh system are initially preset to open under MacWrite, all we need to do is double-click the Digital Edge document icon to access both the document and MacWrite. As we do so, MacWrite asks if we want the document formatted with carriage returns at the ends of lines or at the ends of paragraphs. This is a text-only document and the result of transferring text-only via modem is to place carriage returns at the end of lines (not paragraphs). Since we want the document to look as close as possible to what the author originally intended we tell MacWrite to format the document with carriage returns at the end of lines.

When MacWrite finishes with its conversion, it opens the document as "untitled" and we immediately save it as "Digital Edge Copy."

Now, what we want to do in MacWrite is take out these funny characters. So we select one of them and copy it to the clipboard. We then choose "Change..." from the Search menu. When the Change dialog box appears we paste the character into the "Find What" portion of the box and then press the "Change All" button (see Figure 4-3). MacWrite warns that this is undoable and we tell it to go ahead.

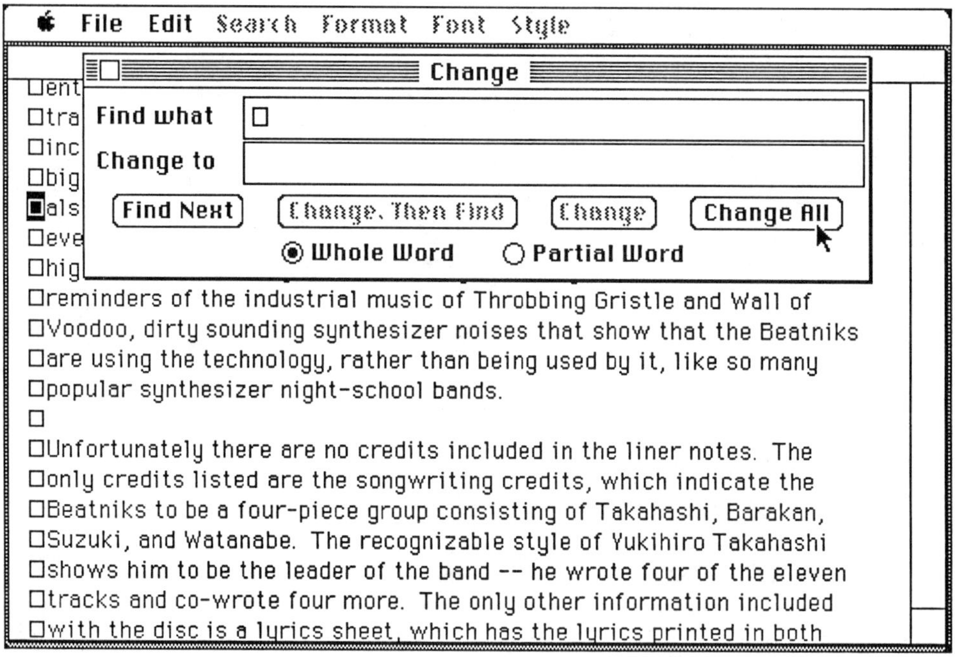

Figure 4-3. Oddball Character in MacWrite's "Change..." Dialog Box.

When the global change is complete, MacWrite positions the cursor at the bottom of the document where we notice another array of box-like characters (see Figure 4-4). We simply darken in both lines of boxes and backspace once to get rid of them. We now save the document again and quit MacWrite.

COMPLETING THE CONVERSION IN MICROSOFT WORD

We now open Microsoft Word, close the untitled window, and open up "Digital Edge Copy." Word tells us it's going to do a conversion on the MacWrite document, and we click "OK." When the conversion is done, Word opens the document in an untitled window. We quickly save the document as "Digital Edge Copy/FINAL." We add the word "FINAL" so that when we look in the mini-finder the next time we want to open this text, we'll know this is the last version we worked with.

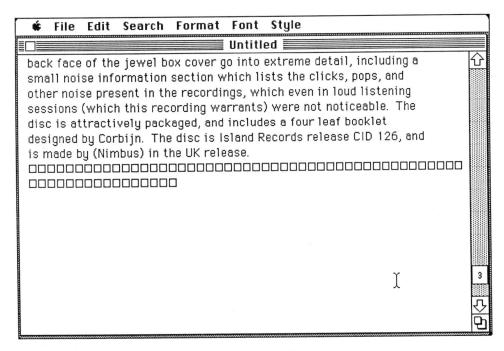

Figure 4-4. Another String of Unknown Characters.

The first thing we do is globally change the font to one that will print elegantly on the LaserWriter. We move the cursor to the far left of the screen where it changes into a right-pointing arrow, press the [Command] key and click once. This selects the entire document. Then we press [Command] [D] to make the font change. We scroll through the font names until we find "Times," click on it and click "OK."

SHOWING FORMAT CHARACTERS

The next thing we want to do with the document is to look at the paragraph markers. We do this by pressing [Command] [Y] which exposes all formatting characters. Ends of paragraphs are indicated with the ¶ symbol, tabs are indicated with an arrow pointing to the right, and spaces are indicated with tiny dots between words. The first thing we notice is that all the lines end in paragraph markers. We anticipated this. We have to somehow convert these back to original paragraphs with only a single marker at the end.

CONVERTING TO THE ORIGINAL PARAGRAPHS

A quick scroll through the document indicates that two paragraph markers in a row mark the end of a true paragraph. We do a global search-and-replace to swap double paragraph markers for double dollar signs or some other such set of characters that do not already exist in the document. To do this we press [Command] [H] to access the "Change..." function from the Search menu. We type "^p^p" in the "Find What" box ("P" tells Word to search for paragraph markers; the "^" is a [Shift] [6]). We type "$$" in the "Change To" box and click on the "Change All" button. When this is complete we close the dialog box and save the document again.

The next global search-and-replace we perform changes all the remaining paragraph markers (now end-of-line markers) to single spaces. To do so, we press [Command] [H] and type a single "^p" into the "Find What:" box and a single press of the spacebar in the "Change To:" box. We click "Change All" and Word goes about cleaning up the document. This can take a while, depending on the size of your document.

Finally, once this is done, we [Tab] to the "Find What:" box, type in "$$", [Tab] to the "Change To:" box and type in "^p" to make true paragraphs where they were in the original document. We click "Change Selection" and when Word completes this procedure our document is nearly converted.

The remaining task takes some time and there is no way to make it go any quicker. We have to convert boldface, italicizations, and such special formats back to the way the author intended. We do this on a case-by-case basis constantly comparing our on-screen text with the author's original.

You may want to continue reformatting the document to concur with your own conventions. At this time it may be appropriate to reset the paragraph indentations and the margins. If your original author used "--" to indicate an em dash, you'll want to search and replace those too.

Copyediting

Once your copy is written or acquired from external sources and made compatible with Microsoft Word formats, you will probably need to copy-edit it. The purpose of this section is not to teach you how to proofread or copyedit. However, this is the time in the desktop publishing process to finalize your copy in whatever way you're accustomed.

You'll probably want to perform some minor global search-and-replace functions to make sure the copy is compatible with proper printing on the LaserWriter. You need not worry about spell-checking the document yet; that is covered in the next section. You simply need to finalize any changes in grammar, usage, issues of audience, personal taste, and editorial concerns at this time using whatever means you are accustomed to. Usually you'll obtain printed versions of all your articles, mark them up, and then enter the changes in Microsoft Word.

Quotes and Apostrophes

Two specific changes to all copy are recommended here. In Microsoft Word, we want to perform a global search-and-replace for two specific typed characters: the inches symbol (") which appears on your keyboard, and is most comfortably typed as a quote symbol, and the feet symbol (') which we'd normally type as an apostrophe. It is possible to type these characters in the original copy, but they are so awkward to type, it is usually easier to convert them later. In any properly constructed LaserWriter font, the keys [Option] [[ ] and [Option] [Shift] [[ ] as well as [Option] [ ]] and [Option] [Shift] [ ]] produce the correct quote and apostrophe characters—(" ") and (' ') respectively. You can see the difference immediately.

CHANGING APOSTROPHES

The simplest way to make this change is to do a global search-and-replace. Accessing the "Change..." function from Microsoft Word with a [Command] [H], we type in the foot symbol ('), [Tab] to the "Change To:" box, and type [Option] [Shift] [ ]] to get the correct apostrophe symbol (') and then, unless we are using the foot symbol elsewhere in this text, we click the "Change All" button.

CHANGING OPEN AND CLOSE QUOTES

Changing from inch marks to the correct quote symbols is a bit more involved. We use the same search-and-replace method as above, typing the (") mark in the "Find What" box. This time we change the left side of the quote first, using the [Option] [[ ] key combination in the "Change To:" box to produce the open quote mark ("). We press the "Find" button to find the first occurrence of an inch symbol and then press "Change, then Find" to find the next one.

When we originally typed these characters both sides of a quoted phrase used the same punctuation symbol ("). To use the correct quote symbols—(") to open the quote and (") to close it—we want to skip the right side (or close quote) without changing it so we press "Find" to move past it to the next left-sided inch symbol.

Alternating in this way, we move through the document changing only the left side of quoted phrases and terms. When we finish this phase, we can change the remaining close quotes by typing a single (") ([Option] [Shift] [[ ]) in the "Change To:" box and, at this point, we can click "Change All" or "Change Selection," whichever appears in the "Change..." dialog box, so long as you are not making any legitimate uses of the inch symbol (e.g., as in the phrase 8.5" x 11"). If you do have inch symbols you wish to keep, you need to make all your changes on a case-by-case basis.

In our Elton John review we made one search-and-replace pass to resolve the differences between the foot symbol and the apostrophe using "Change All" (see Figure 4-5).

We then make our changes by substituting the correct open and close quotes for the inch symbol. We make the first pass on a case-by-case basis, swapping inch marks for open quotes and then make the second pass globally by pressing "Change All."

Each document you plan to use in your publication should be copy-edited and changed in this manner. When you have taken your documents this far, you are then ready to do a spell-check and afterward go on to select type for the final layout preparations.

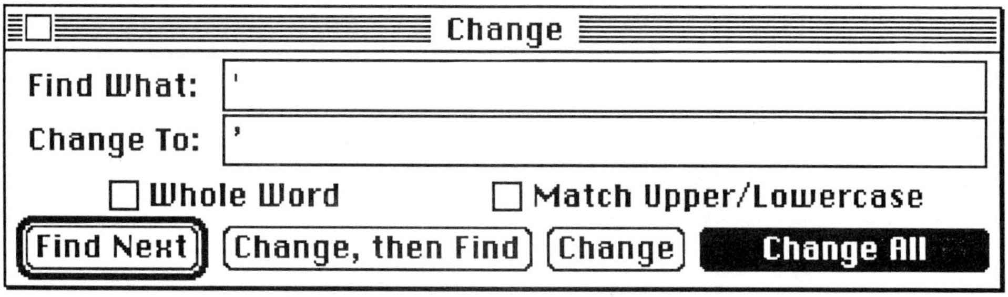

```
┌─────────────────────────────────────────────────────┐
│ ▣ ▤▤▤▤▤▤▤▤▤▤ Change ▤▤▤▤▤▤▤▤▤▤ │
├─────────────────────────────────────────────────────┤
│ Find What:  │ '                                      │
│                                                       │
│ Change To:  │ '                                      │
│                                                       │
│   ☐ Whole Word          ☐ Match Upper/Lowercase      │
│ ┌──────────┐ ┌────────────────┐ ┌────────┐ ┌────────┐│
│ │Find Next │ │Change, then Find│ │ Change │ │Change All││
│ └──────────┘ └────────────────┘ └────────┘ └────────┘│
└─────────────────────────────────────────────────────┘
```

Figure 4-5. Changing the Symbol for Feet into an Apostrophe.

Spell-Check Your Copy

The last thing we do with all our copy before we typeset it is use a spelling checker to check for typos and incorrectly spelled words. There are many spelling checkers for the Macintosh on the market; feel free to use the spelling checker of your choice. For its ease of use, extensive dictionary and bug-free operation, we use MacSpell+, from Creighton Development, Inc. MacSpell+ is installed as a desk accessory in either MacWrite or Microsoft Word (or both). It is used as a desk accessory only with those programs and it only shows up under the menu while we are using one of those two programs. We will show you how we spell-check our Elton John review before we go on to typeset it.

In Microsoft Word, we open the document "Elton John Review" and then pull down the menu and select MacSpell+. MacSpell+ opens its spell checker dialog box and asks us to open a dictionary named "Words," the name of which we double-click to continue. MacSpell+ displays its full dialog box and we click the "Spell Check Document" button (see Figure 4-6). The program makes a few swift moves to set itself up and goes on to spell-check our document. MacSpell+ is fully interactive. As it encounters errors or words not in its dictionary we can make changes by clicking on one of three options: "Accept," "Add to Dictionary," or "Ignore" (see Figure 4-6). We choose "Accept" when we want to edit a word in the "Word Selected:" box to tell MacSpell+ to accept our change. We do this whenever we want to change a word for which MacSpell+ offers no substitute. "Add to Dictionary" is used when MacSpell+ encounters a word not found in its dictionary, and we want to add that word to the dictionary. "Ignore" tells MacSpell+ to ignore this word throughout the spell-checking session.

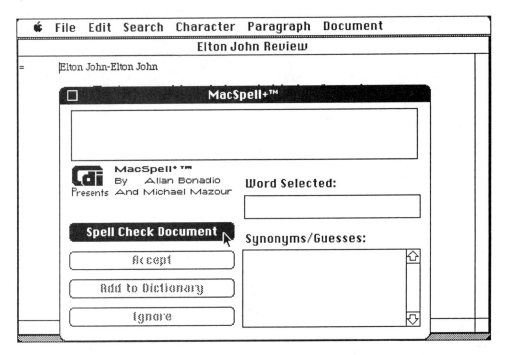

Figure 4-6. MacSpell+ Spell-Checker Window.

The first word MacSpell+ encounters as it spell-checks our review is "Elton." We click "Ignore" and it continues. The next word it picks up, of course, is "John," and since we know several men named "John" and will likely use the word in a document again, we click "Add to Dictionary" and the program continues. The next suspect word it encounters is "transfered" and it guesses we mean "transferred." We click on the word in the "Guesses:" box and MacSpell+ goes into our document —visually we watch it happen—and it changes the correct spelling for the wrong one and then continues on. The next word it encounters is "unmistakeable," which we replace by clicking on the guessed word "unmistakable." It goes on through the review like this. We encounter a few proper names and tell MacSpell+ to ignore these. When we get to the term "CD," which is unknown to the dictionary MacSpell+ uses, we click "Add to Dictionary," as this is a term we use quite often.

When MacSpell+ finishes spell-checking our review it displays its dialog box again and gives us its final word count. MacSpell+ also works well as a synonym finder and has a hyphenation feature. Simply double-click the word you wish to hyphenate or find a synonym for and MacSpell+ will display the proper hyphenation in the "Word Selected:" box and the synonyms in the "Guesses:" box.

Choosing a Font

Our copy for the issue is now in nearly final form. All documents have been created in Microsoft Word or converted to Word's format. We have copyedited and spell-checked the documents so they are now ready to typeset. We can now step into the role of typesetter, but first we have to play the part of art director and make an important decision. What kind of type will we use for the body of our copy?

We follow this rule: *use only one style of type and only one point size*. If we use different typestyles and sizes for the text, our newsletter ends up looking inconsistent and difficult to follow. In general, we use no more than two type styles throughout the publication, and one of these is the body type. Steer clear of using more than three or four different point sizes of the same type throughout the newsletter. The text type will be one size only. In staying with the design goal of "keeping it simple," we avoid complicating things by following these basic rules of thumb that many art directors and designers suggest: no more than two typestyles per publication; no more than three or four point sizes within a typestyle.

Why Type?

Type, in this context, means *typeface:* the printed letters that appear on any page of written material. Even the type you see on a typewritten page is a typeface, albeit not nearly as refined as type that is typeset. The art of typography intimately involves setting type and arranging it on a page. Choosing and using type properly is a task that involves both aesthetic and technical expertise. You have a multitude of choices before you. Never use too many typefaces; you can never use too few.

Take a close look at Figure 4-7. The differences between how each of these letters is shaped is immediately apparent. Notice how the curl at the top of the Bookman "G" differs from that of the Palatino. If you look carefully at the type in several different publications, comparing the letter "a" in one with the letter "a" in another, you'll soon gain familiarity with what a difference typefaces can make.

Garamond   Bookman   Palatino   Avant Garde   Helvetica

Figure 4-7. The Letter "G" in Five LaserWriter Plus Typefaces.

Type comes in all shapes and sizes. You should learn typographic measurement and purchase a good point-and-pica ruler. For *Audio Image* we use the Schaedler Precision Rule which is printed on thin enough material to use with both the screen and paper (although screen measurements can only give you a rough approximation of your final printed results). There are many occasions, where you might like to check something before printing. If you have any doubts about your type selection, talk it over with an experienced graphic designer.

DISPLAY TYPE AND BODY TYPE

There are two distinguishing features for all type. There is *display type* and *body type*. Display type is used for headlines or phrases used in advertising—wherever your copy needs to be prominently displayed, as on a billboard or across a two-page spread in the center of a magazine. Body type is used whenever there is enough text on the page to represent a substantial body of copy—wherever you are concerned with paragraph-length or longer text that requires easy reading. Some styles of type are better suited to one or the other (see Figure 4-8).

SERIF AND SANS SERIF

Another distinguishing feature of type is whether it is *serif* or *sans serif*. Palatino is a serifed font. The body copy for this book has been set in Palatino. Helvetica is sans serif. Serifs are the short lines stemming from the upper and lower strokes of a letter (see Figure 4-9). Serifed type is commonly used in almost everything we read; it is generally preferred for body type because it is the easier to read of the two.

Avant Garde is a fine display type.

> Bookman is an excellent and readable body type. Actually, for creating brochures and such, using Avant Garde for the display type and Bookman for the body type, makes a great combo.

Figure 4-8. Display Type and Body Type.

Sans-serif type is more often used where short phrases or words are used to call out elements of a graphic display. Sans-serif type is also used for captions, short technical guides, and is a common display type.

Figure 4-9. Serif and Sans Serif Type.

What Fonts Are Available

Over ten thousand typefaces have been developed, and several thousand of these are available today. As of this writing, only a handful of these have been converted into PostScript for use with the LaserWriter, but by the beginning of 1987 there will be more than one hundred type families available.

The original LaserWriter provided two common families of type built into the machine: Times and Helvetica. It also provided the typewriter font, Courier, and the specialized Symbol font, which is primarily used with mathematics and scientific notation.

The LaserWriter Plus adds to these the families Palatino, New Century Schoolbook, Helvetica Narrow, ITC Bookman, ITC Avant Garde, ITC Zapf Chancery Italic and ITC Zapf Dingbats (a font family of pictograms and typographic ornaments). Adobe Systems of Palo Alto, California, the makers of the PostScript page-description language, offers several more downloadable type families. There is also a wide array of existing Imagewriter fonts which, even though not truly typeset, can be used as display type. How do we choose?

CHOOSING A TYPEFACE FOR *AUDIO IMAGE*

We can be certain that the body type chosen for *Audio Image* will be a serifed font. Even though we have a LaserWriter Plus and all the font choices it offers, we'd rather stick to something more common (we can't assume that everybody has a LaserWriter Plus but almost everyone should have access to the original LaserWriter). Since the LaserWriter only provides Times or Helvetica, and one is serifed and the other is sans serif, our choice is simple: Times.

CHOOSING A TYPE SIZE FOR *AUDIO IMAGE*

Choosing type size is an arbitrary decision made within the context of some standard typographic principles. In general, we should never make the body type smaller than 9 points and rarely larger than 12. The LaserWriter permits us to scale fonts as small as 4 points and as large as 127 points.

However, matching screen fonts for the Macintosh are usually set at increments of 9, 10, 12, 14, 18, and 24. Increments between these numbers (or smaller than 9 point and larger than 24 point) presents a screen display that is only a rough approximation of what our type will actually look like when printed. Where screen fonts in particular sizes exist, they are usually displayed in the program's font selection dialog box or pull-down menu with the numbers outlined. Of course, we are given the option in PageMaker and Microsoft Word of typing in our own specific type sizes.

Given these options, we have chosen 10 point Times as our type size and style for the body copy used throughout *Audio Image*.

Format for Layout

Now that we have chosen our type we can go on to finalize copy preparation by formatting the copy into typeset galleys. This is a relatively simple procedure involving a series of clearly defined steps. We will use them on our Elton John review in order to demonstrate the process. We recommend that you follow these steps closely in your own publication. The process will be a real time-saver when we get to placing the text in PageMaker.

To format our copy for final layout we need to set the type and size, adjust the margins to line up with the columns in PageMaker, set paragraph indentations, set the leading, and set the size and style for the headings. To give the best letterspacing possible we also want to change "fi" and "fl" to "fi" and "fl" (known as *"ligatures"*) and close up any white space at the ends of sentences. Once these tasks are performed we can hyphenate the text to achieve even tighter letterspacing.

Set Type

In Microsoft Word, with our "Elton John Review" document open, the first thing we do is to select all the text in the document. We move the pointer to the extreme left side of the page, where it turns into an arrow pointing right, and while holding down the [Command] key, click outside the left margin. This selects the entire document.

Our document has already been set in Times but if yours is not, you would now type [Command] [Shift] [E] and press [4] to change it to Times (remember, your system may have a different font-number association than ours). We also want to make it 10 point instead of 12, so with the text still selected, we press [Command] [Shift] [<] to take the type size down one increment to 10 points—Microsoft Word steps the type in increments that are equivalent to the screen font sizes on the System File.

Set Margins

We need to return to PageMaker briefly to carefully measure column width. We quit Microsoft Word, saving our changes, and start up PageMaker by double-clicking the page icon for the Audio Image Layout document. When the document appears on the screen, we zoom in to a 200 percent view of the upper left section of the leftmost column—just underneath the word "Premier Issue"—by holding down the [Option] [Command] keys and clicking the mouse (pointed at that region). We expose the rulers using [Command] [R] and close the toolbox with a [Command] [W] to clear the screen as much as possible. A quick scan, comparing the distance between the inside margin and the right column guide with the marks on the horizontal ruler, reveals that we should use a margin of two and five-sixteenths inches (see Figure 4-10). We make a note of the measurement and quit PageMaker. There's no need to save since all we have changed is our view of the page.

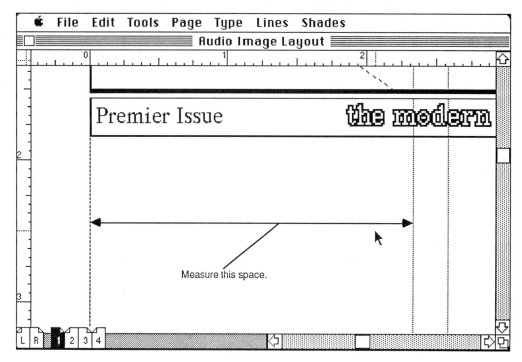

Figure 4-10. Measuring Column Width in PageMaker.

With our measurement in hand, we restart Microsoft Word by double-clicking the Elton John Review document icon. When the document appears on the screen, we again select all the text in the file by pressing the [Command] key and clicking in the leftmost part of the screen. With the text selected, we expose the rulers in Microsoft Word by pressing [Command] [R]. Looking to the right of the ruler, we can pick up the right margin marker by positioning the pointer on top of it, pressing the mouse button, and dragging it left to line up with the two-and-five-sixteenths-inch mark. We let go of the mouse button when the marker is lined up properly and watch Microsoft Word adjust the text accordingly (see Figure 4-11).

Notice that the paragraph indentation has been lost. Adjusting the margins in this way—globally—removes all tabs from the paragraph formats. However, we need to reset the paragraph indentation anyway to maintain consistency with established typographic formats. We do this next.

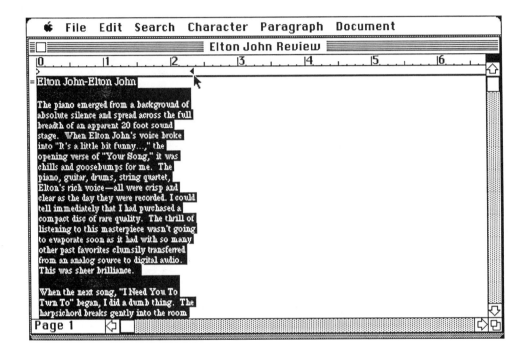

Figure 4-11. Text Adjusted by Microsoft Word.

Set Paragraph Format

Paragraph indentation for typeset publications is handled somewhat differently than it is with material that is simply typed or word processed. The standard typewriter indentation is one-half inch. If you look through books and magazines, you will notice that the paragraph indentation for typeset text is about half that size. Let's look at how typographic measurement is used before going on to adjust paragraph formats.

TYPOGRAPHIC MEASUREMENT

Typesetters use a standard measure known as a *pica* or an *em* which measures 12 points or approximately three-sixteenths of an inch. The commonly used em dash (—) gives you a good idea of how small this is. There are 72 points to an inch and 12 points to a pica or 6 picas to an inch (see Figure 4-12).

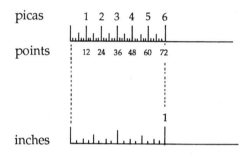

Figure 4-12. Typographic Measurement.

Microsoft Word and PageMaker both permit us to use point and pica rulers on the screen. To do that, we pull down the Edit menu, select "Preferences," click on the "Points" button and click "OK" (see Figure 4-13). You can immediately see the difference in how the ruler is arranged. There are now markers numbering 72, 144, 216, and so forth with smaller measures at half-pica or 6 point increments.

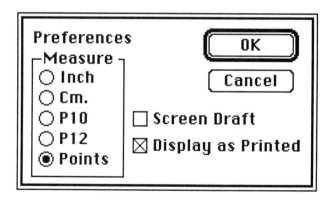

Figure 4-13. "Preferences" Dialog Box in Word.

SETTING PARAGRAPH INDENTATION

We want to set the first line indentation for the second paragraph at one pica (the first paragraph in typeset copy that falls underneath a headline is usually kept flush left). We scroll down to where we can see the second paragraph and then position the cursor anywhere in the paragraph or double-click in the extreme left of the screen to select the paragraph so that changes are made only to that paragraph and not any other. Then we point at the left margin marker, pick up the left indent marker by positioning the pointer on top of it, and drag it out to the second half-pica mark. When we let go of the mouse button, Microsoft Word makes the requisite adjustment to the paragraph (see Figure 4-14).

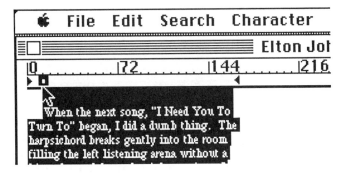

Figure 4-14. Setting the First Line Indent.

MAKING ALL PARAGRAPHS CONFORM TO ONE

We need to change all the paragraphs in the review, but we need not adjust the ruler each time. We can copy formats from one paragraph to the next by simply pointing and clicking the mouse button. To do so, we position the cursor anywhere in the next paragraph and then point to the previous paragraph, positioning the mouse outside the left margin on the far left of the screen—where it turns into a right arrow. Then we hold down the [Option] and [Command] keys together and click. The second paragraph now has the same indentation as the first.

REMOVING OPEN SPACE

In most typeset publications there is no space between paragraphs, so if your copy has spaces between paragraphs, you need to remove them. (We originally used open space when creating our copy because it's easier to copyedit with space between the paragraphs.) With the cursor still positioned anywhere in the paragraph, we press [Command] [M] to open Microsoft Word's paragraph "Formats..." dialog box, tab four times to move to the "Space Before:" box, type "0" and press [Enter]. This removes the open space without disturbing any of our other dimensions.

From here it is a relatively simple process of positioning the cursor inside the paragraphs we want to adjust and copying the formats from the previous paragraph. As before, we move the cursor down to the third paragraph, point to the left of the previous paragraph, hold down [Option] [Command] and click. The third paragraph is now formatted like the second. Scrolling through the document, we make these changes to all paragraphs except the Fact Sheet at the end of our Elton John review. It is fine just as it is.

Set Leading

Leading (pronounced "ledding") is the amount of space between lines of typeset text. Also referred to as "line spacing," the term comes from the old days of hot type when the typesetter used to actually place a point or two of thin lead strips between each printed line of text.

Leading is set using typographical measurement; it is usually set one or two points larger than the point size of the typeface. The general rule of thumb, learned through much research into readability and eyestrain, is to add two points of leading to the point size of your typeface to obtain the proper spacing between lines. If you are using 12 point type, you want 14 point leading (in a type shop this is referred to as "12 on 14"). If you have 10 point type, as we do, you want 12 point leading.

We darken in all our paragraphs from just underneath the "Elton John-Elton John" header all the way to just above the header, "Fact Sheet." We then press [Command] [M] to open the paragraph "Formats" dialog box, tab three times around to the "Line Spacing:" box, type in "12 pt" and click "OK" or press [Enter]. We scroll down and select the last paragraph and repeat this operation. Even if you have preferences set to inches, you can still set the leading in points by typing in "12 pt" —Microsoft Word accepts the abbreviation for points to indicate our preference.

Set Headings

The remaining task is to set the headings in a point size larger than the body type. All we need do is scroll back to the top of the document, position the cursor in the heading "Elton John-Elton John," hold down the [Command] key and click. This selects all the words in the heading. With the heading selected, we press [Command] [>] twice to increase the size of the heading to 14 points. While it is selected, we press [Command] [Shift] [I] to italicize the heading just for a bit of flourish.

Next, we scroll down to the end of the document, select the phrase, "Fact Sheet" and press [Command] [Shift] [>] twice to raise it to 14 points. We also press [Command] [Shift] [B] to make it boldface.

Set Ligatures

Ligatures tie two letters together that would normally have wide letterspacing were they kept separate. In hot type or photocomposed type there are many ligatures built into the font families. For now, two of the most common ligatures—"fi" and "fl"—are built into all LaserWriter fonts and we recommend using them (see Figure 4-15). This compresses the letterspacing of words produced with desktop publishing and makes them easier to read.

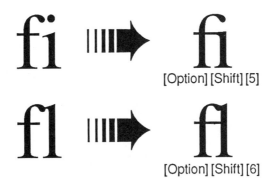

[Option] [Shift] [5]

[Option] [Shift] [6]

Figure 4-15. Ligatures.

This is a simple search-and-replace procedure. We access the "Change..." dialog box in Word by pressing [Command] [H] and type "fi" into the "Find What:" space [Tab] to the "Change To:" box and press

[Option] [Shift] [5] to enter the "fi" character. It shows in the window as a square box because Chicago, the System font, doesn't have ligature characters. We also click in the "Match Upper/Lowercase" box because ligatures only apply to lowercase characters—there aren't any ligatures for "Fi" or "Fl" —then press "Change All."

We repeat the procedure for "fl" by replacing "fi" with "fl" and [Option] [Shift] [5] or "fi" with [Option] [Shift] [6] to get "fl."

Replace Double Space with Single Space

In typesetting, a single space after the period at the end of a sentence is enough. This differs from typing where machinery dictates spacing. We do a quick global search and replace, replacing two spaces with a single space. We simply type two spacebar strokes into the "Find What:" box and a single spacebar stroke in the "Change To:" box. Click "Change All" to make the change universal.

Since we use desktop publishing equipment all the time, we've changed our old typing habits and now type single spaces after periods all the time.

Hyphenate the Text

The last operation to perform is hyphenation. We want to achieve the tightest letterspacing possible in our document so that the eye rarely has to jump between characters and interrupt the flow of reading. It is difficult to scan a column of text if every so often there are huge breaks in the sentences where an unhyphenated polysyllabic word must be pushed onto the next line.

Hyphenation is most important if you plan to justify your columns of text. But even unjustified (also called "ragged") columns are improved when carefully hyphenated.

DISCRETIONARY HYPHENS

The discretionary hyphen, typed with a [Command] [-], permits us to embed an otherwise invisible hyphen between syllables of a word. If that word needs to be broken at the right margin, the hyphen is used. If it doesn't need to be broken, all syllables are kept together. The discretionary hyphen works in all Macintosh word processing and page layout programs (except MockWrite). Any discretionary hyphens we put into our Word document will carry over to PageMaker automatically. The discretionary hyphen permits us to reformat the document using variable column widths without having to remove the old hyphens.

DOING HYPHENATION

There are several programs on the market you can use to help you with hyphenation; it is a feature often included in spell-checking programs. Of course, you can also use the dictionary. We use MacSpell+ to help us hyphenate individual words, one at a time.

Here is the reason we save this step for last. If our text is properly formatted and our column widths are already set up, we can simply browse the right edge of the text looking for polysyllabic words to hyphenate. If we had changed our column widths or hadn't thoroughly copyedited and then had to change the text, we would have to hyphenate that paragraph all over again. We certainly don't want to hyphenate every polysyllabic word in every article.

We summon MacSpell+ from the menu, select the dictionary and then activate the text window in Word (in this case the Elton John review we've been working with all along). Scanning down the right edge of the column, we see the first word we can hyphenate is "opening." We double-click the word to select it, then move the pointer to the bottom of the window and click to activate the MacSpell+ window. After a few seconds, the word "opening" appears under "Word Selected:" shown with a hyphen between the letters "n" and "i." When we click on the hyphen in the word, MacSpell+ goes out to our document and inserts a discretionary hyphen between the "n" and the "i." If we have a longer word, MacSpell+ will show all the hyphens in the word and we can choose exactly where we want it broken.

We continue through the column in this manner, selecting words like "guitar," "immediately," and "evaporate" and letting MacSpell+ provide the proper hyphenation. When we've completed the hyphenation process we save the document and print out the galleys. We are now finished.

We now hold aside the typeset documents, saved on disk, for later placement into the Audio Image Layout document in PageMaker.

Before we do that, however, we need to prepare the art. That's the subject of the next chapter.

Summary

You've covered quite a bit of territory in this chapter. You've seen what it takes to prepare copy for desktop publishing with a Macintosh in several ways. You've learned how you can save time and keystrokes using Microsoft Word's most powerful features. You now know how you can quickly and painlessly convert material created on someone else's computer into formats you can use with the Mac and LaserWriter.

You've also learned something about typography and we hope you are encouraged to learn more. And finally, you've seen what it takes to transform ordinary typing into extraordinary typesetting.

When you do your own publication, it makes sense to prepare your copy in much the same way as we have ours. This way your text is finalized and doesn't require any further changes or heavy editing. When you return to your publication template to do the final layout in PageMaker, you'll find that having all your copy prepared gives you the freedom to try out as many approaches as you like. Preparing copy to this degree paves the way for a smooth and trouble-free desktop publishing experience.

What's Next

In Chapter Five we'll take a close look at how artwork is prepared and how you can take advantage of many different resources to come up with a professionally illustrated publication. You'll learn about digitizers and how electronic drawing makes desktop publishing one of the most sophisticated ways to combine text and graphics on a page. You'll discover how easy it is to create a chart in Microsoft Excel and paste it into any report or brochure. You'll also learn how easy it is to prepare art and make life easier when you do your final electronic pasteup.

Preparing Artwork

5

In this chapter you will learn:

- How the Macintosh treats graphic images
- How to create and transfer artwork
- How to use digitized graphics
- How you can combine resources to produce art

Probably no one needs to be told how important artwork can be in a publication. Illustrations or photographs can convey certain kinds of information much more quickly than words. In addition, artwork vastly improves the visual interest and effectiveness of your page layout. Think of how much more you enjoy a publication that is richly illustrated over one that just contains words.

For some publications, artwork is optional. A quarterly report, for example, might be acceptable with only text and tables of dollar amounts (although it could almost certainly profit from charts and other illustrative graphics). In other types of publications, however, artwork is essential. It's hard to imagine any sort of advertising brochure with no art at all.

This chapter will explore the various ways you can add art to your publication using desktop publishing techniques—primarily, it shows ways to add artwork electronically to your documents. In some circumstances the electronic approach may not be appropriate (such as the reproduction of high-resolution photographs, which is discussed in the chapter on printing). For most artwork, however, the simplest and easiest way to create graphics is to use your Macintosh to develop or capture digital images that can be manipulated with PageMaker in much the same way as the text.

There are many ways to create digital images. This chapter will explore some of the most common: drawing your own images with Mac-

Paint and MacDraw, using the graphics capabilities of number-oriented programs such as Excel, and by digitizing existing images (photocopied line art, for example) with special equipment such as ThunderScan.

The goal of this chapter is not to provide detailed instructions on how to use these graphics-oriented programs and devices. Rather it is to show you the development of some specific art in enough detail that you will finish the chapter with a clear idea of the ways art can be created in an electronic desktop publishing environment. The emphasis here will be on interaction between various art-producing programs. Often it is advantageous to create an image with one program, embellish it with another, and finally move it into a third to combine it with text.

As with text, you should have all your art assembled to your taste and finalized before you do the layout.

This chapter will show you how we created several pieces of art for our premier issue of *Audio Image*. For the Elton John review, we digitized an image of the "Elton John" logo from the album art that accompanies the compact disc. We also include a chart created in Microsoft Excel that evaluates the quality of the disc by various criteria. To augment the article "Pentimento," which discusses how analog recordings are converted into the digital format, we worked up a diagram in MacDraw. For the header on the editorial column, we captured a portrait of *Audio Image's* editor using MacVision. Two ThunderScanned images accompany the column "Industry In-Depth," which discusses the Nimbus record label and the firm's compact discmastering facility in Great Britain. Finally, *Audio Image* is described in the masthead as "An Electric Stylus Publication." Since Electric Stylus has its own unique logo, which was developed in MacPaint using specialized font characters and modified with Fat Bits, we thought you might find it interesting to see how that was developed as well.

How the Mac Treats Graphic Images

Before you move into the hands-on part of this chapter, you might be interested in how graphic images are treated in the Macintosh environment. This is a bit technical; you don't have to know this in order to draw images with the Mac, but if you understand how the Mac treats graphic images, you're in a better position to make choices about what kind of artwork to use and where one kind may be appropriate while another is not. If you already know the difference between a bit map and an object, you can skip this section.

Bit-Mapped Images versus Object-Based Images

MacPaint and MacDraw are both useful for creating and editing art, but in different ways. To understand this difference, you need to look at the two ways in which the Mac stores images. In computer jargon we can say that MacPaint creates bit-mapped images and MacDraw creates object-based images. Now you need to know just what the difference is between a bit map and an object. Understanding this can help you make better art decisions when you're choosing between MacPaint and MacDraw. Look at Figure 5-1; the circle on the left was created with MacPaint, the one on the right with MacDraw. The difference between them is obvious: the MacPaint circle is jagged, while the MacDraw circle is much smoother.

MacPaint
Bit-Map

MacDraw
Object

Figure 5-1. A Circle in MacPaint and a Circle in MacDraw.

MacPaint and Bit Maps

When MacPaint creates a circle, the image is made up of black dots on the screen known as *pixels*. On your screen, these dots or pixels are actually square (as they are on the LaserWriter when printed). MacPaint computes the radius of the circle while you draw it on the screen but once it's drawn, the image on the screen is simply a formation of pixels whose value is either black or white. The fact that it's a circle is forgotten. The same is true of any typing you do in MacPaint; once you've moved on to something else, MacPaint forgets everything about the text, including which font it is, and handles it as only black and white dots on the screen. That's why you can't change text in MacPaint after it's on the screen.

Each bit or pixel is mapped directly from the computer's memory to the video image on your screen. When you print this on a page, the image is simply transformed from a bit-mapped screen image to a bit-mapped printed image. The LaserWriter can enhance the image using a technique called *smoothing* which helps smooth out the rough edges or squared-off look—also called *jaggies*—of the image and helps somewhat to make the circle appear more, shall we say, circular (see Figure 5-2). But, as you can see, it doesn't do a perfect job. LaserWriter smoothing can be turned on or off in the "Page Setup..." dialog box of most Macintosh programs (in PageMaker you use the "Print..." dialog box).

MacPaint
Bit-Map (smoothed)

Figure 5-2. MacPaint Circle Printed with LaserWriter's Smoothing.

MacDraw and Objects

MacDraw handles all this in an entirely different way. A circle drawn in MacDraw is initially computed in the same manner as it is in MacPaint. However, when you move on to do something else, MacDraw remembers not only the locations of the individual bits which make up the circle, but the dimensions of the circle and its location on the screen or page. In other words, MacDraw creates a circle object in memory that tells the program or the printer to draw a circle with these dimensions at this location on the page. Although the circle looks the same as a bit-mapped image on the screen, the printed results are quite different, as you saw in Figure 5-1. Figure 5-3 shows a detailed view of how bit-mapped images and object-based images are stored in the computer's memory. MacDraw images are stored in either the proprietary MacDraw format or the PICT format (used for exporting MacDraw images to PageMaker and other programs). Appendix B discusses what you need to know about managing PICT images for use with PageMaker.

Which One to Use

With MacPaint and other bit-mapped drawing programs, you can achieve a high level of detail. You can turn each individual pixel on or off on the screen one at a time using tools like MacPaint's Fat Bits. In this way, you can create extremely detailed images such as a Grecian urn with flowers in it, a car speeding across a rain-slicked surface, or unique facial expressions. You can create smooth grey-scale transitions that simulate the effects of directional lighting. If you wish to use any existing art in your publication, it can be scanned with a digitizer and captured to the Mac as a bit-mapped image. In short, MacPaint is good for artwork that demands realism, where you want to create a digital representation of objects from the real world.

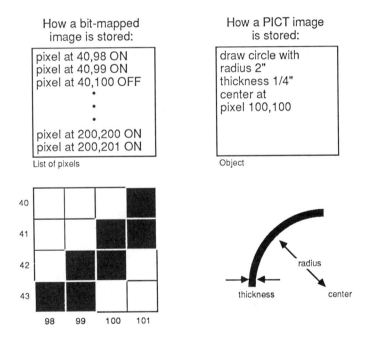

Figure 5-3. How Bit-Mapped and PICT Images Are Stored in Memory.

MacDraw doesn't allow you to turn individual pixels on or off so you can never achieve the level of detail you can with MacPaint but it does permit drawn objects to use true lines, arcs, rectangles, and circles. What you sacrifice in detail is often made up by the smoothness with which images can be rendered. MacDraw enables structured drawings such as diagrams, flow charts, organization charts and simple representational line art. The AppleTalk diagrams in Chapter Two are a good example of the kind of line art you can do with MacDraw.

Throughout this chapter, you'll see how you can use both bit-mapped and object-based images to achieve different effects. You can experiment with combining MacPaint and MacDraw images in Page-Maker to create different effects. Many of the graphics for this book were created this way.

To Smooth or Not to Smooth: How to Eliminate Jaggies

As previously mentioned, the LaserWriter's smoothing routines can help soften the rough edges on bit-mapped images. But smoothing can create moiré effects (an undesirable merging of the dot pattern) that can make complex images confusing. There's a better way if you know how to optimize your use of it.

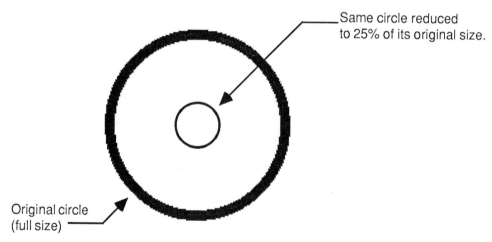

Figure 5-4. Reducing Circles without Smoothing.

The Macintosh video screen displays pixels at 72 dots per inch. The LaserWriter prints at 300 dots per inch. How do these relate? If you multiply 72 by 4 you get 288, which is only 12 dots shy of 300. The jaggies on the LaserWriter image arise because the image is taken lifesize from the Macintosh screen, where each pixel is almost four times as big as it needs to be.

Thus the jaggies can be all but eliminated by drawing or capturing an image at four times the size you want to print at and then printing it at 25 percent of that size from PageMaker or by 20 percent or 30 percent of that size from Microsoft Word. (Word can only scale a reduction in increments of 10 percent.) When it prints on the LaserWriter (without smoothing) the image takes advantage of the printer's 300-dot-per-inch resolution (see Figure 5-4).

Several examples in this chapter take advantage of this reduction process.

Using a Chart from Excel

Let's move onto some concrete examples of images we can generate digitally for inclusion in our publication. The first image we'll consider is that of a chart generated with the Excel spreadsheet program.

Each in-depth review of a compact disc in *Audio Image* rates that disc on a scale of one to ten according to six different criteria: ambience, imaging, LP mixing, CD mastering, dynamic range and noise. For each review we want to graphically present this rating and evaluation. To do so we use Microsoft Excel to create a simple bar chart (see Figure 5-5). Then we copy it and paste it into MacDraw to make it into a PICT image for use with PageMaker.

If you know how to use Excel and plan to pick up charts from the program for your own publications, you can probably duplicate our efforts, given the details in Figure 5-5. Using techniques similar to those described here, you could probably use a chart from Microsoft Chart, Lotus' Jazz, or Paladin's Crunch or Super Crunch.

If you don't plan to use charts from Excel you can probably skip this section (although there is some interesting information here about using MacDraw that anyone might find useful).

Modifying the Chart in Excel

We work on the chart as much as possible while still in Excel. We change the font from Excel's preset selection to Helvetica so that our test prints can be successfully printed on the LaserWriter without font substitution. Another good reason for us to make the font change in Excel is to keep our criteria labels perfectly aligned on the right side. Had we simply copied the chart to MacDraw using the preset font, we would have had to go through a number of successive iterations to change the font and re-align the characters on the right. Excel handles this automatically.

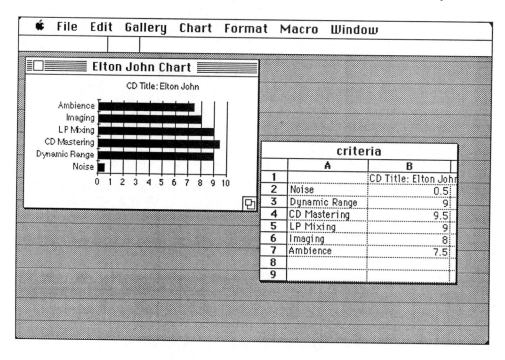

Figure 5-5. Bar Chart Created in Excel.

Moving the Chart to Another Program

There are a few different ways of moving any chart from Excel to PageMaker or any other program; which you use depends on how you plan to use the chart. We can't place an Excel document as a complete file directly into PageMaker. If we simply want to use the chart in PageMaker without making any cosmetic changes to it, we can copy it to the clipboard and, after we start up PageMaker, paste it into our publication directly. If we plan to use the chart at some later date, we can paste it into the scrapbook where it will remain until we need it. Likewise, if we want to use a chart in a Microsoft Word document, we can paste it there directly, after copying it from Excel or the scrapbook.

However, we're not genuinely satisfied with how this chart looks; quite often in desktop publishing it is necessary to alter a chart's appearance in order to suit art direction guidelines. For these kinds of changes we need to make a copy of the chart and paste it into either MacPaint or MacDraw, depending on how artistic we want to get.

For example, we could change the bars so they look like individual compact discs stacked up on top of each other. Or, if we had created a column chart to show the number of water mains in a water district, we might want to make the columns look like water pipes instead of ordinary black columns, and we can use MacPaint or MacDraw to do so. In this specific case, all we want to do is adjust the words "CD Title: Elton John," so we center them to our taste over the chart image.

Excel creates all the component parts of the chart as PICT-formatted objects. Therefore, it transfers nicely to MacDraw, where any part of the drawing can be modified as if it were originally created in MacDraw. If the chart is pasted into MacPaint, it becomes a bit-mapped image and loses all the font and object information. If we wanted to add artistic detail to the chart we usually prefer MacPaint, but since all we want to change is the text, we choose MacDraw.

Moving the Chart to MacDraw

While still in Excel we copy the chart to the clipboard using the "Copy Chart..." function under the Edit menu, and when the dialog box appears, we choose "As Shown on Screen." (This selects the copied image of the chart on the basis of the size of the chart window in Excel.) We then quit Excel and start up MacDraw, where we use "Paste" to import the image.

You can see in Figure 5-6 all the black marks around the various objects in the chart. These are the MacDraw "handles" you could use to grab and reshape the objects if you wanted to make any changes to the chart. You can see how the Excel chart, once pasted into MacDraw, is broken into multiple objects you can manipulate. If we wanted, we could rather easily alter the shape and size of these objects at this point (in MacPaint we would have to do this sort of manipulation laboriously in Fat Bits).

We save the chart with the document name "Elton John Chart/ Draw" and print out a copy on the LaserWriter to thoroughly inspect it. The only modification we want to make is to center the text "CD Title: Elton John" over the entire chart image, including the criteria labels, rather than just the chart portion itself. If you want to learn the details of how images can be "doctored" or improved using MacDraw, read on.

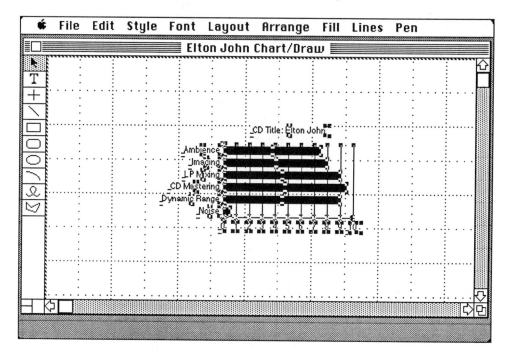

Figure 5-6. Chart Pasted into MacDraw Window.

Grouping and Locking Objects in MacDraw

To position the title accurately, we select all the objects in the chart/label portion of the drawing by positioning the pointer somewhere to the upper left of the chart between the top of the chart and the bottom of the CD title label, dragging down to the lower right of the chart, and releasing the mouse button (see Figure 5-7). This selects all the objects: bars, text, lines, and such. We then press [Command] [G] to make a group of these objects. By grouping these objects together into a single object we can perform operations on the whole image rather than just its component parts.

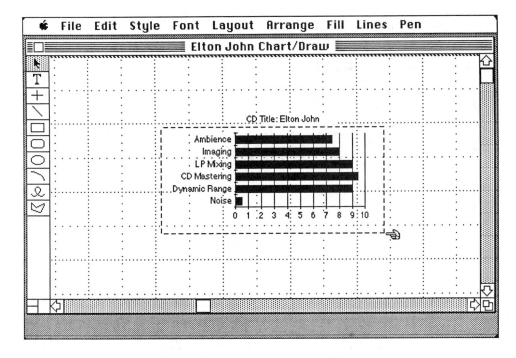

Figure 5-7. Selecting All Objects in a Specific Region.

Next, with the grouped object still selected, we choose "Lock" from the Arrange menu. This locks the image into place on the screen. When we align objects in MacDraw, the objects need a reference point on which to base the alignment. If we tell it to align the objects using their left and right centers, MacDraw will choose a point in the middle of each object and center both objects relative to that center (actually moving each object).

We want the label to be aligned relative to the chart. So we "lock" it into place in the drawing window. This way, when we perform the alignment, only the label moves and not the chart.

Aligning Objects in MacDraw

We select all the objects in the drawing by pressing [Command] [A]. Then we pull down the Arrange menu and choose "Align Objects..." which presents us with a dialog box (see Figure 5-8).

```
┌──────────────────────────────────────────────┐
│                                                │
│   Align Objects:                               │
│      ○ Left Sides    ◉ L/R Centers ○ Right Sides│
│      ○ Tops          ○ T/B Centers ○ Bottoms   │
│   ┌──────────────┐            ┌──────────────┐ │
│   │     OK       │            │    Cancel    │ │
│   └──────────────┘            └──────────────┘ │
│                                                │
└──────────────────────────────────────────────┘
```

Figure 5-8. "Align Objects..." Dialog Box.

We click the "L/R Centers" button to align the center of our label with the center of the chart object. The label is centered (and moved in the drawing) relative to the center of the chart. We save our image with [Command] [S] and print it with the LaserWriter (see Figure 5-9).

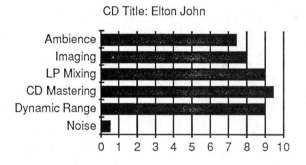

Figure 5-9. Final Version of the Chart.

Saving the Chart as a PICT Image

When we're satisfied with our work, the last thing we do in MacDraw is save the chart as a PICT image (see Appendix B for an explanation of why it is done this way). We press [Command] [A] to select all the objects and press [Command] [C] to copy them. Then we press [Command] [N] to open a new MacDraw window and press [Command] [V] to paste the objects in the new window. When we press [Command] [S] to save we are presented with the "Save document as..." dialog box from MacDraw. We type in "Elton John Chart/PICT," and with the pointer, press the PICT format button. We can now press the "Save" button.

When we return to PageMaker, in Chapter Six, to do the layout, our artwork will be ready to place. At that time we can further adjust its size to fit our space requirements.

Using MacDraw to Create Art

No matter what kind of publication or report you are developing, you will find MacDraw a facile tool with which to create diagrams and line art of all types. The crisp, clean lines it produces on the LaserWriter will suit almost any need for high-definition line art. Once created, the art can easily be copied and pasted into any document.

MacDraw can also be used as a layout tool by itself. Although the letter-spacing is not as tight as that produced by Word or PageMaker, you can combine art and text in MacDraw to create a quick flyer or bulletin board notice in no time at all. Be cautioned however: as of this writing, if you use MacPaint and MacDraw together, the placement of art from MacPaint into MacDraw may not print from the LaserWriter as it appears on the screen. You will need to experiment with positioning MacPaint art relative to MacDraw objects a few times to obtain ideal results. The posters shown in Figure 5-10 were created with MacDraw, combining MacPaint clip-art from Axlon's The Card Shoppe with the messages specified by the client.

Figure 5-10. Two Posters Created in MacDraw.

Creating a Diagram

Using MacDraw, we need to develop a diagram to support our *Audio Image* article titled "Pentimento," which discusses how analog recordings are converted and digitally mastered for production as compact discs. The article discusses the three generations of tape between the original multi-rack recording and the compact disc. Since all analog material transferred to compact disc is technically a digital remastering, which generation of tape is used for this mastering determines the quality of sound on the compact disc. To illustrate the generations of tape involved, we created the diagram shown in Figure 5-11, using MacDraw.

The tape reel symbol we use in the diagram is taken from a LaserWriter Plus typeface called Zapf Dingbats which is full of such symbols and ornaments. If you don't have the Zapf Dingbats font in your System File, you need to install it using the Font/DA Mover. If you don't have a LaserWriter Plus and wish to follow along, you can substitute a half-inch circle, which approximates the size of the tape reels shown in the figures.

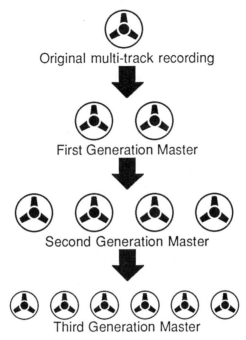

Figure 5-11. An Illustrative Diagram to Accompany an Article.

We begin by selecting the text tool in MacDraw. Before positioning the tool on the drawing page, we choose "Zapf Dingbats" from the Font menu. We then immediately return to the Font menu and choose 48 point type. Now we place the text tool in the top center of the screen and type the tape reel symbol (see Figure 5-12). On the Macintosh keyboard this corresponds to the lowercase foot symbol (') or ⊛. We then select "Center" from the Style menu to center the character.

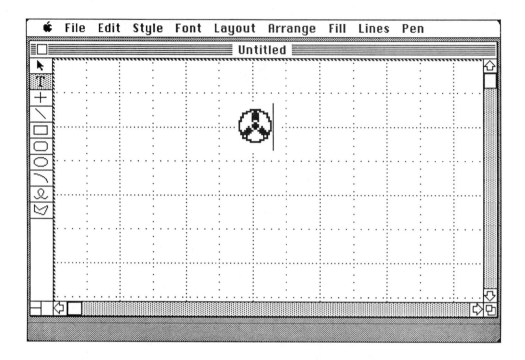

Figure 5-12. 48 Point Tape Reel Symbol as Typed in MacDraw.

Duplicating and Positioning the Symbols

With the tape reel symbol selected, we press [Command] [D] to duplicate it and then drag the duplicate one grid stop to the left and eight stops down the page. With the duplicate still selected, we press [Command] [D] twice to create two more copies of the tape reel and position them at the same relative distance apart. This gives us the basic set of symbols we want to use. Then we go on to duplicate the reels in their appropriate rows (as shown in Figure 5-13). When we get to the last row, we select all six symbols, and from the Font menu, make the reels smaller by selecting 36 point type.

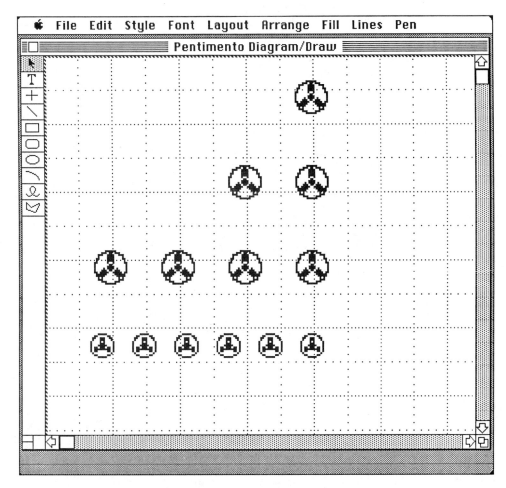

Figure 5-13. Positions for Tape Symbols (Screen Modified).

Using MacDraw's Grid to Construct an Arrow

Each time we start drawing a line with MacDraw in an untitled document window, we notice that our line snaps from point to point as we draw. This is evidence of MacDraw's grid in action. Preset to one-eighth-inch intervals, this grid helps keep objects lined up and accurately positioned. Using MacDraw's "Custom Rulers..." we can adjust the grid to any of 12 divisions corresponding to the minor divisions on the ruler.

The grid can also be turned off (refer to the documentation accompanying MacDraw for further information about using the grid).

Now we select the polygon tool and place it on the page at the nearest grid point somewhere in the upper left portion of the screen (see Figure 5-14). By clicking the mouse button, we begin shaping the arrow. Once we have clicked the button, we only click it again each time we want to establish a fixed angle or line or to change direction in shaping the polygon.

Moving first slightly to the right, we draw the initial angle for the apex of the arrow and click to establish a point. When the grid is in action, clicking causes the line to jump to the nearest grid point. We continue as shown in Figure 5-15 (a 200 percent enlargement), to complete the arrow, clicking to establish points each time we change direction. When we connect the last angle at the bottom of the arrow, MacDraw assumes we've finished the polygon and displays the object with its handles.

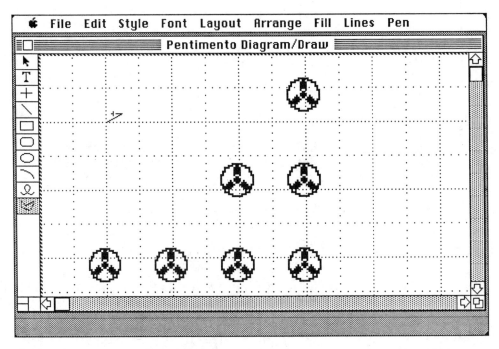

Figure 5-14. Starting the Arrow.

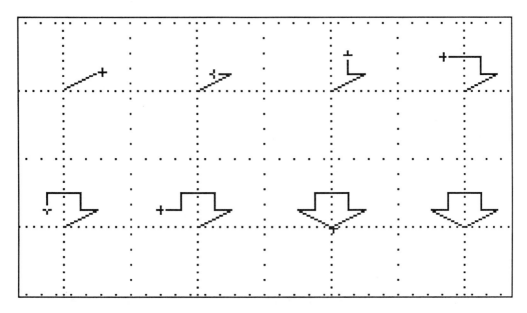

Figure 5-15. Drawing an Arrow Using Eight Grid Points.

Now that we have our arrow, we want to adjust it slightly to conform to our artistic inclinations. With the object still selected, we position the pointer on the top center handle and drag up one grid stop. This elongates the arrow without changing its width (see Figure 5-16).

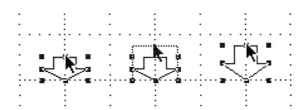

Figure 5-16. Elongating the Arrow.

To finish up, with the arrow still selected, we pull down the Fill menu and choose black to darken the arrow in. Now we make two duplicates of the arrow (for a total of three) by pressing [Command] [D] twice.

Using Text in MacDraw

We want to use four lines of text in the diagram. These are: "Original multi-track recording," "First Generation Master," "Second Generation Master" and "Third Generation Master." The easiest way to enter these into the MacDraw diagram is to use the text tool. We type the first one. Then we duplicate it three times (for a total of four). Then we modify the three copies to suit our requirements.

We select the text tool, pull down the Font menu, choose Helvetica, pull down the Font menu again, and choose 12 point type. Now we scroll the window to the left so we have some white space to type in, on the right, and position our text tool. Before typing, we pull down the Arrange menu and choose "Align To Grid." This makes sure all phrases will be properly aligned to the grid when we later move them around in the drawing. We now type the first phrase. When we're finished we press [Enter] and then press [Command] [D] three times to make duplicates of our phrase.

Picking up each phrase to separate it from the others gives some space to modify it. We reselect the text tool and triple-click the second phrase to highlight the entire phrase. Now we can type, "First Generation Master," and repeat this sequence until the remaining phrases are complete. When we've finished with the last one, we press [Enter] to reselect the pointer.

Making Groups of the Objects

With the text complete, we now want to make grouped objects out of each set of tape reels. This will let us center-align all the elements of the diagram into the final illustration for the article. This process falls together amazingly quickly.

We move the pointer to the upper left of the row of two tape reels. Dragging down and to the right just beneath them selects them. We press [Command] [G] to group these two together into a single object. Scrolling the window so we can see the remaining rows of tape reels, we do the same with each set, selecting the row of four and making a group of them, and finally making a group out of the row of six smaller tapes.

Completing the Diagram

The only remaining task is to center all the objects on the page. We move all our pieces into position as shown in Figure 5-17. Once the phrases and arrows are positioned, we press [Command] [A] to select all the objects in the drawing. Pulling down the Arrange menu we choose "Align Objects..." The alignment dialog box appears and we select "L/R centers."

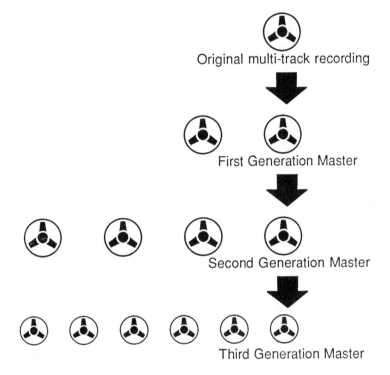

Figure 5-17. Diagram before Using "Align Objects..."

MacDraw immediately centers all the objects relative to one another and our diagram is complete. It now appears as shown in Figure 5-10. We save it, first in MacDraw format and second as "Pentimento Diagram /PICT," using the PICT format for later placement in PageMaker. A printed test version on the LaserWriter reveals no major flaws, so we now feel free to use it in our article.

You will find MacDraw a useful tool for quickly creating diagrams like these that can be used in reports, brochures and overhead projections. You don't have to be an artist to create an elegant and communicative illustration. If you followed along and actually created the diagram or something close to it, you've had a good taste of how easy it is to use MacDraw to produce an illustration. Practice will improve your skill. If you also created the chart in Excel, you now have at least two pieces of art you can use when you reach Chapter Six, where we demonstrate our layout process.

Digitized Images

Suppose you have a company logo you'd like to use with a desktop-published in-house newsletter. You don't want to re-draw it in MacPaint or MacDraw, so how do you acquire it for use on the Macintosh? You digitize it.

Digitization for the Macintosh is a process whereby a camera or other scanning device assesses the various levels of grey in a picture —black and white or color—and transforms that image into numerical data that the computer can understand. Computers are "digital" devices, meaning that everything is ultimately represented to the computer as numbers or digits—at the lowest level, simply ones and zeros or on and off signals.

Digitization takes the image you have outside the computer and makes it into an image that can be used inside the computer and manipulated by drawing programs like MacPaint or by specialized programs supplied with the digitizer. These images can then be added to your layout using simple copy and paste commands, or placed directly into PageMaker as MacPaint documents.

Digitizers come in two flavors. Some, like MacVision, use a video camera to capture your original. Others, like ThunderScan, feed your original through a typewriter-like platen while the scanning head moves back and forth over the surface of the original. In order to do any kind of digitization, you need to use either a video camera device—best suited for three-dimensional objects—or you need to have your original prepared as a two-dimensional object, on paper or photographic stock so that it can be fed into the digitizer. Which type you use—and many people use both—depends on the nature of your original, whether it's three-dimensional or flat, and the quality of art required for your publication.

There is always some loss of resolution when going from photographic or press-quality originals to digitized images. If you want to retain the full image quality of an original photograph for use in your publication, you need to reserve space in your layout for that photograph and have the printer drop it in when you go to press. Chapter Seven, which discusses printers and printing, tells you exactly how to do this.

Super high-resolution digitizers are not available for the Macintosh at this writing, although some very expensive models are being adapted for use in desktop publishing. When these are available, (at upwards of $30,000) you will be able to make use of them through service bureaus and printers.

To capture images for *Audio Image,* we used ThunderScan, from ThunderWare, and MacVision, from Koala Technologies, Inc. There are other digitizers on the market and more are likely to be introduced in the near future. ThunderScan and MacVision are, at the time of this writing, the most popular, readily available, and—perhaps we should mention —easy to use. Their strict adherence to the Macintosh user interface makes them a joy to work with.

ThunderScan

ThunderScan uses the Apple Imagewriter or Imagewriter II printer to scan images into the computer through a connection to the printer port on the back of the Macintosh. The scanning unit fits into the same space as the ink cartridge. The ThunderScan software then manipulates the printer's carriage and paper-feed mechanism to scan the image. It is not our intention to instruct you in how to use ThunderScan. The program that comes with the scanning unit provides many methods for achieving a variety of special effects. You will have to experiment with these yourself to suit your own taste. The main point is how best to use this equipment for desktop publishing purposes and how to use digitized art in a publication.

PREPARING AN IMAGE FOR THUNDERSCAN

Anything you wish to digitize using ThunderScan should be first photocopied on a photocopier with clean glass and fresh toner to obtain the most consistent and highest quality image. This is especially true of four-color material. ThunderScan uses a red LED to reflect light off the page being scanned, and therefore has difficulty assessing the levels of grey in any part of the original that is red. However, a photocopy retains all the information present in the original, including red. Another advantage of photocopying is to guarantee smooth passage through the

Imagewriter. Photos and other thick originals often will not move properly through the printer's transport mechanism.

USING THUNDERSCAN FOR *AUDIO IMAGE*

For our edition of *Audio Image*, we digitized several pieces of art using ThunderScan. All of these images were obtained from the packaging materials accompanying the compact discs being reviewed. We made copies of all the art we anticipated using, aligned each page properly in the Imagewriter, and using the ThunderScan program, defined the area on the page we wanted to scan. We then directed ThunderScan to do its magic and watched the screen as our original art was transformed into digitized images (a fairly slow process, depending on the size of the image). We saved our images as ThunderScan documents; this option saves the entire grey scale for each image. Saving the entire grey scale permits you to use the ThunderScan software at any time to re-halftone or add special effects to images. The images can later be copied to or saved as MacPaint documents.

It is important to note that we scanned all our originals at either 200 percent or 400 percent of their original size. Although the documentation accompanying ThunderScan explains this more thoroughly, we can obtain excellent results when we make ThunderScan scan the image at a substantial percentage larger than its original size. As we pointed out at the beginning of this chapter, when we capture any bit-mapped image at four times its original size, and using the LaserWriter's reduction feature, reduce it to print at 25 percent of the scanned size, it comes out looking very close to the original.

We digitized the "Elton John" logo from the liner notes accompanying the compact disc for use with the Elton John review. We also scanned two other pieces from compact discs manufactured and distributed by Nimbus Records of Great Britain. In our "Industry In-Depth" column, we discuss not only the Nimbus Records, using a Thunder-Scanned image of its logo, but also how compact disc buyers can identify a disc mastered at Nimbus yet distributed by another company—that is, by looking at the inner ring of the disc. To demonstrate this we photo-copied an actual compact disc and digitized (at 400 percent) the area surrounding the inner ring. We will look at each of these later in this chapter.

MacVision

MacVision includes a brightness and contrast control device that attaches to a black-and-white video camera with one cable and the printer port with another. MacVision is operated as a desk accessory that is accessible from the menu, so it can be operated while using any Macintosh application. A more sophisticated version of the MacVision desk accessory, called MoreVision, operates as a stand-alone application and offers enhanced features.

Since it attaches to a video camera, MacVision is particularly sensitive to the lighting used for digitization. The video camera adds to the cost and complexity of the digitization process, but if you have three-dimensional objects that need to be digitized for use in your publication, there is no better way to do it. MacVision is easy to set up and use. It works much quicker than ThunderScan, since the image is continuously sampled by the video camera. However, MacVision works very poorly with two-dimensional or flat objects; for these, ThunderScan is more effective.

We used MacVision to create a portrait of our editor for use with the editorial column header. Once we got the lighting right and the camera properly focused, we clicked the mouse button to capture the portrait. Images are initially saved as a record of a Macintosh screen—the same as pressing [Command] [Shift] [3]—but can later be renamed and used with MacPaint.

We were entirely satisfied with the results and the portrait required minimal modification once created.

Modifying "Elton John" with MacPaint

Once we digitize our images and capture them to disk either as Thunder-Scan documents or MacPaint documents (with MacVision), we need to refine the images to suit our particular needs. To do this, we transform our images into MacPaint documents and modify them in that form.

The image we chose to modify first was the Elton John logo from his album of the same name. Figure 5-18 shows our original image in ThunderScan. It was very close to the original when printed at 25 percent and printed on the LaserWriter. However, we wanted the characters cleaned up a bit to reflect as accurate as possible an impression of the original album artwork. We also wanted the characters reversed from the original, black on white rather than white on black.

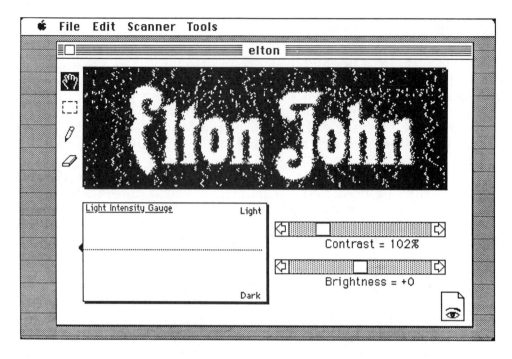

Figure 5-18. Album Art Digitized with ThunderScan.

WORKING WITH FAT BITS

To make these changes, we went into MacPaint with a copy of the Elton John logo, as shown in Figure 5-19. First, we started working in Fat Bits on the "E" in Elton to clean it up. This began as a tedious and painstaking effort but, as you shall see, it gets easier as we go along.

Fat Bits is a wonderful tool for doing detail work on pictures of all sorts. Working with the white space in the "E" is much like carving; we scrape away at the edges with the pencil tool until a smoother image begins to emerge. We can fill in as well as scrape away in order to keep the image consistent (see Figure 5-20).

Working this way in Fat Bits and constantly comparing our work with the original art we were able to clean up all the characters in the word "Elton" to our satisfaction. We measured the widths of each character by counting the number of pixels from edge to edge to keep them consistent as we modified them. We kept a close eye on the miniature view of our drawing in the upper left corner of the screen provided in the Fat Bits window. We filled in all the white dots that cluttered the black space surrounding the words. It took less than an hour to obtain the results shown in Figure 5-21.

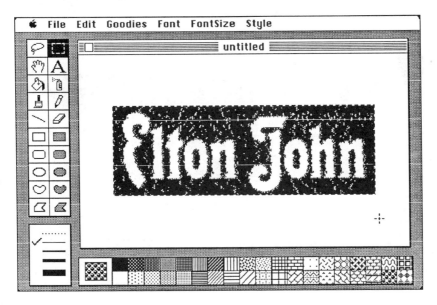

Figure 5-19. Album Art as Pasted into MacPaint.

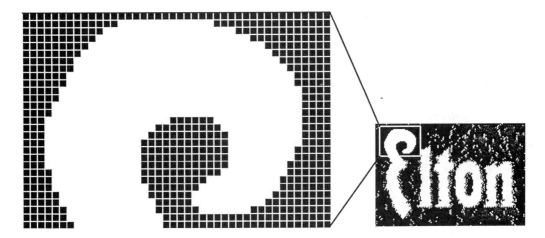

Figure 5-20. Cleaning Up the "E" in Fat Bits.

Figure 5-21. The Word *Elton* Perfected.

COPYING SIMILAR ITEMS

Often Fat Bits is not the most efficient way to clean up an image. It can be a painstakingly slow process. We made use of copying to simplify cleaning up the word John. Now that we had an "o" and an "n" from "Elton," we had all the components we needed.

We lassoed the "n" and positioned it on top of the "n" at the end of "John" and lassoed the "o" and replaced it as well. To form the "h" we took another copy of our "n," clipped off the top serif and positioned the remaining portion over the bottom of the "h" (see Figure 5-22). We cleaned up the lines leading to the top serif on the "h" and positioned our copy of the serif from the "n" on top of that. The only necessary detail work in Fat Bits was on the capital "J."

INVERTING THE IMAGE

To complete the task, we surrounded the Elton John logo with the marquee tool and chose "Invert" from the Edit menu. This gave us the black-on-white image you see in Figure 5-23. We could now use this logo in our layout associated with the review of Elton John's second album now on compact disc.

Figure 5-22. Parts of "n" Lassoed to Refine the "h" in John.

Figure 5-23. Completed Art.

Modifying the Nimbus Logo in MacPaint

We have two digitized images we want to use with the "Industry In-Depth" column about Nimbus Records. The first is the Nimbus logo, which required only minor modification. Figure 5-24 shows the company logo as digitized with ThunderScan. The second is the inner disc circlet that shows where the name "Nimbus Records" appears on compact discs mastered and manufactured by the company. The second image took considerably more work to finalize.

Figure 5-24. Nimbus Records' Logo Digitized in MacPaint.

From ThunderScan we saved the image shown in Figure 5-24 as a MacPaint document and cleaned up the image with the eraser in MacPaint. This didn't take much work at all. Just to test things out though, since we had scanned the image at 400 percent its original size, we decided to print a test version at 25 percent. Since MacPaint doesn't permit scaling of pictures, we quickly placed the image in PageMaker and printed it from there (see Figure 5-25). We were pleasantly surprised to see that it looked almost as good as the original.

Developing the Compact Disc Image

The Nimbus name on the compact disc circlet was surprisingly difficult to capture. Too much light reflected off the disc to get a decent image with either MacVision or a regular 35-millimeter camera. Had we in-vested in expensive close-up photography, we might have been able to get a more accurate image but, considering the budget we have for *Audio Image*, we were very happy with our photocopy and ThunderScan image (see Figure 5-26).

Figure 5-25. Nimbus' Logo Cleaned Up.

If you skip ahead to Figure 5-28, you'll see how much we had to trim the original image. We used PageMaker, MacDraw, and MacPaint loaded into Switcher operating on our Macintosh Plus. (See Appendix A for some tips on using Switcher for desktop publishing.) Switcher lets you load more than one program at a time into memory and then "switch" between them. With the programs loaded into Switcher, you can use the keyboard or the mouse to change from one to the other.

Figure 5-27 shows the steps involved to achieve the final image. The objective here was to clear away enough of the background material in the original ThunderScanned image, so that we ended up with a clear circular image. We had to somehow define where the background stopped and the circle began.

This is how we did it. The first step was to create a mask which would overlay the circlet image and define its circular shape. We couldn't fit the entire image (originally scanned at 400 percent) into any program where we could view it all at once except PageMaker. We put the MacPaint image we had made in ThunderScan onto a blank page in PageMaker and, using the oval tool, we drew out a circle that outlined the image (Step 1 in Figure 5-27).

In PageMaker this circle object is black and the one we want needs to be white (reversed). There's no way to change the pen color in Page-Maker so we copied the encircling outline to the clipboard and switched over to MacDraw. We pasted the image into MacDraw, thickened the line width from the Lines menu and changed the pen color to white from the Pen menu (Step 2).

Figure 5-26. Digitized Inner Circlet of a Nimbus-Mastered Compact Disc.

We copied the new circle object and switched back to PageMaker, where we pasted the object on top of our compact disc image (Step 3). After making a few minor adjustments to it we began the next phase.

There was no way to get the entire image back into MacPaint all at once so we zoomed into actual size and made six separate screen snapshots ([Command] [Shift] [3]) of various regions of the image. Switching to MacPaint, we cleaned up each of these using MacPaint's eraser and pencil tool (Step 4). Then we copied all the segments to a new MacPaint document and assembled them into the image you see in Figure 5-28.

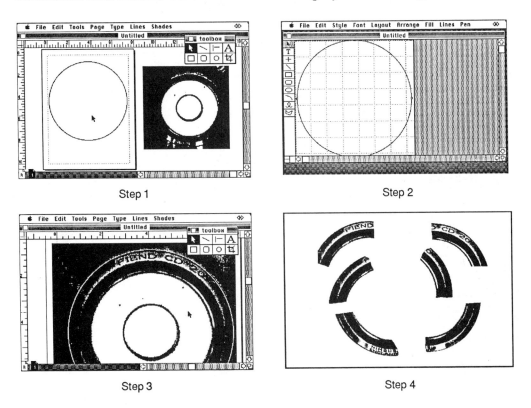

Step 1   Step 2

Step 3   Step 4

Figure 5-27. Modifying Digitized Image of Compact Disc Inner Circlet.

Figure 5-28. Final Version of Inner Circlet Ready for Newsletter.

The Editor's MacVision Portrait

All we needed to do with the MacVision portrait of *Audio Image's* editor was erase around the edges in MacPaint to clean out the background. Once we had erased enough of the background, we lassoed the portrait, pasted it into a new MacPaint window and saved it (see Figure 5-29). MacVision images are just as easy to manipulate in MacPaint as are ThunderScanned images. However, we required no further modifications of the image (see Figure 5-30).

All in all we are quite satisfied with the results of our digitization. We found the tools interesting and exciting to use. You'll probably enjoy experimenting with digitized images also.

The Electric
Stylus Logo

On the masthead for *Audio Image,* we plan to print the phrase, "An Electric Stylus Publication." Electric Stylus is the newsletter publisher's company, which, in effect, sponsors *Audio Image* and other publications. To show you how you can mix art from different sources using MacPaint, we'll explain how the Electric Stylus logo was assembled.

Figure 5-29. Cleaning up the Editor's Portrait in MacPaint.

Figure 5-30. Editor's Portrait Ready for Use in *Audio Image*.

We took an existing font, Mos Eisley from Miles Computing's "Mac The Knife, Volume Two: Fonts," replaced the "l" in "Electric" with a character from Apple's own Taliesin font (which comes with MacDraw) and modified a character in Fat Bits (the "y" in "Stylus") to produce the results you see in Figure 5-31. This sort of endeavor is easy, yet can yield pleasing and original results. Producing art in this way is one of the enjoyable things about using the Macintosh for desktop publishing. You can bring almost all of your publishing efforts in-house and come up with creative results—*use your imagination*. That's what art is all about.

Electronic Clip-Art

In traditional publishing, clip-art is a mainstay among art directors and graphic designers. Clip-art is traditionally available either as press-on transfers or in paperbound books of reproducible art that contain numerous ornaments, borders, cartoon sketches, animals, and familiar objects such as cars, bouncing balls, scissors, and the like. The art is clipped from these sources using scissors or an X-Acto® knife and pasted into the publication where needed.

Ever since the Macintosh was introduced with MacPaint, companies have rushed to market a number of disks full of electronic clip-art (see Figure 5-32 for some examples). Electronic clip-art can be lassoed in MacPaint and copied to the clipboard for electronic pasting in your publication. Some of the most popular packages are from Miles Computing of Van Nuys, California, makers of the "Mac The Knife" series (Volumes, I, II and III) and T/Maker of Mountain View, California, makers of the "Click-Art" series ("Click-Art," "Click-Art Letters," and "Click-Art Publications"). Another fine collection called The Card Shoppe comes from Axlon of Sunnyvale, California. Originally conceived as a kit for assembling greeting cards, the clip-art in this package is useful in many other ways as well.

Perhaps the most interesting collection of clip-art is the Mac-Memories Series from ImageWorld of Eugene, Oregon. Nearly all of these images are captured from turn-of-the-century catalogs, book plates, advertisements and such; their older, antique style of art reproduces well on the LaserWriter. Many of the MacMemories images are full-page MacPaint documents. When reduced as part of a publication in Page-Maker, they print with incredible detail.

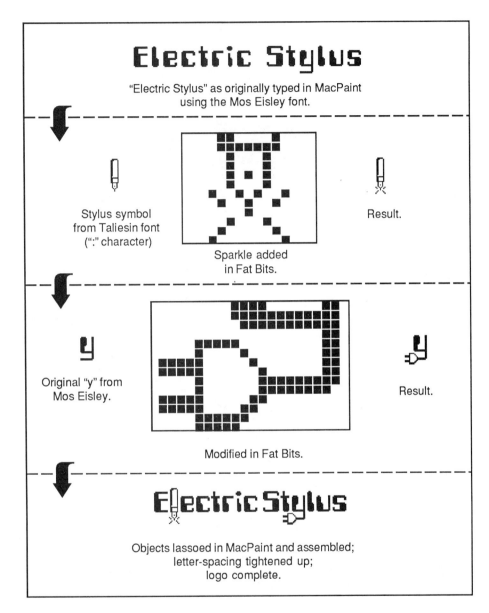

Electric Stylus

"Electric Stylus" as originally typed in MacPaint using the Mos Eisley font.

Stylus symbol from Taliesin font (":" character)

Sparkle added in Fat Bits.

Result.

Original "y" from Mos Eisley.

Modified in Fat Bits.

Result.

Electric Stylus

Objects lassoed in MacPaint and assembled; letter-spacing tightened up; logo complete.

Figure 5-31. How the Electric Stylus Logo Was Created.

Perhaps the most interesting collection of clip-art is the Mac-Memories Series from ImageWorld of Eugene, Oregon. Nearly all of these images are captured from turn-of-the-century catalogs, book plates, advertisements and such; their older, antique style of art reproduces well on the LaserWriter. Many of the MacMemories images are full-page MacPaint documents. When reduced as part of a publication in Page-Maker, they print with incredible detail.

Hanging fuchias from MacMemories Series

Animals from Mac The Knife, Vol. 1

Sailing ship from The Card Shoppe

Cameo Portraits from Click Art

Figure 5-32. Clip-Art Sampler.

Almost all electronic clip-art is constructed for use with MacPaint. Some of the pictures are digitized from real life and refined by the manu-facturer's artists; the rest are hand-drawn in MacPaint. (Some useful clip-art is also available via information utilities like Compuserve, GEnie, and The Source in their respective on-line Macintosh clubs and confer-ences.)

You will have to assess your own needs for this kind of art solution; oftentimes it is very handy to fill a space on a page or make the page more visually interesting. But, as we've cautioned before, you can easily overdo it. If you use too much of this kind of art on a page you will confuse your readers and mislead them as to the content of the page. But used appropriately, it can provide just the right touch.

Another consideration is how well this art prints on a LaserWriter —for that matter, how any MacPaint art prints on the LaserWriter. As we mentioned earlier, the Macintosh screen displays characters and images at a resolution of 72 dots (pixels) per inch while the LaserWriter prints at 300 dots per inch. This represents quite a difference in resolution. If your art is reduced by using PageMaker's reduction skills—as we will do in Chapter Six—many of the resolution problems disappear. You also have the option of smoothing the clip-art, in this way removing or softening the jaggies from MacPaint. For some art this works well, for others it does not. You will have to experiment and see which pieces are suitable and which are not.

All in all, though, electronic clip-art for the Macintosh can provide quick solutions to illustration problems. The art in the posters shown in Figure 5-10 was assembled entirely from electronic clip-art. As you create art from various sources, you'll want to assemble your own disk volumes of reusable clip-art.

Summary

Getting the artwork ready is another major phase in developing a publication. In this chapter you have discovered how a chart can be moved into any Macintosh program—Microsoft Word, MacDraw, or PageMaker. You have followed along as we drew a diagram in MacDraw to use with an article. If you performed both of these steps with us, you now have some art with which you can simulate the placement of art into a publication, as we will do in Chapter Six. Of course, you may not wish to duplicate our efforts exactly. Feel free to use some of your own art. Just make sure it approximates the same size and shape as ours and you'll have no trouble following along.

We discussed digitized images and pointed out both the advantages and pitfalls of capturing art digitally. You now know how such images can be refined using the Macintosh's drawing tools. You also learned how art can be created by combining pieces from various sources, as we developed the Electric Stylus logo. Finally, electronic clip-art gives you a means of obtaining art from outside sources and a basis for evaluating the worth of such art.

Whether you use these specific techniques or not, the important point is that you have your art planned and developed before you attempt your layout. You want to have all the pieces ready, copy and art alike, as you go on to assemble your publication in PageMaker. You'll see in Chapter Six, how this makes the entire layout process much easier and less confusing.

What's Next

In Chapter Six you'll follow along as we use PageMaker to do the page composition and layout for *Audio Image*. In the process, you'll discover some important rules of thumb you can apply to your own publication, both in designing the page composition and in your use of PageMaker. We'll do the entire electronic pasteup of our first page in typical hands-on fashion. You'll also learn how some interesting effects can be achieved by taking PageMaker to the limit.

Page Composition and Layout

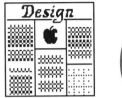

6

In this chapter you will learn:

- Page composition and layout fundamentals
- Placement of text and graphics
- Manipulating text and graphics
- Contour-fitting text around irregular shapes

In the preceding sections you've seen how to create text, artwork and a template to provide the basic framework for a publication. In this chapter we'll put it all together. We'll show you in detail the steps we took to combine the various elements into the completed pages of the *Audio Image* newsletter, shown in Figures 6-1 through 6-4, on the following pages.

For you to follow along in this chapter, it is important that you have actually created some of the text and graphic elements described in the previous chapters in this book—at least those which appear on the first page of the newsletter. Of course, the elements you've created need not be exactly the same as the ones we've done. You may have written different text, or created different graphic images. However, it will be helpful if your text and images are roughly the same size as those we use, so that you'll be able to follow along step-by-step as we combine the elements into a finished page.

In order to follow the discussion in this chapter it is also important that you have some prior experience with PageMaker. The creation of the template described in Chapter Three is a good start. You should also have experimented with PageMaker on your own, worked through the tutorial and read through the remainder of the PageMaker manual. If you encounter a term or procedure that is unfamiliar, you should feel free to refer to the manual for further information.

Elton John

The piano emerged from a background of absolute silence and spread across the full breadth of an apparent 20 foot sound stage. When Elton John's voice broke into "It's a little bit funny...," the opening verse of "Your Song," it was chills and goosebumps for me. The piano, guitar, drums, string quartet, Elton's rich voice —all were crisp and clear as the day they were recorded. I could tell immediately that I had purchased a compact disc of rare quality. The thrill of listening to this masterpiece wasn't going to evaporate soon as it had with so many other past favorites clumsily transferred from an analog source to digital audio. This was sheer brilliance.

When the next song, "I Need You To Turn To" began, I did a dumb thing. The harpsichord breaks gently into the room filling the left listening arena without a hint of sound from the right speaker. I thought there was something wrong with it. I rushed over and put my ear up to it and, you guessed it, about this time Elton John starts singing and I almost went deaf. But that's the startling thing about this disc—as little extraneous noise as I have heard on any compact disc to date (excluding most digital recordings). After he finishes singing the first verse, the guitar gently breaks into the right of the listening room. Another verse and the lush orchestration of Paul Buckmaster overwhelms you.

By the time "Take Me To The Pilot" finishes—with its slight echo on voice, swirling orchestra effect and Caleb Quaye's funky guitar riffs—you suddenly realize this is one of your favorite albums and how wonderful it is to be able to listen to it and really *hear* it, the way Gus Dudgeon, the producer, must have heard it the day they finished mixing.

"Sixty Years On" is a special case in point. From the first bee-buzzing of the cellos at the beginning to the sudden decay and introduction of the harp, you know you've wandered into a sonic wonderland of undeniable beauty. What dimension! The masterful arrangement of the strings by Paul Buckmaster —who graces all of Elton John's early albums —transforms this into a performance rivaling any of today's modern string quartets. This isn't one of those set pieces where the strings are brought in to bolster a poorly written pop melody. Here they shine through as an unmistakable part of the music, not an afterthought. The strings are mixed tight and share equal footing with the other instruments —piano, guitar and drums alike.

But this is not meant to be a performance review. You already know if you like this album or not. If you do, you are in for one of the most pleasant surprises compact disc technology has to offer. With no informative code in evidence anywhere on the package, we can only assume the disc was digitally mastered (*Audio Image* is checking into this) and, most likely, mastered from the original mix down tape. There are obviously very few generations of oxide between the source and your ears. Speaking of oxide, for a tape made 17 years ago, this one must have been watched over with extreme care. Only the slightest hint of hiss—difficult to discern with even the most critical of ears—was evident in any of the songs (see Evaluation Chart).

This attests to the continuing high level of excellence and superior attention to detail evidenced throughout Nimbus Records' repertoire of analog to digital masterings (see **Industry In-Depth** column, this issue). We can only hope that with the opening of their second CD plant that they are able to maintain the same level of quality.

This, Elton John's second album, is available as an import on the DJM label (British). Don't get it confused with the domestic release. It won't be nearly as good. Compared with the rest of *Audio Image's* Elton John collection which includes *Tumbleweed Connection, Madman Across the Water*, and *Goodbye Yellow Brick Road*, all on MCA, this is by far the best. It is, for now, the benchmark against which all other digitally mastered analog recordings will live or die on our CD player. The accompanying booklet is complete with lyrics, accompanist credits and color photos—a thorough reconstruction of the album sleeve right down to the purple print on the names of the songs. ◉

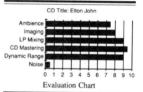

Evaluation Chart

Fact Sheet:

Title: **Elton John**. Artist: Elton John, vocals and piano. Lyrics: Bernie Taupin. Arranger and Conductor: Paul Buckmaster. Producer: Gus Dudgeon. Label: DJM. Disc mastering: Nimbus Records. Mastering Facility: Great Britain. Original album copyright, 1970.

> ### Inside This Issue:
>
> *How to identify Nimbus' discs...see page 2.*
>
> *Find out what "digitally mastered analog recording" really means...see page 3.*
>
> *What's new from Japan & Germany...see page 3.*
>
> *And, find out why we created Audio Image...see page 2.*

Page 1

Figure 6-1. Page One of *Audio Image*.

EDITORIAL
Why Create *Audio Image*?
by Kevin Rardin

Audio Image was created for the discriminating compact disc listener. Like us, you are impressed with the awesome sound compact discs have brought into our listening rooms. All of a sudden music sounds like it never has before—clear, crisp, full and *loud* —and there's that wonderful absolute silence between tracks that lets you know that nothing but a beam of light is touching the disc. We can all agree that the compact disc is a genuine technological breakthrough for stereo sound.

However, these little discs in their "jewel" boxes cost a pretty penny. Quite frankly, after the initial sheen and awe has worn off, your ears settle down and get quite used to the compact disc sound as a standard. Just listening to the car radio can become an intolerable experience.

And, after your ears are sensitized, you begin to notice some strange things about those CD's. Why, gosh, there's an awful lot of hiss in that song, or how come the bass sounds muffled on one recording and tight and thumpy on another. But hey, give the band a break, those noises were in there all along. They're built into the analog recording process.

On the other hand, the compact disc gives us something only the high-end audiophiles can call a common experience and that's what's called, "imaging." Now, by simply going from black vinyl to silver plastic, the sound comes from all corners of the room. Maybe this is a first for you...or maybe this kind of sonic experience is what you *demand* out of your system.

Either way, *Audio Image* is here to let

you know which discs are the best and how they got that way. We accept no paid advertising and we aren't tied to any advertiser's point of view.

The emphasis here is on sound, not performance. You can read Rolling Stone or Stereo Review to find out who likes a certain piece of music. But who's going to tell you whether it sounds good on CD? *Audio Image* is. And we'll tell you as much about that sound as we can. Does it image? Is it ambient? Does it expoit the full CD dynamic range?

And we also plan to take you behind the scenes, so you'll know how to make enlightened CD purchasing decisions. *Audio Image* will take you on tours of compact disc pressing plants and mastering facilities. We'll interview topnotch recording engineers so you'll know what goes on in a recording studio to get the sound just right. You'll discover which labels to trust and which ones to avoid and find the little known secrets of who's doing what, when and where. ☺

INDUSTRY IN-DEPTH
Nimbus Records

In the ever constant quest for compact discs of superior sound quality, *Audio Image* has stumbled upon a little known record company based in Wales (Great Britain) whose name, appropriately enough, is Nimbus. Nimbus Records is well-known in Britain as a classical recording company and also better known there for their CD mastering and manufacturing facility. The entire operation including recording studios, concert halls, LP and CD mastering and manufacturing facilities are housed on an estate in the Welsh countryside known as Wyastone Leys. Nimbus commitment to quality sound is evident in listening to any of their own classical music discs or the

discs they have mastered and pressed for other labels—mostly pop.

Their own titles can be idenitified by the quaint art nouveau logo, a sample of which accompanies this article.

However, discovering which discs they've mastered for other labels is somewhat less obvious. To date, *Audio Image* has found Nimbus' mastered discs on the DJM, Virgin and Island labels. However, all of these labels make use of other mastering and pressing facilities in Germany and Japan whose sound quality can't compete with those assembled by Nimbus. So you have to look carefully at the inner ring on the CD to find the words, "Nimbus England" imprinted (see figure).

We've been extremely happy with the compact discs on Nimbus that we've been

Inside ring from a Nimbus' mastered compact disc—notice the words, "Nimbus England."

able to find here in the U.S. These include two reviewed in this issue of *Audio Image*, Propaganda and Elton John. Other titles mastered by Nimbus that we like are The Stranglers' **Aural Sculpture**, Mike Oldfield's **Tubular Bells** and Orchestral Manœuvres In The Dark (OMD) recent album, **Crush**. ☺

---

audio image safe bets

- Kate Bush: **Hounds Of Love** (EMI Records, Ltd.)
- Chicago: **Chicago 17** (Warner Bros.)
- Dire Straits: **Brothers In Arms** (Vertigo/Phonogram)
- Arne Domnérus, et. al.: **Jazz At The Pawn Shop** (Proprius/AudioSource®)
- Michael Hedges: **Aerial Boundaries** (Windham Hill)
- Jimi Hendrix: **Electric Ladyland** (Polydor)
- Jean-Michel Jarre: **Zoolook** (Disques Dreyfus)
- Trevor Pinnock & The English Concert: **Pachelbel Canon & Gigue** (Archiv/Polydor)
- John Wallace & The Philharmonia Orchestra: **Man—The Measure of All Things** (Nimbus Records)

Page 2

Figure 6-2. Page Two of *Audio Image*.

Pentimento

by Kevin Rardin

"Pentimento" is a word used in the art and museum circles to describe the process of refurbishing and preserving a classic work of art—making it new again. One of the central concerns of *Audio Image*'s reviews is a constant evaluation of the care taken in transferring older modern "classics" like **Tubular Bells** and **Dark Side of the Moon** to the new digital format. We take very seriously the caveat on the back of some compact disc packages that warns, "The music on this compact disc was originally recorded on analog equipment...Because of its high resolution, however, the compact disc can reveal limitations of the source tape." And you can bet there are real and audible limitations.

The pentimento process for converting analog recording to the digital compact disc format isn't easy. Some record companies take it seriously and some are just trying to get those discs to market as fast as they can. In order to fully understand the meaning of the phrase, "digitally mastered analog recording" you have to know something about how records are made and the various changes that take place between the recording studio and your local CD store.

The "master" is the source tape used to create all commercially available records, tapes and compact discs. There are, however, several generations of "masters" and which one is used for the digital mastering of a CD is very important to how good that CD sounds.

A recording typically begins in a recording studio. Many classical recordings are made in the concert hall where the orchestra usually practices and performs. Several microphones are used to record the music onto a multi-track tape. A multi-track tape can have anywhere from 8 to 48 tracks on it and may physically measure anywhere from 1/8" to 1" wide.

Once the multi-track recording is made, any planned overdubs are then introduced onto the tape. Once the overdubbing is complete or if there are no overdubs and everyone's happy with the multi-track recording, the next step is mixing the tracks to achieve their various stereo effects.

This is a complicated process which *Audio Image* plans to cover in depth in

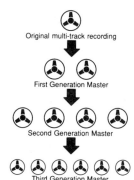

Original multi-track recording

First Generation Master

Second Generation Master

Third Generation Master

future issues. However, understand that this tape, the mix master, is, in most recording circles, considered the first generation master tape (see diagram). Sometimes a "safety" tape is made simultaneously along with the mix master, so there may be, in fact, two mix masters.

From the mix master, a second generation of masters is spawned. Three or four dub tapes are made by tape librarians of the mix master tape. It is commonly understood that up to 400% of the original recorded sound is lost in this transfer from mix master to dub. The mix master is put in a storage vault and the dub tapes are distributed to other facilities to begin preparations for making actual records and tapes. However, there are more than a few LP, tape and CD pressing plants

working on these projects, so yet a third generation tape is made.

The third generation tape made from the dub tape is usually compressed and equalized for the specific format it will be used with: vinyl record, cassette tape or compact disc. Several of these third generation "masters" are made; however many are needed to supply the numerous pressing plants throughout the world. This tape is still considered by the recording industry as a master tape. You can imagine, though, how much sound quality is lost in the translation, given the nature of tape formulations, the decay of iron oxides, and recording equipment involved. We are now four steps from our multi-track recording and into three generations of master tapes.

You should be aware that *most* digitally mastered analog recordings for compact disc are made from this third generation tape. If we're lucky the digital master will be made from a dub tape. Companies like Mobile Fidelity and Audio-Source specialize in the use of original vault masters to create their digitally mastered CDs.

A careful and critical listening of CD's on mid-fi or high-end equipment will tell you from which generation the digital master was made. Listen to a disc that you *know* was mastered from a vault original. Then listen to one you have doubts about. Rest assured, you will be able to tell the difference.

When we can determine it and trust the source of our information, *Audio Image* will let you know, in our reviews, from which generation an analog source tape was acquired for digital mastering. ◎

Beatniks & Propaganda: Intense!

by John Relph

One of the most interesting and provocative discs currently available is the 1985 release by the Japanese formation The Beatniks entitled **Exitentialism** (*sic*). The music is distinctly Japanese: traditional harmonies work with more modern rhythms and textures including influences from the lush arrangements of post-war american big band music to the Beatles. This diversity in musical styles is also reflected in lyrics that address current concerns including the ever-present nuclear threat, overcrowding of cities, and the **EXITENTIALISM** hectic high-pressure **THE BEATNIKS** lifestyle that is today's society. There are also reminders of the industrial music of Throbbing Gristle and Wall of Voodoo, dirty sounding synthesizer noises that show that the Beatniks are using the technology, rather than being used by it, like so many popular synthesizer night-school bands.

Unfortunately there are no credits included in the liner notes. The only credits listed are the songwriting credits, which indicate the Beatniks to be a four-piece group con-

See page 4

Figure 6-3. Page Three of *Audio Image.*

BEATNIKS & PROPAGANDA

sisting of Takahashi, Barakan, Suzuki, and Watanabe. The recognizable style of Yukihiro Takahashi shows him to be the leader of the band— he wrote four of the eleven tracks and co-wrote four more. The only other information included with the disc is a lyrics sheet, which has the lyrics printed in both the language in which the songs were performed and in Japanese, as is usual practice in Japanese releases. The songs move easily from French to English and back again, with only a smattering of Japanese thrown in as if in token recognition of the band's origin. This effort is defnitely an international one, though it is also purely Japanese in essence.

The production is excellent throughout. The disc has been digitally mastered and there is little hiss, evincing a very clear analog recording. The mix is both tight and spacious, with very good imaging and interesting movement across the channels. The performance is exceptional. Takahashi's drumming is both inventive and precise, never overly flashy, always supremely competent. The synthesizers never seem to take over the music, but are used to provide a spare background upon which are flashed percussives, sometimes drumlike, sometimes merely noises, sometimes bouncing back and forth from channel to channel as if disembodied. In the two instrumental tracks featured on this disc, the noises are reminiscent of The Residents' **Mark of the Mole**, or some of Jean-Michel Jarre's city-influenced works. However, though synthesizers are heavily used, most of the

drums are not synthesized, and acoustic piano and guitar are found in a good number of the selections.

Altogether, The Beatniks' mastery of different styles, their thoughtful and competent instrumentation, and their fine production made this disc a wonderful find and quite enjoyable to listen to. The disc is produced by VAP, Inc., Tokyo, Japan, number 80018-32.

Another fine disc which I happened upon almost by accident is the 1985 Propaganda release **a secret wish**. This German band is co-ordinated by Zang Tuum Tumb, otherwise known as ZTT. ZTT has released a series of singles and albums called the "Wishful Action Series", of which **a secret wish** is number 13. Other releases in this series have included a picture disc ostensibly performed by, but not credited to, Propaganda, and previous versions of various pieces on this release. Incidentally, the compact disc version of this release contains performances which are not on the album release, and vice versa. Propaganda is a four piece band consisting of Michael Mertens, Suzanne Freytag, Claudia Brücken, and Ralf Dorper. Mertens writes the music, Dorper, the lyrics. Propaganda's sound is a more mainstream presentation than that of The Beatniks. Produced by S.J. Lipson, mixed by Lipson and Trevor Horn, this disc shows evidence of Horn's influence, especially in the clear mix like that of Yes' **90125**. Lipson and Horn, as well as Steve Howe and other artists, also played some instruments on this release.

Propaganda is well aware of the connotations that their name carries, and the packaging of the disc is filled with various quotations and written pieces on various subjects. The band seems to be reasonably well educated, as it appears that they wrote most of the text included in the accompanying booklet. Indeed, the first selection on the disc is a version of Edgar Allan Poe's "A Dream Within a Dream," the refrain of which opens and closes **a secret wish** although this is not the same version as that performed by the Alan Parsons Project on their **Edgar Allan Poe: Tales of Mystery and**

Imagination release. The photography of the band is done by Anton Corbijn, who also did the photography on the Police's **Synchronicity** and U2's **War**.

While the presentation is more mainstream, there are still more experimental elements present in their music. A drum solo, rarely heard nowadays, graces the middle section of the nine minute long "A Dream Within a Dream." Two versions of the same song are performed, entitled "Jewel" and "Duel;" one more punk, one more pop, respectively. The former has overtones of the group 999, with scratchy vocals that almost sound screamed, while the latter sounds more like recent Human League, complete with stock synthesizer licks and "nice" female vocals. Much of the music reflects their German origin, and sounds much like what little German dance music that has made it over the ocean to America, such as Falco or Peter Schilling.

This disc is entirely digital. The recording notes included on the back face of the jewel box cover go into extreme detail, including a small "noise information" section which lists the clicks, pops, and other noise present in the recordings, which even in loud listening sessions (which this recording warrants) are not noticeable. The disc is attractively packaged, and includes a four leaf booklet designed by Corbijn. The disc is Island Records release CID 126, and is made by Nimbus in the UK release. ◉

---

audio image

Vol. 1, No. 1—Premier Issue
Fall, 1986

Editor & Publisher:
Kevin Michael Rardin
Office Management:
Lynn Maya-Ray
Contributors:
John Relph, Warren Sirota

Audio Image is published once each quarter for $18.00 per year by Electric Stylus, P.O. Box 621, Palo Alto, California 94302-0621.

An **E|ectric Stylus** Publication
TM & © 1986, Electric Stylus
All Rights Reserved

Page 4

Editor's Quarterly Gramophone Award

Aqualung
by
Jethro Tull
(Chrysalis)

If you want to hear the guitar solos on this album like you've never heard them before, then buy it. However, the rest of the music is obscured by tape hiss resulting from—we think—numerous overdubs. We are hopeful that some company like Nimbus or Mobile Fidelity will acquire the first generation master and do a better job. If you have to have it, be prepared for a bitter dissappointment. We were. —*Editor* ◉

Figure 6-4. Page Four of *Audio Image*.

Page Composition
and Layout Basics

In this chapter we will show you step-by-step how we created our publication and how our design decisions evolved. When you're ready to do your own publication, you'll need to make similar design decisions about what kind of layout you want.

Page composition is an art. If you have no previous experience, it's doubtful that you'll be able to sit down at your Mac and create layouts that rival those of the best graphic artists. However, there's no reason why, after reading this book and experimenting a bit, you can't come up with a satisfactory design. This section mentions a few of the fundamental rules used by graphic designers and art directors. Needless to say, entire books have been written about design, so we can only scratch the surface. Our advice is this: read the chapter, try your own layout and then, if you have any question—and maybe even if you're completely satisfied—take it to one or two people who know something about design and ask for their opinion. That's what we did and it paid off handsomely.

Before you start, you should have a clear picture in your mind of what you want your publication to look like. Is it two-column or three-column? How do you envision the placement of artwork to support the copy? Will you use heads and subheads? Ask yourself as many questions about your publication as possible and visualize your answers. Having a strong visual image of how you want your publication to look makes your use of any page layout tool, including PageMaker, much easier.

If necessary, take pencil and paper in hand and sketch out several possible dummy pages. Likewise, you can print your galleys from Microsoft Word, cut them up and play with the page composition until you have a good idea of what you want to do in PageMaker. Or, you can create dummy pages in PageMaker using your actual copy and art.

If you find yourself at a loss for ideas, look at other publications in the same professional or occupational field as yours. For elegance and simplicity of design, we often referred to *Time* magazine and the *New York Times Book Review* to inspire our page design efforts. If you see something you like, such as a headline with white letters on a black background, duplicate the effect in PageMaker and see if it works. If it does, great. If it doesn't, go on to try something else.

The remainder of this section suggests fundamental methods and techniques for turning Macintosh desktop publishing tools to your advantage and avoiding the pitfalls of careless page composition and layout. Once you've achieved a level of satisfaction with the page composition and layout, you'll still need to spend a fair amount of time fine-tuning the publication. If you want an effective publication that truly communicates, attention to detail is extremely important.

Simplicity

As previously mentioned, perhaps the most important advice graphic artists give to beginners is to keep it simple. Nothing looks worse than a complex design executed by a novice. Don't use too many design elements and try to combine them in simple ways. Stick to one or two fonts and a very few sizes of type. When in doubt about whether to add a new element, don't. A page with four or five type sizes, two different kinds of boxes enclosing text, several pieces of art—some with boxes, some not—will most likely look so chaotic and jumbled that potential readers won't be able to read it. If your design is too simple you run the risk of creating a routine layout, but this is preferable to being too complex and confusing the reader.

As you do more design work you'll begin to develop a feeling for what works and what doesn't. After your third or fourth publication you'll have the confidence to try more complex designs. But don't push it—it's always better to err on the side of simplicity.

Symmetry, Asymmetry and Visual Interest

Symmetry is fundamental to design—whether created by man or found in nature. Look around you. The left side of most objects are mirror images of the right. The tiger's stripes fall equally from the center of its back onto its sides. Similarly, the words on the title page of a book are often centered on the page so equal amounts of type fall on the left and right. Symmetry is natural and it is the starting point from which all basic design proceeds.

Symmetry can also be very boring, especially if looked at time and again, page after page. Asymmetry is introduced into the design to create visual interest. Every so often we want to break up the established order of things to make the page more interesting to look at. But be careful, this can get out of hand very quickly. Remember that we start with symmetry and perfect symmetry is our base.

In Chapter Three, you saw the basic symmetrical layout of a logo centered on the page over three columns. Fold the page in half and you'll see the left mirrors the right. Although we won't stray far from that basic design rule, we suggest that you should be prepared, as you go about planning your page composition and layout, to upset the balance once in awhile. Holding too tightly to the idea of perfect symmetry can lead to a tedious page layout. Ignoring symmetry altogether, though, only creates confusion.

The trick here is to strike a balance between symmetry and asymmetry in such a way as to make the page interesting to view. Symmetry always prevails throughout the publication. Asymmetry is delicately introduced into the publication, here and there, to keep the eye moving and to avoid monotony. You'll see how we used symmetry and asymmetry to create visual interest in *Audio Image* as we proceed in this chapter.

Page Layout Rules of Thumb

Before we get into the details of using PageMaker, we'll show you some of the rules used by graphic designers to help ensure the most effective layout process.

POSITION YOUR LARGEST BLOCKS OF COPY FIRST

Regardless of what kind of publication you are assembling, you will invariably have a mix of long articles and short ones. If you don't, you should definitely consider creating articles of varying length because they give you much more flexibility when it comes to page composition and layout.

You want to position your largest pieces first. You probably have a lead article or introductory piece that you want to position prominently. Place your articles in descending order of consequence, with the most important first.

With PageMaker, as you'll see, this is a very straightforward process. Using the "Place..." command, you simply flow the text into the columns for as many columns as needed. Keep in mind how you want to position your accompanying art. If necessary, large pieces of art should be positioned at the same time as the article.

WORK IN LARGE ARTWORK NEXT

Once you've placed your major articles, you will want to work in your most prominent and bulky illustrations or photo blocks. You will need to adjust the copy to fit around the artwork and vice versa. Using the text handles in PageMaker, you can easily adjust the text, place the art and reflow the text either around or past the illustration.

USE AN ODD NUMBER OF VISUAL ELEMENTS PER PAGE

In order to achieve a good balance between copy and artwork, you should try to use an odd number of visual elements per page. Elements can include, but are not limited to, illustrations, photos and diagrams. It is much easier to achieve a balanced and pleasing design if you use 1, 3 or 5 art elements per page.

USE RULER GUIDES TO KEEP THINGS LINED UP

As you move through your publication, flowing text and placing art, use PageMaker's horizontal and vertical ruler guides to keep things lined up. If two elements—text or graphics—end up positioned vertically or horizontally relative to one another, pull in a ruler guide from the ruler and make sure the elements line up exactly. Likewise, if you are moving column guides on the page or temporarily adjusting them, use a vertical ruler guide as a place marker so you can return to the same position later. Ruler guides are also useful in lining up text across the page or setting text so they line up with an adjacent art element.

WORK IN HEADS AND SUBHEADS

Heads (or topic headlines) and subheads are positioned after your major text and art have been placed. Your heads and subheads should be written, edited and finalized before you position them on the page. Each line of a head should contain at least two words; never just one. Once they are written, you can easily decide how they should be typeset. As you make decisions about typesetting your heads and subheads, look ahead through the publication and carefully analyze the number of words in each. Will the head fit on a single line or will the lines be stacked on top of one another?

In general, subheads are usually typeset using the same point size as the body copy or slightly larger (a point or two). Heads are set proportionately larger than the body type. You should be careful, however, to make sure the proportions are appealing. Heads and subheads shouldn't dominate the article.

If heads and subheads are set in a different typeface from the body copy, special care should be taken that they are not more than a few points larger than the body copy. The difference in typestyle draws enough attention to the head; widely varying type sizes confuse the matter.

Heads and subheads are often set in boldface. They can also be spread across columns. If you wish to use underlined heads and subheads, make sure you do not use lowercase characters with descenders such as "p," "y," "g," "j," or "q." On the LaserWriter, the descenders are scored through and do not render a professional appearance. In most circumstances it is unwise to use underlining at all with lowercase characters; it is a carry-over from type-writing and, with the ability to use boldface and italics for emphasis, underlining is rarely called for. All uppercase headlines are often underlined, however, but this is generally just another way of adding a rule to the line of type.

It is unwise to set a headline in boldface, italicize it and have it under-lined all at once. This is simply too much for the eye to deal with.

Once you've made all these decisions, stick to them. Every head and subhead should share the same style and format throughout the pubication.

AVOID CONTINUATIONS

As much as possible, avoid continuations between articles (that is, having to say "continued on page 3"). The most satisfying way to read something is to start at the beginning and read all the way through to the end. Continuing from one page to the next is all right and if the publication is tabloid, or newspaper style, you can continue front-page items on the back page, so the reader can simply flip the publication over to continue reading. Continuations that spread, in bits and pieces, throughout the publication should be avoided.

COPYEDIT TO ADJUST COLUMN LENGTH AND TO AVOID WIDOWS

As you go along positioning articles and flowing them into columns with PageMaker, you'll inevitably run up against two difficult situations. For one, the column of text may simply not fit where and how you'd like. The other is the occurrence of a "widow" at the top of a column or page and sometimes at the end of paragraphs. "Widow" is a typographical term that refers to the last line of a paragraph that appears at the top of a column. Widows are unacceptable and must be avoided.

Another less serious orphan-like effect may occur on the last line at the end of a paragraph where a single monosyllabic word appears. This too should be avoided, but not necessarily at all costs. If the word is polysyllabic and flows well into the column width, let it be.

To resolve these discrepancies, be prepared to copyedit and make editing decisions as you go along, since you must often alter the original copy to make it fit. In fact, if the publication is being laid out against a tight deadline, make sure your authors are available for phone consultation during the layout phase.

For the sake of consistency with the original copy, you should return to Microsoft Word to make any editorial changes, especially if they involve more than a few characters. If you are doing dummy pages in PageMaker and plan to lay out the entire publication over again from start to finish one last time (a well-advised practice), you most definitely want to make sure your original copy reflects any copyediting made for the sake of column adjustments.

FILL IN WITH SHORTER PIECES

Once all the major portions of the copy and artwork are positioned on the pages, you can use brief articles, lists and smaller artwork to fill in spaces where a column is not full to the bottom of the page. You should always have shorter pieces available to use. This may be impractical when doing a report or a book. However, nearly any other kind of publication can benefit from the availability of shorter pieces both to fill space and to create visual interest.

USING RULES

Last, but certainly not least, is the use of rules (a rule is a line used for graphic effect). PageMaker provides several single-width line and double line rules in the Lines menu. These may be used, sparingly, to separate articles and to create visual interest on the page. In general you should use only one or two different rule weights or rule styles per publication.

Doing the Layout: Page One

Now we're ready to show you the layout process step-by-step, completely making up the first page. Let's start with the blank template developed in

Chapter Three. If you've typed in the Elton John article and modified it as shown in Chapter Four and created the chart as shown in Chapter Five (or created text and graphics of about the same size and shape), you should be able to duplicate our efforts.

You should understand that the page layout we do here is the result of an evolutionary process that involved at least two complete passes. The first time through we roughed out the page layout to the best of our ability and then took the results to a graphic designer for consultation. The designer's advice helped shape what you see here.

The only major change that occurred as a result of our earlier efforts had to do with fitting copy into columns. On the first pass, when we placed articles in columns, we ran over the page boundaries by a sentence or two—not enough to cause a major redesign but too much to fix with simple copyediting. The adjustment we made to compensate for this was to decrease the leading in all our articles by a half point (from 12 point to 11.5 point). Since both PageMaker and Microsoft Word support half-point leading this is no problem and is, in fact, a common solution to properly fitting copy on the page.

We return to Microsoft Word and change the line spacing or leading from 12 point to 11.5 point for each article. We select all the text in the document, press [Command] [M], tab over to "Line Spacing," type in "11.5 pt" and then press [Enter]. We repeat this procedure for all our articles.

Sizing Artwork

Most of our artwork was digitized with ThunderScan at 400 percent of its original size, cleaned up and saved as MacPaint documents. As we mentioned before, this is a useful technique, since we can reduce the art by 25 percent in PageMaker and obtain something very close to the original. Since we'll be using the art throughout our publication, we start out using a blank page in PageMaker to reduce all our digitized art and save it to the Macintosh scrapbook. But there's a trick to getting those 25 percent reductions just right.

In PageMaker, we select "New" from the File menu and press [Enter] to accept the default margins (this is a temporary page that will be tossed out when we're finished). Once the page is displayed on the Macintosh screen, we select "Place..." from the File menu and choose the "Nimbus Logo" MacPaint document. When the MacPaint document icon appears, we position it in the upper left corner of the page, aligning it with the margin guides and click the mouse button (see Figure 6-5).

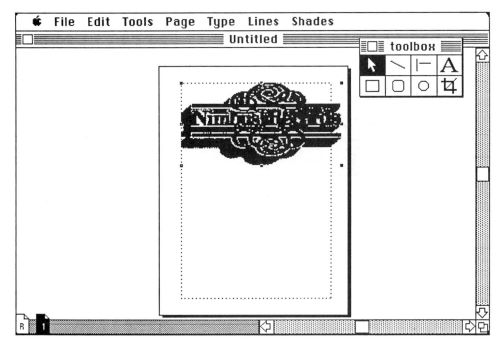

Figure 6-5. Nimbus Logo Pasted into PageMaker.

You notice immediately that it more than fills in the page. Our first goal is to reduce the size of the image, both horizontally and vertically, so it is 25 percent of the size it is now. This is a two-step process. First, we zoom in to actual size near the bottom center handle of the image and exposing the rulers with [Command] [R], drag out a vertical ruler guide from the vertical ruler and position it in the center of the middle bottom handle (see Figure 6-6).

Scrolling up and to the left, we do the same with the middle left handle pulling out a horizontal ruler guide and positioning it so it aligns with the center. Then we position the cursor on the lower right handle and holding down the [Shift] key, press the mouse button and drag the image so it shrinks to within the square bounded by the ruler guides in the upper left of the page (see Figure 6-7). Holding down the [Shift] key guarantees that the reduction in PageMaker will be proportionate.

This reduces the image by 50 percent, both horizontally and vertically. Now we reposition the ruler guides to align with the bottom center and left center handles and reduce the image one more time to fit within this new square. We now have an image that is 25 percent of its original size (see

Figure 6-8). We copy the reduced image to the clipboard, access the scrap-book and paste it there for future use.

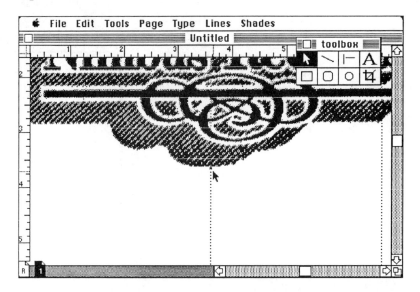

Figure 6-6. Vertical Ruler Guide Aligned above Middle Bottom Handle.

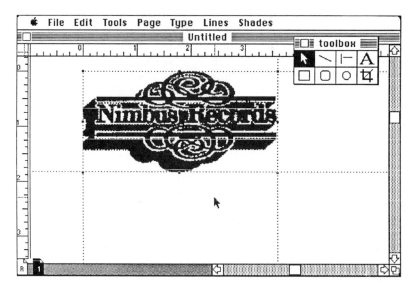

Figure 6-7. Image Reduced to 50 Percent Original Size.

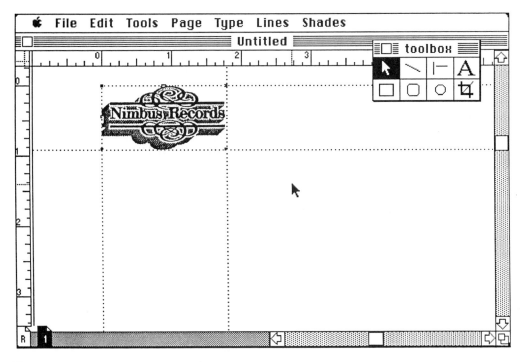

Figure 6-8. Image Reduced to 25 Percent Original Size.

We repeat this same procedure for each digitized image we use in the issue; for *Audio Image* this includes the Elton John logo, the editor's portrait, the inside ring from the Nimbus compact disc and the art that accompanies the "Digital Edge" column. If the piece was originally scanned at 200 percent we only reduce it by half. When we finish, all our art is neatly assembled and ready to use in the pages of the scrapbook. (If you're using a 512K Macintosh without a hard disk, you may be better off doing these reductions in PageMaker using your actual publication and simply moving them to the pasteboard until you're ready to use them.)

At this point, we are ready to start composing the page and actually placing elements on it.

Positioning the Logo

Returning to the original Audio Image Layout document in PageMaker, the first thing we do is select "Preferences..." from the Edit menu and choose the picas-and-points-scale ruler. Since almost all of the publication consists of type, and type is measured in picas and points, we prefer to use typographical measurements, even when positioning artwork.

Next we access the scrapbook, scrolling through it until we find our reduced Elton John logo and copy it to the clipboard (you probably don't have this particular piece of art, but you could create a similar piece or use PageMaker's rectangle tool and the Shades menu to draw a filled black box that approximates the size of the logo).

We zoom in to actual size and press [Command] [V] to paste the logo onto the page. Then we pick it up by positioning the pointer on top of it, pressing the mouse button and carefully dragging it on the page to just underneath the bottom rule of the subtitle (see Figure 6-9). (We may adjust this later to fit more proportionately between the bottom rule and the article but for now we leave it about half a pica below the bottom rule, centered between the left margin and the right column guide.) We keep an eye on the ruler as we do this. Grey lines representing the top and bottom dimensions of our image appear on the vertical ruler and similar lines corresponding to the left and right dimensions appear on the horizontal ruler. As we move the image, these lines move and allow us to align the image right where we want it.

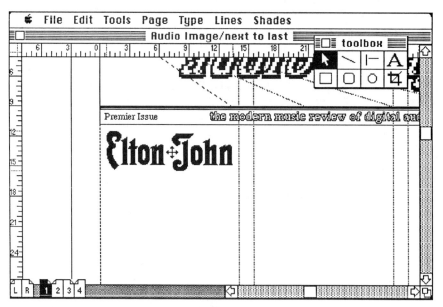

Figure 6-9. Positioning the Elton John Logo.

Flowing the Copy

Now we want to position the lead article copy on page one. First we press [Command] [F] to fit the page in the window. We flow the copy into the columns by selecting "Place…" from the File menu and then choosing the "Elton John Review" (or comparable) document. When we click the "Place" button (or press [Enter]), the text icon appears in place of the pointer and we position it just under the Elton John logo. Notice whenever we move the text icon near the left margin guide that it tends to be pulled toward the guide as if by a magnet. This is evidence of PageMaker's *snap-to* guides, which are a great help in making sure everything lines up neatly.

We click the mouse button and the article flows into the column. Since we prepared the copy to fit these same column dimensions in Microsoft Word, there are no surprises at this step. When we zoom in to actual size near the bottom of the first column, we notice that the copy has overrun our master horizontal ruler guide, which is set 3 picas above the bottom-of-page margin guide (see Figure 6-10). This is normal. PageMaker assumes the bottom margin as the ultimate guide and knows nothing of our intention to end our columns 3 picas above it.

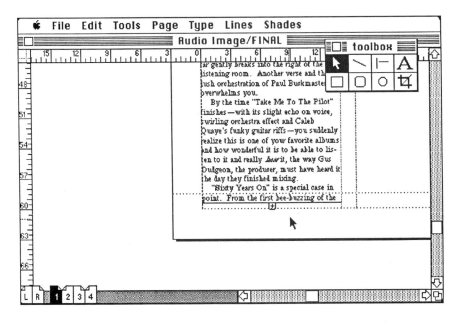

Figure 6-10. Text Flows beyond Ruler Guide.

Positioning the pointer on top of the + handle and pressing the mouse button, we drag it up one line so that the line beginning "'Sixty Years On' is a special..." is the last line in the column. With the pointer still positioned on top of the + handle, we click once and the text icon is displayed. The remainder of the article is represented by this icon. We scroll up to the top center of the page and, keeping an eye on the ruler, position the text icon so it aligns with the vertical ruler at a point approximately a half pica beneath the bottom rule of the subtitle and click the mouse button in the second column (see Figure 6-11).

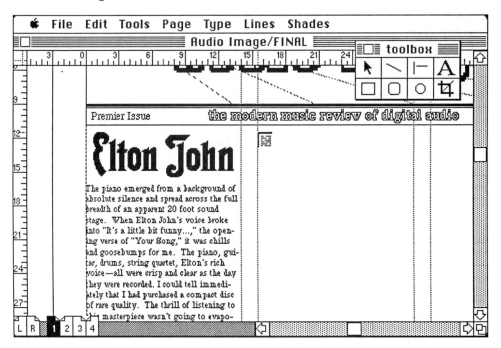

Figure 6-11. Placing the Second Column.

As we did at the end of column one, we now scroll down to the bottom of column two, adjust the column length to align with our ruler guide, then click on the + handle to pick up the rest of the article and place it at the top of the third column. We place it, like the second column, a half pica down from the bottom rule of the subtitle frame. When it finishes flowing into the column, the # handle appears, indicating there is no further text to place (see Figure 6-12).

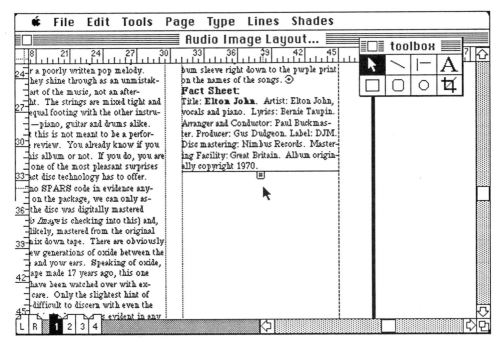

Figure 6-12. The # Handle Shows the End of Our Text.

Carefully Aligning the Text

In order to achieve the finest page compositon possible, we want to make sure our typeset text is aligned carefully across the page. So far we have simply placed the text on the page in a somewhat imprecise manner. Now we want to make sure all the text is aligned across the page. A line in column one should sit on the same base line (an imaginary line connecting the bottoms of capital letters) as the adjacent line in column two.

We do this by picking up the text with the pointer and positioning it at the bottom of the column so that the + handle lines up with the master ruler guide, set 3 picas above the bottom page margin. With the text still in actual size, we press the [Option] key, changing the pointer to a hand and move the page until we can see the lower part of column one in the window (see Figure 6-13).

We then position the pointer anywhere in the column of text, press the mouse button and drag the column up slightly. When we release the mouse button, the + handle marking the bottom of the column should snap into place (see Figure 6-14). Scrolling up to the top of the column and taking a quick look reveals that there is still plenty of white space surrounding the art.

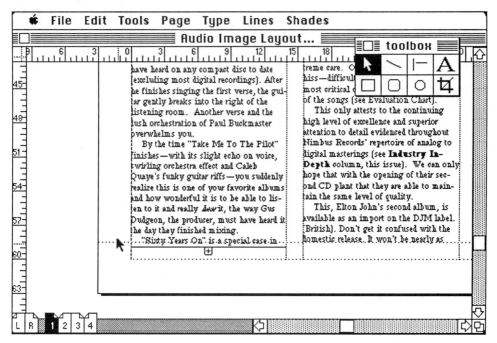

Figure 6-13. Bottom of Column One.

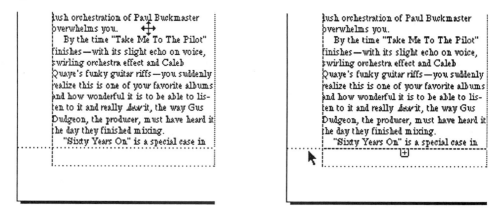

Figure 6-14. Aligning Text with Horizontal Ruler Guide.

We scroll back down the page to see the bottom of column two and repeat the text alignment procedure. When we scan the lines in the two columns we can see that they are properly aligned.

Now we need to line up the third column with the first two. Column three doesn't end at the bottom of the page, so we must align it with the top of column two. We click on column two to expose the + handle, then pull down a horizontal ruler guide from the ruler and line it up so it precisely covers the line attached to the + handle. We click on the third column, pick up the top + handle and align it with the ruler guide (see Figure 6-15).

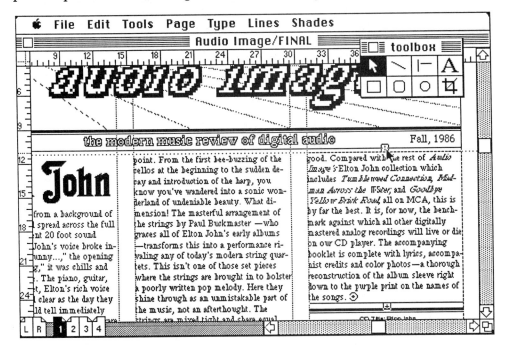

Figure 6-15. Aligning Text in Third Column.

This aligns the text as perfectly as possible and gives the publication a very professional look. We do this with all the columns for all the text in our newsletter.

Positioning the Evaluation Chart

Now we position the compact disc evaluation chart we originally developed in Microsoft Excel. But first, we need to move the text for the "Fact Sheet" out of the way. We do this by positioning the pointer on top of the # handle and dragging up to just above the words, "Fact Sheet." We let go and our fact sheet is safe beneath what is now represented as a + handle.

Next, we lay in a rule from the Lines menu. We select the straight line tool from the Toolbox and then go to the Lines menu and select the 10th line from the top (see Figure 6-16). Positioning the cross-hair pointer so it's lined up with the 25-pica point on the vertical ruler we draw our line across until it touches the right margin.

Figure 6-16. Choosing a Rule Weight.

We now select "Place..." from the File menu and choose the "Elton John Chart/PICT" document. The pointer changes into the MacDraw document icon. We position it in the third column at the 26-pica point on the ruler and click. This places the chart in the column. It exceeds the column boundary and we need to reduce it to bring it within the column dimensions.

We do this by positioning the pointer on top of the lower right handle, holding down the [Shift] key (for proportionate reduction), pressing the mouse button and dragging towards the upper left corner until the image frame snaps within the column guides (see Figure 6-17). When printed on the LaserWriter, it will be proportionately reduced and easy to read.

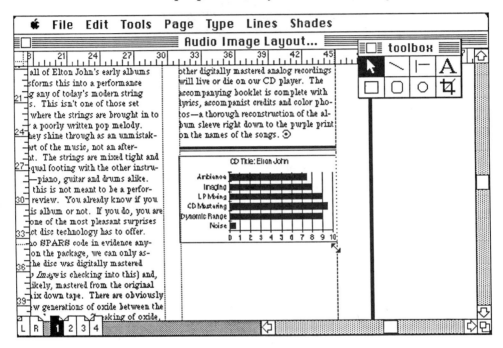

Figure 6-17. Proportionately Reducing the Chart.

Two items remain for us to accomplish: writing the caption for this chart and adding the bottom rule. To write a caption we select the text tool from the Toolbox, position it on the inner left column guide bordering column three and click the mouse to set it down. Before we type anything we press [Command] [T] to select Type Specs and change from 12 point to 10 point. We click "OK" (or press [Enter]) to exit the dialog box and then pull down the Type menu, choosing "Align Center." Then we type the caption, in this case, "Evaluation Chart."

To finish, we select the perpendicular line tool from the Toolbox, position the cross-hair pointer beneath the caption and draw the bottom rule. The chart is complete (see Figure 6-18) and we can go on to place the "Fact Sheet" beneath it and then make a shadowed box for a feature called "Inside This Issue."

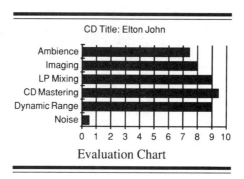

Figure 6-18. Evaluation Chart as Printed in *Audio Image.*

Continuing the "Fact Sheet"

We now scroll back up the page until the end of the Elton John article is in view. We select it by clicking once anywhere on the text. Positioning the pointer on top of the + handle, we click once to pick up the "Fact Sheet" text (still included in the text block above the chart) and then scroll down so there is some white space on the screen underneath the chart. Positioning the text icon near the column guide on the left of the third column, we click and the "Fact Sheet" flows into the column. Now we position it relative to the chart so that approximately 16 picas of space remain at the bottom of column three for our "Inside This Issue" element.

Making "Inside This Issue"

Creating "Inside This Issue"—an element common to most newsletters —involved a few basic steps. First we wrote the copy using MockWrite (see below). Then we drew the *drop shadow* portion of the box, copied it and pasted the copy on top of the original box, changing the grey shade in the process. Then we adjusted the column guides, left and right and flowed the copy between them.

USING MOCKWRITE

There are many occasions when we want to create a short block of text and place it in PageMaker. Since we don't want to make a habit of using PageMaker as a word processor, except for short pieces like captions, we use MockWrite. This simple text processor is a desk accessory and can thus be accessed from the ⌘ menu once installed. We compose all the text for "Inside This Issue" using MockWrite and save it to disk with the name "Inside this issue/text." This creates a text-only document that we later typeset and format in PageMaker.

DRAWING THE DROP-SHADOW IMAGE

Next we draw the background box by selecting the rounded-corner tool from PageMaker's Toolbox. We knew in advance we'd want to use the full point line weight, so we check that off on the Lines menu. Positioning the cross-hair cursor on the inner left column guide bordering column three at the 44-pica mark on the ruler, we drag down and across to the bottom horizontal ruler guide. We line up the right side of the box with the 44.5-pica mark on the top ruler. The box ends one-half pica above and a half pica in from the lower right corner where the ruler guide meets the right page margin. The box measures down the left side from the 44-pica mark to the 58-pica mark and across from the 31-pica mark to the 44.5-pica mark.

The box drawn, we select it by clicking anywhere on it and choose "Rounded Corners..." from the Tools menu and select our preferred rounded corner (see Figure 6-19). Now we copy the box shape to the clipboard for temporary storage.

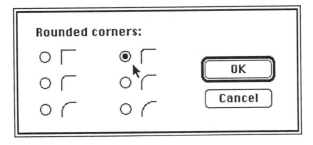

Figure 6-19. "Rounded Corners..." Dialog Box.

With the box still selected we choose black from the Shades menu to fill it. Then we paste the copy from the clipboard, aligning the copy of the box with the lower right corner of the page. With the copy selected we choose a 10-percent grey screen from the Shades menu.

SETTING THE TEXT

The next part, setting the text, involves repositioning the column guides. Since our drop-shadowed box fits squarely within the column boundaries, we want the text to flow within margins slightly narrower than those of the screened box. To do this we adjust the column guides.

We want precise measurements here, so we zoom into a 200 percent view of our box. Positioning the pointer in the middle of the left column guide, we press the mouse button and drag it over so the right line of the guide lines up with the 32-pica mark on the ruler (see Figure 6-20). We do likewise with the outside page margin, dragging it in to line up with the 44.5-pica mark. Now we're ready to flow in our text.

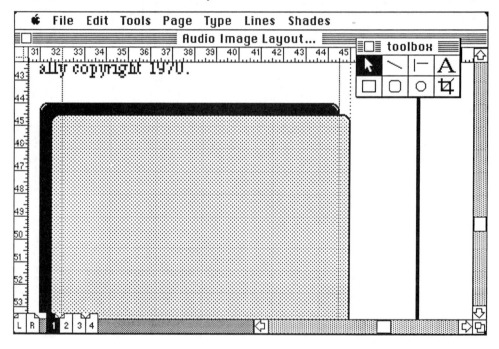

Figure 6-20. Adjusting Column Guides at 200 Percent Enlargement.

The copy for "Inside This Issue" is saved to disk as a text-only document, which carries no character or typeface formatting information.

We can select boldface, italic and 12 point Times from "Type Specs..." before placing the text so that when we place it, using the Place command from the File menu, it will follow those guidelines. It flows neatly within the new boundaries of our drop-shadowed box; however, it overruns the page boundary, lengthwise.

We want to make a few alterations to adjust for this as well as increase the point size of the title "Inside This Issue." We triple-click the line "Inside This Issue" and select "14 pt" from Type Specs. We don't really need a full space between these lines, so we'll adjust each one so that it uses 6 point leading instead of PageMaker's automatic leading. To do this we triple-click in the line space between our top line and the next ("How to identify..."). We access Type Specs, tab to the leading box, type "6" and press [Enter]. We repeat this for each blank line between items and find that it brings the text block well within the frame of our drop-shadowed box (see Figure 6-21).

Inside This Issue:

**How to identify Nimbus'
discs...see page 2.**

**Find out what "digitally
mastered analog
recording" really
means...see page 3.**

**What's new from Japan &
Germany...see page 3.**

**And, find out why we
created Audio Image...see
page 2.**

Figure 6-21. "Inside This Issue" as Printed in *Audio Image*.

Now page one of *Audio Image* looks just the way we want it. Using these techniques you should be able to compose pages in any multi-column publication with PageMaker. You should notice that it really didn't take long to lay out this page. That's the benefit of having all the materials ready to go and well-prepared in advance. The work we did in the earlier chapters has paid off. If we wanted, we could easily recompose this page in a matter of minutes to achieve different design goals with little trouble.

Additional
Page Elements

Assuming you've carefully looked at our complete newsletter (shown in Figures 6-1 through 6-4), you may be interested in how certain effects were achieved, such as positioning and framing the digitized image of *Audio Image's* editor, keeping heads and subheads consistent in size and proportion, balancing text so that it meets at the bottom of a two- or three-column spread and contour-fitting text around artwork.

You should find it easy to transfer the techniques talked about here to publications of your own design.

Positioning the Editor's Digitized Photo

Positioning the photo at the top of page two was fairly easy to accomplish. Even though the image, captured with MacVision, wasn't originally scanned at 400 percent, we can still reduce it by 25 percent of its original scanned size (using techniques described earlier) and print a sample on the LaserWriter Plus. After reducing it, we move it onto the pasteboard for later use.

When we begin laying out the editorial, we simply pick up the reduced art with the pointer and position it in the upper left corner where the top page margin meets the inside page margin. We then select the square-corner tool, check "Hairline" in the Lines menu and draw a box to frame the digitized photo. Using PageMaker this way makes it almost too easy. If you have experience working with layout, you can imagine what we would have had to do using traditional pasteup methods.

Making Heads and Subheads

Heads and subheads are used in almost any informative publication. "By-lines"—lines that say who wrote the article—are also used in those publications where authorial credit is given. Once you've established a model for one combination of head, subhead and by-line, you should use that same setup each time an article calls for it. This maintains the publication's consistent look and provides a single visual cue your readers can use to determine where any article begins.

For *Audio Image* we created the subhead, head and by-line combination shown in Figure 6-22. We create the text block once and then use a copy of that for each additional subhead, head and by-line our articles require. To change the text from that of the copy, we simply triple-click the line we want to change, type in the new text and position it in on the page.

To create the model subhead and head for the editorial, we select the text tool from the Toolbox, position the cursor on the pasteboard, press [Command] [U] to underline, type the subhead "Editorial" and press [Return]. We then press [Command][P] to make the type plain (cancels underline), press [Command] [T] to access "Type Specs..." to set the head in 24 point type, [Tab] to "Leading" and type "28" (increases the space between the head and by-line) and press [Enter]. We type, "Why Create," press [Command] [I] for italic, then *Audio Image,* press [Command] [P] for plain text, type the question mark and press [Return] to move to the next line. We again access "Type Specs..." with a [Command] [T], type "12" to return to 12 point text, [Tab] to "Leading" and type "auto" to return to automatic leading. Then we press [Enter], press [Command] [I] for italics and type "by Kevin Rardin."

We reselect the pointer from the Toolbox, pick up the text block and drag it into position next to the photo. With the text block selected, we press [Command] [C] to make a copy, press [Command] [V] to paste it back into the page, pick up the copy and place it anywhere on the pasteboard for future use. Then, whenever we need to add a subhead, head and by-line, it's ready for us to copy and use over again.

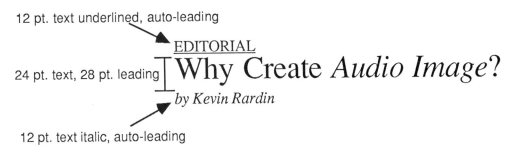

12 pt. text underlined, auto-leading

EDITORIAL

24 pt. text, 28 pt. leading Why Create *Audio Image?*

by Kevin Rardin

12 pt. text italic, auto-leading

Figure 6-22. Subhead, Head and By-Line Created for Editorial.

Balancing Text

One of the genuine advantages of using desktop publishing tools like PageMaker is that we have the ability to play with the text and graphics on the page until we get the arrangement just right. When we positioned the "Pentimento" article on page 3, it was a simple procedure to place it in the first column underneath the subhead and head. Then we picked up what was left behind the + handle and flowed it beneath the diagram. Still more of the text remained and this was placed at the top of the third column. However, our intention here was to leave enough space in the two bottom right columns to position the beginning of our "Digital Edge" column.

We balanced the "Pentimento" article in columns two and three so the two adjacent sentences at the end of each column would meet on the same line. To do this we simply moved the + handle up on the page and watched as the third column filled out. PageMaker does this automatically. As long as it doesn't run into an obstacle, such as a rule or a graphic, it will automatically reflow the text until it ends, each time another column is adjusted. We can almost always balance the text in two or more columns by simply lifting the + handle in one column and watching as PageMaker reflows the text in the next column or columns. After a few adjustments, it comes out nicely balanced. In some cases, we may have to edit a line here or there to make sure all columns end on adjacent lines. When we finished balancing the text in columns two and three of page three, the two adjacent sentence fragments which read "few LP, tape and CD pressing plants" and "was acquired for digital mastering" are positioned on the same line across from each other. The column ends evenly across the page, we can place a rule underneath them to establish a visual cue to end the article and begin the next article underneath the rule (see Figure 6-3).

Placing the "Pentimento" Diagram

By now you should be familiar with the diagram we created with MacDraw in Chapter Five to accompany the "Pentimento" article. We ran into an unusual problem that may or may not occur when you are using MacDraw artwork. This has happened more than once in our experience. When we originally placed the diagram in PageMaker, the top and right of the figure are cropped (see Figure 6-23). We tried to use the cropping tool to pull the diagram boundaries away from the cropped edges, in effect "uncropping" the missing parts (a technique that sometime works when part of the drawing is missing), but this didn't work.

Original multi-track recording

First Generation Master

Second Generation Master

Third Generation Master

Figure 6-23. Problematic Diagram (with Unintentionally Cropped Edges).

Experience dictated that we try another way of moving the diagram into PageMaker. We quit PageMaker and returned to MacDraw, to open our original diagram document. We selected all objects in the diagram, making a group of them ([Command] [G]) and copied the diagram to the clipboard. Then we returned to the layout document in PageMaker and pasted the diagram on the page. At this point, our diagram appeared the way we had originally constructed it. We positioned the diagram at the top of column two on page 3 and reduced it to fit within the column boundaries using the [Shift] key/corner-handle drag combination.

Contour Fitting

One of the major strengths of desktop publishing is it gives us the power to compose pages using text and graphics in ways that would be very costly were we to use traditional publishing or typesetting methods. Contour fitting is a case in point. This effect is used frequently in advertising; less often in magazine editorial layouts and newsletters. The typeset text is adjusted on the page so that it fits snugly against the contours of a graphic shape. This makes for an interesting visual image and is very popular among designers and art directors. However, unless we know exactly what we are doing, we can spend excessive amounts of money on typesetting to achieve this effect. With PageMaker it's comparatively easy.

We use two PageMaker techniques to contour fit. The first of these permitted us to fit the text around the Nimbus logo in a visually pleasing way. (We used a similar technique with our "Digital Edge" column.) The second, more advanced method, used in the same article (middle column of page 4, see Figure 6-4), fitted text to the right-hand contour of a shape captured from the album art for the German band, Propaganda.

The Nimbus Logo

With PageMaker, it is easiest to contour fit text around an object by adjusting the column guides to create space around the object in the form of a square or rectangle. To flow our text around the Nimbus logo on page 2 of *Audio Image*, we first flow the complete text for the article into the three columns, then place additional artwork and the caption in the third column.

Next we position the logo in the center of the text in columns one and two (see Figure 6-24). Vertically, we have to estimate what our column length might be when we accommodate the two narrower columns and center the logo art accordingly. Then we select the text in column one and using the + handle, adjust the text upwards in the column until we have sufficient space above the logo. We do likewise with the text in column two.

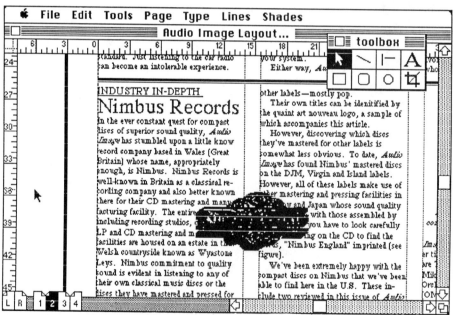

Figure 6-24. Initial Placement of the Nimbus Logo.

Next, we adjust the column guide so its left side lines up with the 8.5-pica point and flow the text into the narrow column to the left of the logo (see Figure 6-25). We then select Copy Master Guides from the Page menu and PageMaker copies back the original formats from our right master page. We lift the text handle back up to leave an equal space below the logo, click the + handle and flow the copy into the column.

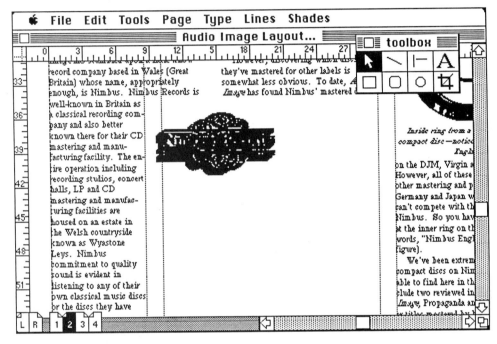

Figure 6-25. Column Adjusted to Flow Text on Left Side of Image.

We repeat this entire procedure on the right of the logo, adjusting our column guide so its right side is positioned at the 21-pica position on the ruler and flow the text into the narrow space. We recopy the master guides and reflow the remainder of the column. To finish up we balance the ends of each column until they line up evenly across all three adjacent columns.

To get all these blocks of copy to match up with equal line spacing we pull in horizontal ruler guides to line up with the bottom + handles of the first copy block as well as the second bit of copy in the narrow column left of the logo. We adjust the empty handles at the tops of each block of copy so they line up with the ruler guides and this makes all the pieces of copy align properly (see Figure 6-26).

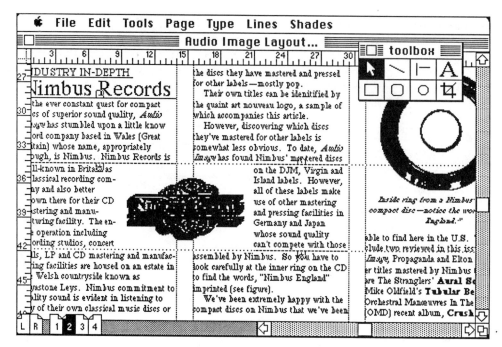

Figure 6-26. Aligning Ruler Guides with Text Handles.

We weren't totally satisfied with this visual image. We had a nice square line of text bordering the right of the logo and a jagged line on the left. Since we used nonjustified or ragged right columns throughout our publication, we couldn't avoid this initially but we wanted to justify this one piece of text on the left of the logo in order to give cleaner lines. There is a trick to this.

On the first try we simply selected the text and chose "Justify" from the Type menu. This, however, justified the entire column—not what we wanted. We copied only the text in the narrow column to the left of the logo to the clipboard ([Command] [C]) and then typed backspace to remove it from the placed text altogether. We positioned the text tool cursor in the pasteboard and pasted our text there, making it a wholly separate and individual piece of text. We selected it and chose "Justify" from the Type menu.

Then we scrolled back to the image area surrounding the Nimbus logo and repositioned the column guide at the 8.5-pica mark. We pulled the # handle up to meet the empty handle on our bit of text and clicked the + handle to re-place the text at its original location. We clicked underneath the last block of copy ending with the words, "...enough, is Nimbus. Nimbus Records is..." and our justified text flowed neatly into the space provided. We adjusted the empty handle to line up with the ruler guide, added some discretionary hyphens ([Command] [-]) and got everything just the way we wanted it (see Figure 6-27).

INDUSTRY IN-DEPTH

Nimbus Records

In the ever constant quest for compact discs of superior sound quality, *Audio Image* has stumbled upon a little known record company based in Wales (Great Britain) whose name, appropriately enough, is Nimbus. Nimbus Records is well-known in Britain as a classical recording company and also better known there for their CD mastering and manufacturing facility. The entire operation including recording studios, concert halls, LP and CD mastering and manufacturing facilities are housed on an estate in the Welsh countryside known as Wyastone Leys. Nimbus commitment to quality sound is evident in listening to any of their own classical music discs or the

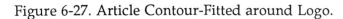

discs they have mastered and pressed for other labels—mostly pop.

Their own titles can be idenitified by the quaint art nouveau logo, a sample of which accompanies this article.

However, discovering which discs they've mastered for other labels is somewhat less obvious. To date, *Audio Image* has found Nimbus' mastered discs on the DJM, Virgin and Island labels. However, all of these labels make use of other mastering and pressing facilities in Germany and Japan whose sound quality can't compete with those assembled by Nimbus. So you have to look carefully at the inner ring on the CD to find the words, "Nimbus England" imprinted (see figure).

We've been extremely happy with the compact discs on Nimbus that we've been

Figure 6-27. Article Contour-Fitted around Logo.

Flowing Text between Two Art Elements

We can break free of the three-column layout to create visual interest and introduce an asymmetrical element into an otherwise symmetrical page, as we did when we composed the page for our "Digital Edge" article. To do so, we pull a vertical ruler guide to align with the right side of column two's column guide, reset the column guides from three to two using the Tools menu and position the right side of the new, single-column guide to align with the vertical ruler guide. At this point we position the subhead, head and by-line and try positioning our art in several different places to decide how we wish to flow the text between the two art items.

When we flow the text for an article into a page, it will cease flowing when it runs into the art items. To fix this, we position the outside margin so it is approximately a half pica to the left of the "Beatniks" art and then adjust the left column guide so it is approximately a half pica to the right of "Exitentialism" (sic). After selecting our text, we click on the + handle and flow the text between the two objects. We then put the margin and column guides back to their original positions and continue flowing our text.

Contour Fitting a Specific Shape

Since the image we planned to use with the review of Propaganda's album was so curvilinear, we shall contour fit the article to the true shape of the image as much as possible. Earlier we had experimented with contour fitting text to a shape by padding spaces at the beginning of each line on the right side of an image (this may be too complex an effect to attempt if you're just starting out—be warned it can look odd if not executed correctly).

As with placing the Nimbus logo, we adjust text using the various handles and then position the image so that it protrudes slightly into the gutter between columns one and two on page four (see Figure 6-28). Then we adjust the right side of the left margin guide to align with the innermost curve on the figure. We continue flowing the text into that space. We then position the text tool cursor at the beginning of each line and type a space or two so that we have approximately six points of space between the form and the first character. Where necessary we add an optional hyphen to tighten up the type. We proceed with this until we reach the bottom of the figure and then restore the original column guides. We flow the remainder of the article into the column.

It would be more difficult to achieve this effect on the left side of the image, as you'd have to use carriage returns rather than spaces but it can be done, if you wish to take the time. However, it is easier to plan the placement of your artwork so you can do this on the right side of the image.

Contour fitting can add a nice touch to a publication. You have just seen two ways of doing it. Feel free to experiment with other techniques.

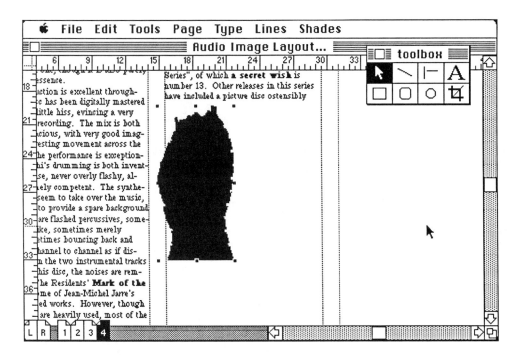

Figure 6-28. Adjusting Column to Align Text with Image.

Summary

You can use any of these techniques with your own publication whether it's a newsletter, a brochure or a report. Page composition and layout using PageMaker will vary from publication to publication but the methods described here will apply to a wide variety of formats. Try them yourself.

Most important, avoid the look of an amateur. After you've created some documents with desktop publishing using the Macintosh, your confidence will increase. There is definitely a learning curve, however. Don't expect to begin on one day and come up with a professional-looking publication the next.

Study the page composition and layout fundamentals at the beginning of this chapter. Remember what we said about simplicity and symmetry. Read the books and subscribe to the magazines in the recommended reading list at the end of this book. Learn to work with typographic measurement. All of this will help you prepare the most professional publication you can.

This chapter has shown you the basics. You've learned how to place text and manipulate graphics. You've learned to balance text and properly align text in adjacent columns. And you've learned a few special effects like how to do contour fitting. Experimentation is encouraged. None of this is learned overnight. Try new things. But keep it simple and consistent. If you use an 18 point headline on page one, use 18 point headlines throughout the publication. If you choose a rule weight for one situation, try to use the same rule weight for all similar situations.

All in all, the simplest approach is best. When in doubt, consult a professional. When you've gained some confidence, try new things but take small steps. You'll be surprised, six months from now, how capable and professional you and your publications have become.

What's Next

Now that your page composition and layout are electronically pasted up and ready to go, you need to print it. Chapter Seven tells you nearly everything you'd ever want to know about printing. You'll discover what you need to know about printing methods, types of paper, preparing your publication for printing and how to work with a printer. Most important, you'll learn what it takes to turn your publication into a printed product ready for distribution to your intended audience.

Printing

7

In this chapter you will learn:

- Fundamentals of the printing process
- Paper and ink characteristics in printing
- How to prepare your publication for the printer
- The importance of your relationship with the printer

Now that we've finished creating our publication using desktop publishing techniques, we're ready to send it out to be printed. This is the moment of truth: will it turn out the way we expected? What unknown pitfalls await us? This chapter discusses the process of transforming our publication from a single original into hundreds or thousands of copies. Printing is a complex process; this chapter will only be able to cover some of its more fundamental aspects, especially those that are most relevant to desktop publishing, with only an occasional glance at other aspects.

There are three main sections in this chapter. The first section briefly covers some of the background of the printing process. If you're already familiar with printing, you can skip this part. The second section tells you how to prepare your desktop published copy for the printer and focuses specifically on the connection between desktop publishing and printing. The third section discusses your relationship with the print shop. This is probably the most important part of the chapter: if you can find a friendly and helpful printer, and learn how to get along with him or her, your printing task will be made far simpler.

As noted at the beginning of this book, you should read this chapter and consult a printer *before* you create your own publication. There are many ways that the specifics of printing will influence your final design; so

201

if you commit yourself to too many decisions concerning the appearance of your publication before you consult a printer, you may be in for some inconvenient surprises. For instance, you may pick a paper size that is expensive and wasteful to produce, or plan for a number of pages that cannot be bound using the process you want.

The assumption in this chapter is that you will probably be taking the original of your publication to an independent shop to have it printed using an offset printing process; that's the most usual approach and it's how we print *Audio Image*. However, there are other possibilities, which we'll point out as we go along.

Printing Fundamentals

Printing has evolved over hundreds of years and has developed its own vocabulary and specialized techniques. There is a bewildering array of printing processes, of papers and inks and of ways to bind your publication. However, only some of the techniques lend themselves to the publications you will be creating with desktop publishing.

The Different Printing Processes

Offset printing (more correctly called *offset lithography*), which is the most common printing process today, was not the first method of printing invented, nor is it the simplest. In order to understand offset printing, it's probably a good idea to know something about other kinds of printing as well, especially letterpress, the original printing process.

LETTERPRESS

Letterpress is the famous process invented by Gutenberg in the fifteenth century. It works on the same principle your rubber address stamp does: you bang the stamp down on the stamp pad, the ink covers the raised letters but not the space in between and then you transfer the inked image to your envelope by banging the stamp down again. Gutenberg's press worked in much the same way (see Figure 7-1), except that each letter and punctuation mark was separate, so when one job was complete, the letters could be taken apart and used again to print entirely different words and sentences. This is the so-called *movable type* that constituted Gutenberg's revolution in printing.

The dominant form of printing until the 1960s, letterpress was used for everything from books to newspapers. In large shops the type was cast from molten lead as it was needed and the process achieved a high degree of mechanization and efficiency.

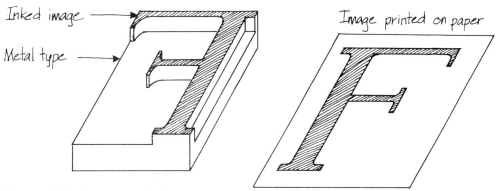

Figure 7-1. Gutenberg's Press.

Letterpress printing produces a very dark image because a denser ink can be used than is possible with offset printing. Also, the letters are actually pressed into the paper, resulting in a more elegant look than offset. However, letterpress is comparatively slow and expensive. Art is difficult to create, since each photograph or drawing must be etched into a metal plate. Letterpress is used nowadays mostly for specialized printing where appearance is more important than cost.

OFFSET LITHOGRAPHY

Offset lithography is the most popular process today. The name is rather intimidating; like many printing terms its meaning has evolved over the years. Lithography was invented in the nineteenth century. It was a method of printing using stone plates (*Lith* means stone in Greek, *graphie* means writing). An image was applied to the stone plate using a grease pencil. The stone was then dampened; it absorbed water everywhere but where the grease had been applied. Ink was then applied to the stone, where it adhered to the grease, but not to the dampened part of the stone. The inked image could then be transferred to paper, as shown in Figure 7-2.

Modern lithography uses a similar process but the stone plates have given way to metal sheets that are specially treated to retain some of the characteristics of stone. (Stone plates are still used for some fine art prints.) Metal plates are easier to use because they can be wrapped around a drum, which can then rotate over a continuous stream of paper, like a car tire leaving tracks on the road. The composition of the ink and the balance between ink, water and grease is critical in offset printing. Until special inks were created in the 1960s the process was not suitable for high-volume printing.

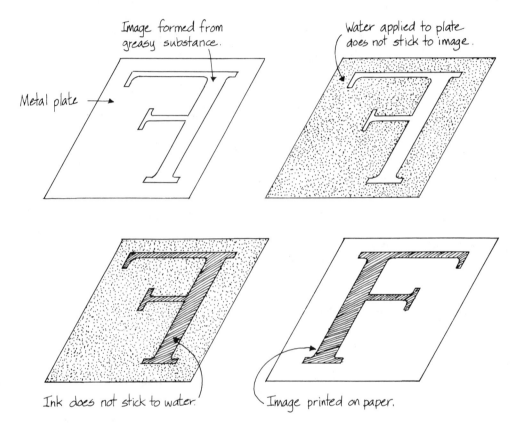

Figure 7-2. Inked Image Transferred to Paper.

The "offset" part of offset lithography comes from one of the more recent enhancements to the process. Instead of the image going directly from the metal plate to the paper, it is first transferred to a drum around which is wrapped a rubber sheet or *blanket,* as shown in Figure 7-3. The rubber protects the litho plate from the abrasiveness of the paper and keeps water from being transferred from the plate to the paper. Thus a wider variety of papers can be used and the process is easier to control.

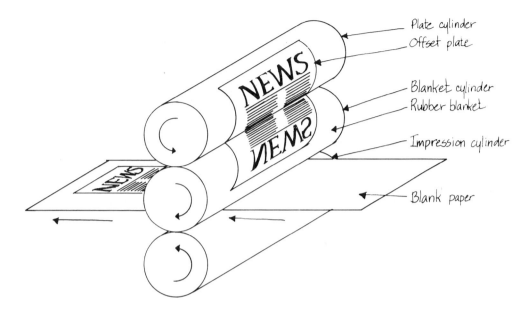

Figure 7-3. Image Wrapped with Rubber Sheet.

Offset printing is fast, easy and comparatively cheap. It reproduces both art and type very well and can handle almost any kind of printing job. One of its few disadvantages is that the ink is not quite as dense as it can be in letterpress printing.

You will probably use offset printing for your publication. It is available in almost any printshop and lends itself well to material produced by desktop publishing methods.

QUICK PRINTING

A specialized form of offset printing is called *quick printing*. This is really just offset printing optimized for rapid and inexpensive processing of small jobs. Often a paper litho plate is used instead of a metal one. The paper plate will not last through as many copies as a metal one, but for small jobs this doesn't matter. Quick printers also usually require certain fixed paper sizes and inks, often black only. Depending on the complexity of your publication and the number of copies you need, quick printing may or may not be appropriate.

GRAVURE

One more common printing process should be mentioned: gravure, which is usually used for high-volume color printing.

Where letterpress uses raised letters that are inked to create the image, gravure uses an image that is depressed into the metal printing plate. When the plate is inked, ink fills the depressions, but is wiped off the smooth non-image part of the plate. When the paper is pressed against the plate, ink from the depressed part of the plate forms the image on the paper. The process is shown in Figure 7-4.

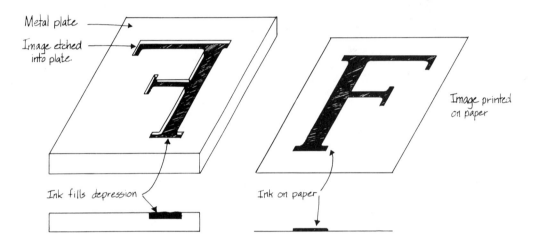

Figure 7-4. Ink-Forming Image.

Gravure is often used for color printing because the inks used in the process can be formulated to dry very quickly. The Sunday newspaper magazine section was often called the "roto gravure section" because it was printed using a gravure process. Gravure is also used for a variety of high-volume color printing jobs such as catalogs and posters and also for certain fine-art reproductions.

PHOTOCOPYING

For small jobs using standard letter- or legal-size paper, photocopying using a standard office copying machine can be a perfectly acceptable alternative to offset printing. However, it does have a number of important limitations.

In photocopying you are restricted to a few paper sizes and limited to types of binding that handle single sheets. The process is slower per copy than offset printing and thus prohibitively expensive for large runs. It also does not reproduce art, especially photographs and other continuous-tone material, very well.

However, for a few hundred copies of a simple job, it can be very acceptable and if you have a photocopying machine in your office the convenience of using it can often outweigh other considerations.

Paper

One of the first decisions you will need to make about your publication is the type of paper to print it on and the size to use. (Note that we are talking here about the paper the copies will be printed on; the paper to use in your LaserWriter to create the original will be covered in the next section, on preparing your publication for the printer.)

In most cases you will decide on a paper after consultation with your printer. This section will briefly review the major considerations involved in this decision.

TYPES OF PAPER

You might think one piece of paper was much like another, but in fact different papers can have a wide variety of differing characteristics.

Bond paper is commonly used for correspondence and business forms. It is lighter than papers used for books. Its name derives from its original use for printing stocks and bonds.

Book papers, as the name implies, are used in books, but they are also used in brochures, booklets, newsletters and many other publications. Book papers have a smooth surface, while *text* paper is similar but textured in a variety of ways. You will most likely use a book or text paper for your desktop publication. We chose book paper for *Audio Image*.

Cover papers are of heavier stock than book papers; this is the paper used for the covers of paperback books.

Bristol papers are heavier still; they are used for posters, postcards, packaging and similar items.

CHARACTERISTICS OF PAPER

Within each of the categories noted above, paper can vary depending on a variety of characteristics.

First, paper comes in certain standard sizes. One standard size is called the "basis size" because it forms the basis of calculating the weight of the paper. Different kinds of paper have different basis sizes. For instance, bond paper has a basis size of 17" by 22", book paper of 25" by 35" and cover paper of 20" by 26". (Note that you can cut exactly four 8.5" by 11" pages from one sheet of bond paper.) Paper manufacturers also produce other standard sizes. The size of the paper to be used is directly related to the size of the press: a single sheet should fit exactly into the press. Before deciding on the dimensions of your publication you need to consider whether it fits one of the standard paper sizes. Usually a sheet of paper will be folded into a signature to make 4, 8, 16 or 32 pages of the final publication. An 8-page signature is shown in Figure 7-5.

As you can see from the figure, the dimensions of the sheets used by the printer should be close to even multiples of the page size you select for your publication. For instance, you can fold a 25" by 35" sheet into pages 6.25 by 8.75 (dividing each dimension by 4). Thus this is an efficient page size. But if you pick a page size that fits awkwardly into the paper size the printer is using, you'll waste paper and increase the cost of your publication. This is something you should discuss with your printer: he or she will tell you what size paper is available for a particular process and what page size it is appropriate for.

Many publications, such as books, are trimmed after they are printed and bound. Usually about one-eighth to one-quarter of an inch is trimmed off from the edges so that the pages come out even. This may need to be taken into account when you calculate page size.

Paper can be special-ordered in nonstandard sizes, but this will be more expensive than using one of the commonly stocked sizes.

Paper is also characterized by weight. You've heard of paper referred to as "20-pound bond." What does this mean? Paper weight is based on the weight of 500 sheets (a "ream"), each sheet being the basis size of the paper. Thus, since the basis size of bond paper is 17" by 22", the phrase "20-pound bond" means that 500 sheets of this paper, each measuring 17" by 22", will weigh 20 pounds.

You'll select a weight of paper based on a variety of factors. For instance, if you're going to send your publication through the mail, you'll be more inclined toward a lighter paper, while if you want to convey a particularly elegant impression, you'll choose a heavier paper.

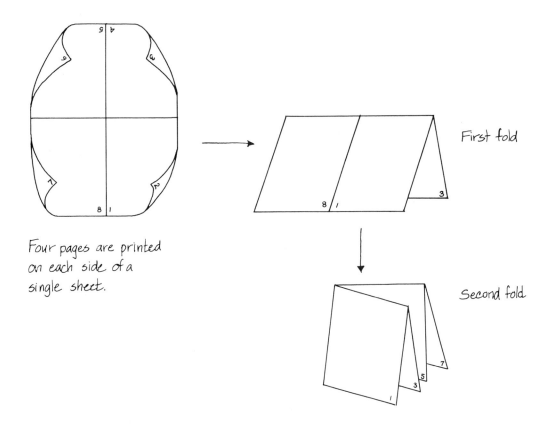

Four pages are printed
on each side of a
single sheet.

First fold

Second fold

Figure 7-5. An 8-page Signature.

Paper can also be coated. Actually all paper used in offset printing must be coated to prevent distortion when the paper is dampened in the printing process. However, special coatings are often used in addition, especially if it is necessary to retain fine detail in the printing process. In desktop publishing this will probably not be the case unless you plan to use photographs (which we'll discuss shortly).

Other characteristics of paper are its opacity, bulk, grain and finish. Opacity is the extent to which printing on one side will show through on the other side. Bulk is the fluffiness of the paper: a paper with greater bulk may weigh the same, but will be thicker. Grain is the orientation of the tiny cellulose (wood) fibers that make up the paper. Grain is important if your paper will be folded: a fold running with the grain will be smooth and easy to make, whereas one running across the grain will be rougher and will tend to break the paper. The grain in book pages should be parallel with the spine so the pages will open easily and lie flat. Grain is an important consideration in brochures, which should be designed so the folds are parallel with the grain. Finish is the final step in producing the paper. The surface of the paper can be given texture or made smoother. Both coated and uncoated papers come in a variety of finishes, depending on the degree of smoothness.

You will usually buy paper from the printer; that is, it will be included in the cost of the printing. However, it is also possible to buy the paper separately from a supplier and furnish it to the printer for the job. The economics of your situation will dictate which is best.

Inks

Again, the printer will help you decide what sort of ink to choose. Usually you'll want black. However, it is also possible to use colored ink. The printer will have sample colors, or you can specify colors using the PANTONE® Matching System, a set of standardized colors available from art dealers.

Special inks include fluorescent inks (useful for posters), metallic inks and high-gloss inks. Once your publication is printed, it can be coated in certain areas with varnish or lacquer to give it a shiny look. Book covers are often completely varnished.

Binding

There are a wide variety of ways to bind printed pages, each appropriate to a different kind of publication. For simple newsletters and the like you may not need any binding at all: an eight- or twelve-page publication can do very well with the pages simply folded together. And, if you're doing only a few copies of an in-house publication, ordinary stapling may work fine. However, for larger publications and larger runs, you'll need a more sophisticated binding process.

LOOSELEAF BINDING

Types of looseleaf binding include the plastic comb, where a series of plastic circles passes through holes punched in the pages; wire-o and spiral, where wire is wound through the pages and rings such as those used in looseleaf notebooks. Some of the most common types of looseleaf binding are shown in Figure 7-6.

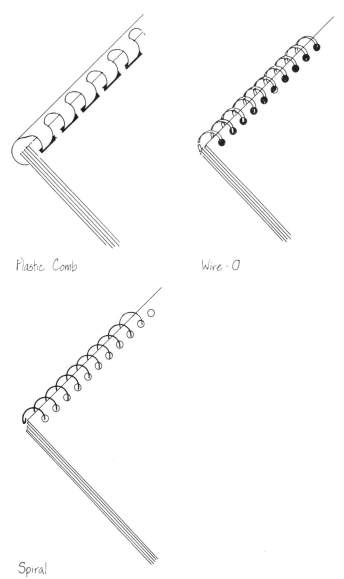

Figure 7-6. Examples of Looseleaf Bindings.

Looseleaf binding is useful for publications like manuals and instruction books. It has the advantage that the pages (usually) lie flat when the book is opened. The disadvantage is that there is no spine to put a title on, so you can't tell what book it is when it's on the shelf. For this reason looseleaf binding is seldom used in books sold in bookstores, although the spine of the plastic comb can sometimes be printed with a title.

Specialized machines are used to punch the holes in the publication and insert the plastic comb or wire binding.

STITCHING

Stitching refers to using metal staples to hold the publication together. This is a commonly-used system and lends itself well to newsletters, reports, small booklets and the like.

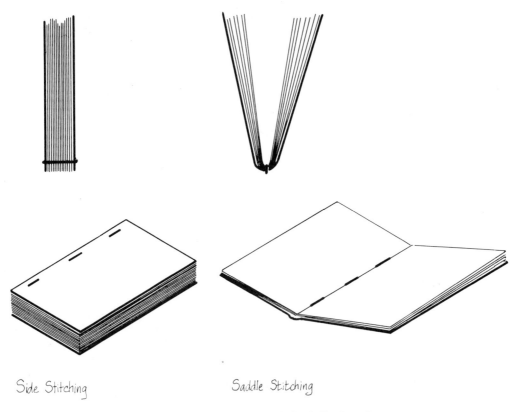

Side Stitching   Saddle Stitching

Figure 7-7. Examples of Side Stitching and Saddle Stitching.

There are two main types of stitching: *side stitching* and *saddle stitching;* they are shown in Figure 7-7. In side stitching the staples go through the pages from the side. The trouble with this system is that it's difficult to get the pages to lie flat when the booklet is open. A more satisfactory approach is the saddle stitch. Here the staples pass through the center of the pages, from the outside to the inside. For this method there must be an even number of sheets, each with four pages. Thus the number of pages in the publication must be divisible by four. If there are too many pages this system doesn't work, since the publication won't stay flat when it is closed.

PERFECT BINDING

So-called "perfect" binding is the system used for paperback books. It can be used for books of almost any size and if well done it is quite durable.

To produce this binding, signatures, often of 16 pages, are folded and the folds along the spine are trimmed off. The trimmed spine is then roughened and clamped together. Glue is applied and the cover is then wrapped around the signatures. The process is shown in Figure 7-8. Once binding is completed, the edges of the pages are trimmed to a uniform size; this is called the "trim size."

CASE BINDING

This is the system used in hardcover books. It is the most durable and has the best appearance.

Usually the signatures are sewn together. They are then glued to a strip of cloth and trimmed. Finally the outside pages are then glued to the inside of the cover. This process is shown in Figure 7-9.

OTHER BINDERY OPTIONS

The bindery can also perform a number of other tasks for you. For instance, you may want to have a coupon in your publication, with perforations around the edge so it is easy to tear out. The bindery can put perforations anywhere on the page. You can also have your pages embossed. An embossed image is raised from the surface of the paper; this can give your work a quality touch. Debossing is similar, except that the image is pressed into the paper.

WHO DOES THE BINDING?

Usually the printer will do the binding. However, many printers do not have the equipment necessary for certain types of binding. In this case the printer can either contract directly with a bindery, or you can take delivery of the printed material and bring it to the bindery yourself.

We decided we wanted *Audio Image* to be saddle-stitched. This means that every issue has to have a number of pages which is divisible by four; in our case this did not present too much of a problem, as we anticipate using either 8 or 12 pages. Our printer was able to do the binding and included it in the bid for the printing job.

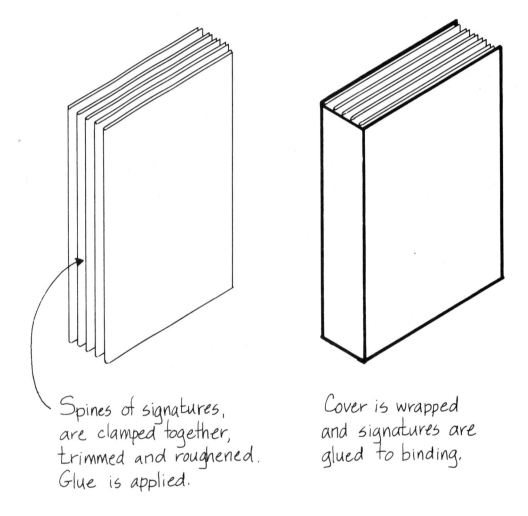

Spines of signatures, are clamped together, trimmed and roughened. Glue is applied.

Cover is wrapped and signatures are glued to binding.

Figure 7-8. Example of Perfect Binding.

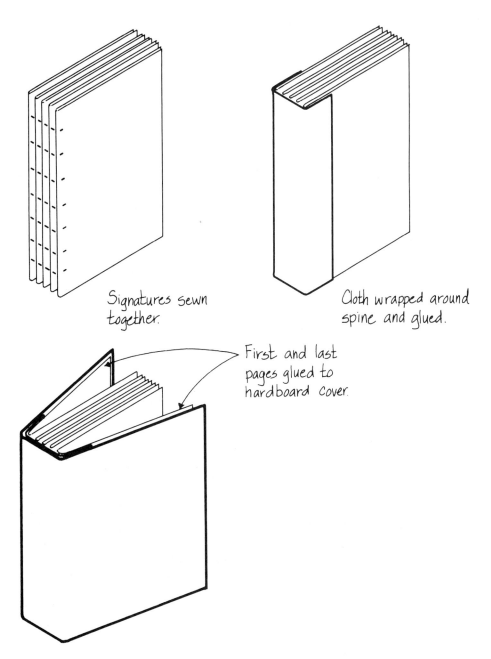

Signatures sewn together.

Cloth wrapped around spine and glued.

First and last pages glued to hardboard cover.

Figure 7-9. Process of Case Binding.

Preparing Your Publication
for the Printer

Now that you know a little about the various options available in the printing process, you'll probably want to know the specifics of how you prepare your publication for the printer.

Camera-Ready Mechanicals

Almost all printing starts with a photographic process: the material to be printed is first photographed by a special, very large camera called a *process* or *copy* camera. In standard offset printing the camera produces a negative of the material to be photographed. This negative is then used to produce the offset plate that is used in the press. In quick printing the negative may not be used; the image goes directly from the original copy onto a paper printing plate.

Your goal, as the producer of your publication, is to create the copy that is to be photographed by the printer. Because what you give to the printer should be completely prepared to be photographed, it is called *camera-ready art*, or *camera-ready mechanicals*, or simply *mechanicals*. (The word "mechanical" arose because in traditional printing all the items to be photographed had to be mechanically pasted together.)

The raw material for the mechanicals can come from several sources. In desktop publishing it will consist primarily of the output from the laser printer. However, you may also have photographs, or other items that you do not want to digitize and that must be added or "dropped in" separately.

THE MECHANICS OF MECHANICALS

The simplest mechanicals are the sheets of paper that come out of the laser printer. For most purposes these are all you'll ever need as camera-ready art, since your desktop publishing system has already prepared them for printing. You bring a stack of these sheets (along with any photos you might have) to the printer, who you tell what you want done with them. No further preparation is necessary. This is also true for the photographic stock that is the output of Linotronic imagesetters, which will be discussed later in this chapter.

However, there can be disadvantages to giving your printer single sheets of paper, especially if you have to mail your mechanicals to a magazine (for advertisements) or to a printer in another town. In transit the sheets can be torn or become dog-eared and the pages are more easily smudged in handling. It is also easier for single sheets to be lost. And, if you need to paste down separate photos or line art, you will not have a firm backing to work with. For these reasons camera-ready art can be prepared on pasteup boards—often called simply *boards*. These are pieces of heavy cardboard, available from art stores and graphics supply houses in a range of sizes. A typical board with two pages pasted up is shown in Figure 7-10.

The pages can be attached to the boards with either contact cement, tape or wax made specifically for this purpose. The most common of these is wax. It is heated in a special gun, like a hot glue gun and flows in a thin layer onto the board. The paper or photo can then be pressed down onto the wax, which holds it firmly in place. If you later decide to move it, you simply peel it off and press it down in another location. If you plan to pasteup your pages this way often, you can invest in a molten wax machine that lets you put a thin layer of wax on the back of whatever you want to paste down. This gives you a bit more freedom to adjust and rearrange things on the board.

Pasteup is an acquired skill. You may want to simply take the whole project to a professional pasteup artist (an option we'll discuss shortly). However, if you want to do it yourself, keep in mind that the items you want to paste onto the boards must be cut to the right size with a sharp knife and positioned on the board at precise locations. Every element must be aligned so it is perfectly straight—vertically and horizontally—relative to the page margins.

Doing pasteup this way requires the right equipment. A drafting table with a straight-edge on the left-hand side, a T-square and a triangle will permit you to draw and cut along lines that are truly vertical and horizontal; this is essential if your work is to look professional. You'll also need an X-Acto® knife with several different blades and a special cutting surface that won't dull the blades or wear out with continued use. All these items are available from your local art supply store or graphics supply house.

USING OUTSIDE PASTEUP ARTISTS

While the principles of pasteup are easy to understand, it takes considerable experience to do a really first-class job. If your printing situation demands more pasteup than you've been able to achieve with PageMaker and it looks to you like the job is more than you want to undertake yourself, don't hesitate to call on a specialist. Your printer or graphics designer can probably recommend one. A professional pasteup artist may charge between $25 and $40 per hour and can probably put together a not-too-complicated quarter-column ad, say, in half an hour. This can be a worthwhile investment.

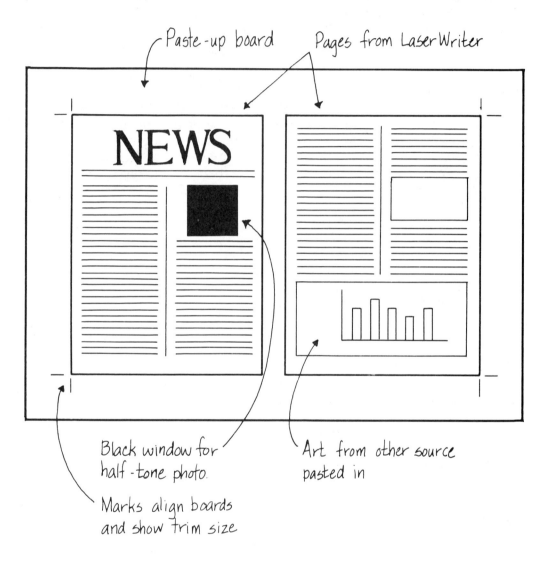

Figure 7-10. Sample of a Pasteup Board.

However, if you have a lengthy publication, you can quickly overrun your budget by using outside pasteup artists and designers and can end up not realizing the true benefits of desktop publishing: economy, simplicity and control. One of the principal ways the advantages of desktop publishing are achieved is by doing the pasteup electronically with PageMaker, so to do it by hand will in many cases be a step in the wrong direction. We mention the possibility here only because you should be aware of the alternatives if you have special needs or if your publication requires special handling or shipping.

CHANGING IMAGE SIZE FOR INCREASED RESOLUTION

When printers photograph your camera-ready art with a copy camera, it is possible for them to change the size of the resulting image. In fact, it is almost as easy to change the size as to keep it the same. You can often take advantage of this fact to improve the quality of your publication.

The characters produced by your laser printer are not as perfect as those produced by traditional typesetting. The 300-dots-per-inch resolution available from the laser printer is good, but not as good as the 1,000 dots per inch typically available by other methods.

If your publication uses a page size that is smaller than the 8.5 by 11 inches size that the laser printer produces, you may be able to start off by producing a larger image than you need and then have it photostatted down by the printer. The easiest way to do this is simply to make everything in your publication larger: use a larger layout, larger type and larger illustrations. For example, suppose you are designing a publication with 4" by 5.5" pages. Instead of creating pages this size, make them 8.5" by 11". Then, if you were planning to use 12 point type, use 24 point instead. In short, make the entire layout twice as large as you want the final result to be. Then have the printer reduce this image to 50 percent of its original size in the process camera. It will be the size you want and the resolution of the type will have been doubled with very little increased effort or expense. Also, if there is any dirt on your original pages, it has been reduced to half its size by the camera; this helps to produce clean copy.

Larger original images cannot be expanded this much or they will be too large for the 8.5" by 11" page size of the LaserWriter; but even making an image 125 percent larger than you want and then photostatting it down the same amount, will increase resolution. This technique is especially appropriate for books, which typically have a smaller page size than 8.5" by 11". Very small items, like business cards, can be expanded even more, yielding an image resolution that equals that of traditional typesetting methods.

Optimizing the Output of the LaserWriter

Since the LaserWriter is the primary device used to generate your camera-ready copy, you should know how to get the best results from it. Care taken with the output of your LaserWriter will have a direct and important impact on the quality of the final work. Primarily you should pay attention to the kind of paper you use and the replaceable cartridges used by the LaserWriter.

PAPER

The paper you use in the LaserWriter is very important to the quality of the final output. First, it should be a coated paper with a smooth matte finish so that the image produced by the LaserWriter is as sharp as possible. On rough uncoated paper the ink at the edges of the characters may bleed into the white areas adjacent to the characters. The paper should also be as white and as opaque as possible so the photographed image will have high contrast; this will yield crisper results.

Paper with these characteristics must be special-ordered; ordinary photocopying paper is not good enough. Your local print shop or graphic arts shop may be able to tell you where to obtain such paper in your locality. Copying machine manufacturers, such as IBM and Xerox, also carry papers suitable for the purpose.

Of course, there is no need to use this paper for your day-to-day LaserWriter output, only for output that will constitute your originals in the printing process.

CARTRIDGES

It is also important that the cartridge used in your LaserWriter is not too old. This will ensure that your image is as dark as possible. If your image is not dark enough, the copy camera will have trouble reproducing it and the final results will suffer. Actually, for the best printing, the cartridge should not be *too* new, since the image density of a brand new cartridge will be changing too rapidly. A cartridge that has already produced 100 to 200 pages is ideal. It's a good idea to keep one cartridge for day-to-day printing and another that you use only for final copy. Of course, if you are producing a long document, like a book, you may need to use several cartridges during the course of production. Don't wait too long to change to the new cartridge, or the difference in density between the old and new cartridge will be noticeable.

Alternatives to the LaserWriter

You can enhance the quality of camera-ready art by printing it on a high-end, expensive laser imagesetter, or you can use printers which exceed the capabilities of the LaserWriter and improve your ability to mass produce publications yourself. The LaserWriter prints pages at 300 dots per inch. It is a light-duty printer with a limited machine life. The output of the Laser-Writer pales when compared with the Linotronic 100 and 300 imagesetters which can produce high-resolution black-and-white images. If you'd like to mass produce publications in volume directly from a laser printer, you should know about the heavy-duty PostScript printers which are available. This section addresses those topics.

LINOTYPE LINOTRONIC IMAGESETTERS

If you really want high-quality output, with the best resolution and the densest blacks possible, you should seek out a print shop or service bureau that will print single sheets using an Linotronic imagesetter. Manufactured by the Linotype Company, a name virtually synon-ymous with typesetting and printwork for decades. These high-end imagesetters let you create camera-ready mechanicals on photographic stock directly from PageMaker, MacWrite, Microsoft Word or other Macintosh files just as you would with the LaserWriter. The Linotronic 100 imagesetter prints at 1,270 dots per inch; the Linotronic 300 imagesetter prints at twice that: 2,540 dots per inch. What this means to you is that you can create camera-ready art with blackness densities rivalling anything produced with traditional typesetting and pasteup methods. As with any other desktop published document, both type and graphics are printed together on the same page with little or no pasteup required.

When you are preparing material to be taken to a printer for mass production, the blackness of your original art will make a great difference. Each typeset character will be even and black, your line art will have consistent blackness in all regions no matter how dense. Grey values are more consistent and fine print attains its highest level of legibility. Although the LaserWriter is a fine output device on its own, you can tell from the numbers alone what a difference the Linotronic imagesetters can make: there's a lot of black to be gained moving from 300 to 1,200 dots per inch, even more when you go to 2,500. By way of comparison, the camera-ready art for the first page of each chapter in this book was printed on the Linotronic 300 imagesetter; all other pages were created with the LaserWriter.

Although the Linotronic printers use laser technology similar to the LaserWriter to create type and graphics on the page, they do so using a photographic process rather than a xerographic process: no ink is deposited on the page. A PostScript is within the printer and then exposed on photographic paper through a lens, much as a black-and-white negative image is in an enlarger to create a photo in a darkroom. The photo stock on which the page is imaged is rolled into a sealed container attached to the Linotronic. To create the camera-ready output, the container is taken to a developer where the paper is fed in and the page image is developed. This process creates a high resolution black-and-white page image on photographic stock, which is the equivalent of true typesetting. In the case of the Linotronic 300 imagesetter, the black-and-white image quality actually exceeds the capability of most phototypesetting equipment, which, normally creates type at around 1,200 dots per inch.

The trade-off for this increased quality is, as you may imagine, cost—and time. You'll have to pay between $8 and $15 per page for the output from the Linotronic. Images can take much longer to process—anywhere from 15 minutes for a single page up to a full hour for a complex publication layout of only a few pages. This can be an expensive option for lengthy publications, although volume pricing can lower the cost. Linotronic camera-ready art for a 300-page book may cost only $3 to $5 a page where the imagesetter output for a two-page flyer may cost $30. Prices may fall as more shops acquire these machines and the market becomes more competitive. Check around before you decide where to have your camera-ready mechanicals prepared using Linotronic equipment.

The camera-ready mechanicals for *Audio Image* were produced on the Linotronic 100 at $9.75 per page for a total cost of $39. Future issues consisting of 8 to 12 pages each will cost between $78 and $117 to produce the camera-ready mechanicals on Linotronic equipment. This is well within our budget per issue. A 300-page book, on the other hand, could cost anywhere from $1,000 to $2,000 for Linotronic mechanicals and could easily be cost-prohibitive. Typesetting, of course, would cost much more than this; many factors need to be taken into account. If you want the highest possible print quality combined with the ease of page composition desktop publishing offers, the Linotronic imagesetters are of definite value and should be sought out.

LASER PRINTERS USED FOR VOLUME PRODUCTION

Wherever there is a lack in the marketplace someone hurries to fill it and this is certainly the case with laser printing technology. The LaserWriter is generally considered a light-duty machine good for desktop publishing installations with no more than five workstations per printer. The LaserWriter can easily produce up to 3,000 pages per month and has a machine-life of 100,000 pages. It is not meant to be used as a high-volume production-oriented output device. Additionally, it does not print pages on 11 by 17 inch paper. We have found three printer manufacturers who make machines which exceed the limitations of the LaserWriter in one way or another. If your needs for desktop publishing require either more memory, a heavier duty machine or tabloid size output, you should consider using one of these printers. The following are PostScript printers like the LaserWriter which connect to your Macintosh via AppleTalk; they all create images at 300 dots per inch.

The *Dataproducts LZR-2665* laser printer offers both 11 by 17 inch page output as well as an increased duty cycle. The LZR-2665 will print up to 60,000 copies per month and has a machine life in excess of 3 million page images. It has 2.5 megabytes of RAM, which allows it to create tabloid size images as well as handle downloadable fonts. It has two paper trays which are selectable using "Page Setup..." in any Macintosh program. This means you can use letter and legal size pages without changing paper trays, or you can have preprinted letterhead in one tray and follow-up paper in the other.

The *Texas Instruments OmniLaser 2108* and *2115* laser printers offer increased machine life, more memory for downloadable fonts and increased paper handling capability. The machine life of the OmniLaser 2108 is rated at 600,000 prints; the OmniLaser 2115 is rated at over 1.5 million page images. The 2108 model has 250 sheet paper input and output trays; the 2115 has two 250 sheet input trays and a single 500 sheet output tray. As the model numbers indicate, these machines can deliver printed pages at 8 and 15 pages per minute.

The *QMS PS-800* laser printer sports a full 2 megabytes of memory and is, in every other respect, similar to the Apple LaserWriter. However, with the additional memory it can compute the image for one page while it prints another and is capable of handling more downloadable fonts.

Each of these printers offers enhanced features beyond the capabilities of the LaserWriter and may do better work for you in a desktop publishing environment. The Dataproducts LZR-2665 is, at this writing, much costlier than the LaserWriter; the others are competitively priced with the LaserWriter and LaserWriter Plus. You should be able to rent time or pay a price per page on any of these machines at service bureaus or printers who have them, just the same way you would rent time on a LaserWriter or Linotronic.

Drop-in Photographs

As we noted before, there will be times when you don't want to use the LaserWriter to produce an image. Although (as the example in *Audio Image* shows) you can achieve perfectly acceptable photographic effects using ThunderScan or MacVision, the result has a certain large-grain look that may not work for some images. While it is not bad for portraits, especially if the somewhat modern look of the large pixels is appropriate to the publication, photos requiring more detail, such as landscapes and architectural views, should be processed separately and taken to the printer with your LaserWriter pages (or pasted onto your mechanicals, if you are doing your own pasteup).

Here's a quick summary of how photographs are prepared for printing.

HALFTONES

A black-and-white photograph is actually composed of many different shades of grey. However, the printing process can generate only black-and-white images (black ink on white paper). Thus a photograph must be transformed from an image with greys into an image with only black-and-white before it can be printed. This is accomplished using what is called a *halftone,* as shown in Figure 7-11. The original photo is rephotographed, but with a screen, which has an even pattern of small dots placed over it. The result, when recorded on high-contrast film, is an image that no longer consists of different greys, but of a pattern of dots: larger dots where the original image was darker, smaller dots where it was lighter. The photographs in any magazine are examples of such reproduction: the dots are obvious under a magnifying glass.

If you plan to use non-digitized photographs, they will need to be converted to halftone form, using this screening process. At the same time they are screened they can also be easily resized to fit your publication.

WHEN TO SCREEN

There are two approaches to screening your photos. Most simply, you can take the original photos to your printer at the same time you take your LaserWriter pages and have the printer screen them and *drop them in* to the

LaserWriter pages just before printing. Or you can take the originals to a graphic arts shop, have them screened and resized and give these screen shots to your printer to drop in. (If you're doing your own pasteup, you can paste these screened shots into your mechanicals before you take the mechanicals to the printer.)

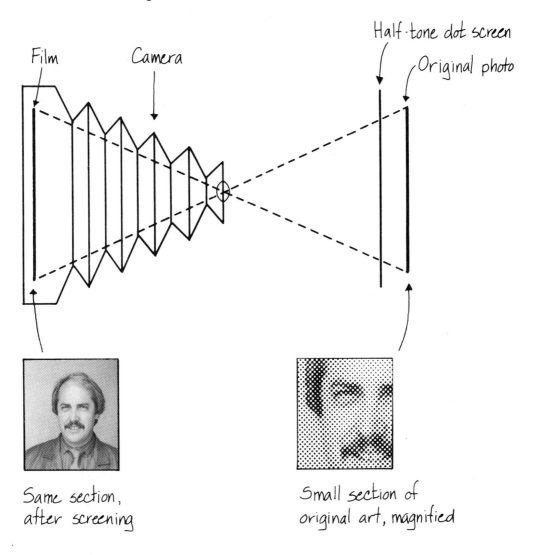

Figure 7-11. Example of a Halftone.

There are pros and cons to both systems. If you let your printer screen the photos you can assume that he or she will do it in such a way as to be compatible with his or her particular printing process. On the other hand, by getting your photos screened as a separate step you can retain more control over the production process and ensure that it turns out the way you want. This is another issue you can discuss with your printer. If he or she is confident he or she can handle your photos, having the printer do them may be easier.

HALFTONE WINDOWS

If you plan to use photographs in your publication, you will need to provide space on your LaserWriter pages for them. In traditional pasteup this is done by pasting down squares of red acetate called "rubylith." The red color photographs turn black in the printer's copy camera, making it easy to insert the photos into the clear spaces that resulted in the negative image of the mechanical.

However, it is easier to let the LaserWriter produce the black squares for you than to try to paste down the acetate. Creating black squares is simple in PageMaker: simply make them the size you want your photograph to be and position them in the right places.

When you give the mechanicals and the photographs to the printer you must use a system you both understand so that he or she will know which photo goes where. You can draw on the mechanicals with a special colored pencil called *non repro blue*; this color will not be picked up by the process camera. This can be useful if your pictures do not have clear captions as part of the copy. Also, make sure that each photo is clearly labeled on the back.

You will also need to tell the printer how large to make each photo and how to crop it (trim off unwanted parts). Different printers use different systems; this is something you should discuss with your printer before you prepare your work.

OTHER DROP-IN ART

You may have other pieces of art that are neither digitized nor photographs. Examples might be tables or other items cut from existing materials, pen-and-ink drawings (pencil sketches are best treated as photographs to retain the different grey levels), or standard items such as an existing company logo that you can print in advance and drop in to various places in your publication. If any of these items are the wrong size, they can be enlarged or reduced photographically, in the same way as photographs. This sort of art, which does not have grey levels, is often called "line art." Again, you have two choices with such items. You can give them to the printer to add to the mechanical or to the negative. Or, if you don't mind doing some pasteup yourself, you can paste them onto your LaserWriter pages or mechanicals.

You don't want to use a black box to show the position of line art. Simply leave an appropriate amount of white space. However, you must show the printer exactly where you want each item to go; consult with your printer about the best way to do this.

Using a Second Color

Up to now we have assumed that your publication will be in one color (black or whatever ink color you choose). Using color printing, in the sense of reproducing full-color photographs, is a highly complex process, well beyond the scope of this book; it is also not something you would probably want to do in a desktop publishing environment, where one of the objects is to produce a publication as inexpensively as possible.

However, it is possible to use a second color in your publication without too much extra complexity. A second color can be used in a variety of ways: as a background for your company's logo, as a background for figures or charts, or as boxes or borders around material that needs special emphasis. A second color lends substantial visual interest to a publication. Of course, it is also more expensive. When you use a second color, your publication must be run through the press twice, once for each color and as a consequence the printing cost is substantially greater.

If you use two colors you must indicate to the printer how the two colors are to fit together on the final publication. For simple jobs, where blocks of color will be printed over parts of the text, this is often done with tissue-paper overlays. A sheet of tissue paper is taped to the top of the mechanical so that it lies flat on the page but can be lifted up. The areas that are to be printed in the second color are marked on the tissue paper.

For more complex jobs, where some copy is to be printed in one color and some in another, one approach is to create two separate mechanicals, one for each color. Two copies of the page can be generated with the laser printer. On one copy, all the text that will be in one color is cut away, while on the other copy the text in the opposite color is cut away. To ensure that the two copies are in registration when they are printed, registration marks are placed on the boards. You'll learn more about registration in the next section.

Alignment

Whether it uses two colors or only one, the content of your publication must be positioned in the same place on each page; that is, the margins must be the same. Otherwise the printer will have trouble getting the image on the same position of the final pages. If you are giving the printer sheets of paper as they come out of the laser printer, achieving this kind of alignment is straightforward. All you need do is ensure that each page layout is always positioned at exactly the same place on the paper relative to the upper lefthand corner of each sheet of paper, as shown in Figure 7-12. PageMaker or Microsoft Word will automatically generate pages with consistently similar margins. On the LaserWriter, manual feed will produce the most accurate registration, but for long documents this may be too tedious. In this case the registration produced by the paper tray feed mechanism should be good enough for most purposes.

If you are doing your own pasteup using boards, it's usual to put small crosses, drawn in non repro blue, at the corners of the page borders, as registration marks. When you paste down your page elements, be careful that each element is precisely positioned relative to the registration marks. The printer will use the marks to position each page on the printing plate so that your copy always falls in the same area of each page.

Imposition

You've already learned that a large, single sheet of paper is usually used to print several pages of the final publication at once and then folded so the pages form a signature, which is then bound into the finished publication. Because several pages are printed at once, they are photographed at the same time by the process camera to make the negatives or printing plate. When the signature is folded, all pages must be aligned properly for binding. So when they are photographed they must be arranged so each page is the correct distance from the others, top to top and side to side. The relationship of the pages to each other in a signature is called *imposition* and the sheet holding all the pages of a signature is called an *imposition sheet*.

For example, an eight-page newsletter with 8.5" by 11" pages would have pages 1, 8, 4 and 5 printed on a single imposition sheet. Pages 1 and 8 would be positioned side by side, with page 8 on the left and 1 on the right. Pages 4 and 5 would be positioned upside down with their tops adjacent to the tops of 1 and 8, with 5 on the left and 4 on the right. On the next imposition sheet—used for the back side of the paper—pages 2 and 7 would be opposite one another and 3 and 6 would be upside down with their tops meeting the tops of 2 and 7. Once the plate is shot, these pages end up printing back to back and are then folded to make the signature.

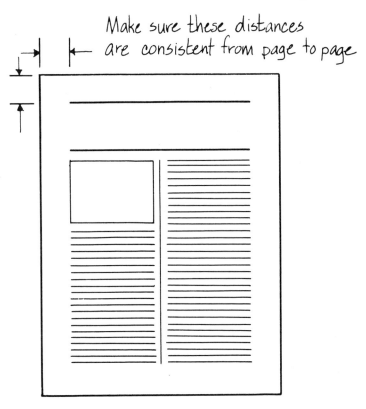

Figure 7-12. Alignment of Page Layout.

For larger publications, such as books, the signatures are often larger, 16 pages or more. It is common to create only a single pasteup board per page and let the printer shoot these separately and make an imposition from the negatives of each page.

In any case the alignment of your pages is critical to correct imposition. If you are giving the printer single sheets from the LaserWriter, make sure, as we explained above, that each layout is in the same relationship to the upper left corner of the page. If you are doing your own pasteup, make sure that your layouts have the same position relative to the registration marks on the boards.

You should discuss imposition carefully with your printer before starting out. If you do your own pasteup, your printer can give you sample imposition sheets against which to check your alignment before you bring in the job.

Proofs

If you are using standard offset printing, the printer will usually furnish you with proofs of your publication before printing begins. (Quick printers will usually not do this, although some may if you ask them.) The printer photographs your copy, creates the printing plates and produces one copy—the proof, but does not actually start the presses rolling. (The proof may be printed in blue ink, like a blueprint, called a *blueline*.) At this point you have the opportunity to look over the proof to see if there are any mistakes. Hopefully *you* will not have made any mistakes in the early stages of the preparation of your copy that you have not discovered until this point. If you have made mistakes that are not the printer's fault, the printer will fix them, but at your expense.

If printers make mistakes that are clearly their fault, they will correct them at no charge to you. (We'll have more to say about this in the next section.) Occasionally, the printer will have made an error in registration, imposition or some other area. Now is the time to catch all these errors; once the printing is done, it's too late. You will be asked to sign your approval of the proofs and if a critical error exists on the proofs that you should have seen, you will have to have the job done over, at your expense.

Preparing *Audio Image*

For the premier edition of our newsletter we used the Linotronic 100 image sector to print our final layout directly from PageMaker. This gave us the blackest image and the cleanest type possible using today's desktop publishing technology. We turned the resulting pages over to the printer and let him or her do the rest. We didn't use pasteup boards because the printer was nearby and we could deliver the pages ourselves. We chose a fine book paper with a lengthwise grain so that our copies could be folded neatly.

Once we signed off the proofs, we told the printer to go ahead with an initial run of 2,000 copies. The printer did the folding (no binding was required for four pages) and delivered the copies to us in bundles, which we loaded into the back of our car.

For future editions of *Audio Image*, which will run from 8 to 12 pages, we plan to use saddle stitching for the binding. We'll use the same paper and now that we've had satisfactory results, probably will continue to use the same print shop.

Your Relationship with the Printer

As you have probably gathered from the earlier sections of this chapter, printing is probably the most complex element of desktop publishing. There are a great many decisions to be made and considerable opportunity for miscommunication. Your relationship with the printer is the most important part of achieving a satisfactory final product. You may know a lot about the printing process, but if you don't achieve a good working relationship with the printer, the results may not be what you had in mind. On the other hand, you may be inexperienced in printing, but if you find a printer who is sympathetic to your needs you can achieve outstanding results.

Finding the Right Printer

As with most things, it pays to shop around (assuming you live in a town big enough to give you this luxury).

Print shops can be too large and too small. A shop which is too large will be busy with big orders for big clients and may not take the time to give your job the care it needs. On the other hand, a shop that is too small may not have all the equipment needed for your job. For instance, if you need your publication bound, you should check to see if your printer can handle the job using the technique you favor. Keeping most or all of the project in one shop can help cut costs.

Check the quality of the printer's work; look at samples that are similar to what you want to have done. Is it what you had in mind? Can someone else do it better, or for less money? Get references from the printer and call them to see if they were satisfied with the work.

Take a careful look at the person you will be dealing with at the shop. In a small shop it may be the owner, but in a larger shop it will be an employee who is hired specifically to deal with customers, a salesperson, often called a printer's representative or *rep*. Will this person take the time to explain exactly how you should prepare your mechanicals? You can't expect a complete course in printing, but you should be able to get careful answers to your questions about what the printer requires and what options are available. If the salesperson is too rushed or impatient to deal with you, try elsewhere.

This salesperson will be the intermediary between you and your job and the resources of the shop. There will inevitably be scheduling conflicts with other jobs: you want someone representing your job who is on your side, who cares whether your job gets done, who will fight to get your job done even if there are other jobs waiting. Have you found the right person?

To make realistic commitments to you about how long the job will take and how much it will cost, the salesperson must be familiar with the printing process and the operation of the shop. Ask how the process will be carried out. Do they seem to know what's happening? Ask what pitfalls are the common problems that can be avoided with a little foresight. Does the person have reasonable answers?

Ideally you should interview a half-dozen or so printers before deciding on the one you want. Talking to this many printers will give you a better idea of the kind of printing services available, what they offer and which one is best suited to your needs. You shouldn't necessarily choose the printer with the lowest bid; choose the one you can work with the best.

Nailing Down the Details

Once you've chosen a printer, you need to ensure that both you and the printer know what to expect so there will be no surprises. Make sure you know exactly what the printer needs from you. What form should the mechanicals be in? How should photographs be handled? Make sure the printer knows exactly what final results you want and is able to provide them. You should agree on the ink, the paper, the binding, the number of copies and most importantly, the price.

SCHEDULING AND PROOFS

An important point is how long the job will take. Usually you will have a deadline; you must also impose a deadline on the printer. Make sure the printer knows what the deadline is and agrees to it; both the day and the time should be specified. You should not be charged for overtime unless you agree beforehand. The other side of the coin is that you must get the mechanicals to the printer on time. Again, both the day and the time should be specified. The printer will usually reserve time for your job; if you're late, you'll miss the time slot assigned to you. Thus if you're a day late turning in your mechanicals, the printer may be delayed a week in finishing your job. Make sure you understand what will happen if you're late. Find out what the printer will do for you if he or she is late.

Agree with the printer when proofs will be available. Again, the printer has a responsibility to have the proofs ready on time, but you have one to examine them promptly; otherwise the job may be held up. Must you look at the proofs in the printshop, or can you take them away? If the president of your company, who can't make it to the shop, must approve them before printing, this can be an important issue. If your printshop considers you an important customer, they may pick up and deliver both the job and proofs.

OVERRUNS AND UNDERRUNS

When printers tell you how many copies they are going to print, it is usually understood that they mean plus or minus 10 percent. You will pay for all the copies printed, whether it is more or less than you actually ordered. If you require a fixed minimum, it should be understood that they may deliver up to 20 percent more than this number.

DELIVERY

Agree how the printed copies will get from the printshop to you. Will you pick them up? Will the shop deliver them, or ship them elsewhere for mailing or distribution? You should also know how your copies will be packaged. They can be bundled, boxed, banded, shrink wrapped, or left in piles on a pallet. Make sure you receive your job with a packing slip or invoice telling how many copies you're getting.

TERMS

Make sure that you know how much the job is going to cost and how and when the printer expects to receive payment. You should also know how long you have to return the job if you find a defect that affects the printed copies. As soon as possible after receiving the copies, check a representative sample for such faults as smudged ink, faults in the binding, areas not printed, excessive variation in ink density and bad registration. Such faults are the printer's responsibility; the printer should correct them at no extra charge.

PLATES AND NEGATIVES

Usually the printer will keep the plates and negatives created for your job. You should let the printer know whether you're going to be using them again, so they can be stored if necessary.

SPECIFICATIONS

Especially for larger jobs, you can create a sheet listing the specifications for your job. This would include the trim size, number of copies, type of paper and ink, number of pages and number of photographs, binding, packing, delivery and so forth. This is a useful starting place in arriving at an understanding with the printer and can also be used as a basis for competitive bids. On smaller jobs the salesperson will merely write the details of the job on the shop's standard form.

PSYCHOLOGY

Remember that the printer is in business to make money, while you're using desktop publishing in order to save money (among other reasons). The printer may therefore be predisposed to suggest ways of doing things that shift more of the job toward him or her than you really need. Many printshops, after all, do their own typesetting, or work closely with a typesetter, so the very fact that you're using desktop publishing—being your own typesetter and electronic pasteup person—constitutes a potential threat to the printer. They may try to make up for some of the business they've lost by suggesting they perform more pasteup, or more work in the stripping process (where the different elements of the publication are combined photographically). There's nothing wrong with such suggestions; just be clear about what you want—with yourself and with the printer.

Summary

If you have never dealt with the printing process before, it may seem as if there is a huge amount of detail to be learned and dealt with. Actually, what you need to know to complete a particular job is fairly simple. Once you've done the first issue of your publication, the others will be easy.

Don't hesitate to ask for help if you need it. Your printer and graphic designer will have people who can help you through the rough spots.

If you already know about printing, you've seen that desktop publishing has few surprises: mostly a desktop publishing job is a simple print job—that's why you've decided to use desktop publishing in the first place.

Appendix A:
Using Switcher

Apple's Switcher is a facile tool for desktop publishing that lets you load more than one program into memory at a time and "switch" between them. Using Switcher you need not quit one program and return to the desktop in order to use another. You can have Microsoft Word and MacDraw loaded into memory at the same time—when you write copy you use Word; when creating a drawing, you press [Command] [ ]] and Switcher pans the window to the right and you're free to use MacDraw.

Every time you switch between programs the contents of the clipboard are carried along and this is where the power of Switcher really begins to emerge. Suppose you're working up an illustration in MacPaint and you want to add typeset labels to parts of the drawing using MacDraw. Without Switcher you'd have to copy the image to the clipboard, quit MacPaint, wait to return to the desktop, and then start MacDraw. And what if when you got to MacDraw, the image didn't turn out quite the way you wanted? You'd have to quit, return to MacPaint and start all over.

With Switcher, you'd simply copy the image to the clipboard, switch to MacDraw in a single motion, paste the image there and do your labels. If you wanted to make changes to the original MacPaint image, you could pan back to MacPaint, make your changes, make another copy, and pan back to MacDraw.

Switcher is sold through authorized Apple dealers as the Switcher Construction Set and includes complete documentation. This appendix won't teach you how to operate Switcher—we'll leave that up to you and the excellent manual that accompanies the program. What we want to show you is how you can optimize Switcher in a desktop publishing environment. We do not recommend using Switcher for desktop publishing without a hard disk.

Memory Management and Partitions

Switcher can raise the level of performance for both you and your Macintosh. However, the number of programs you can load into Switcher at any one time is dependent on how much memory your Macintosh has. Each program you use on a Macintosh, in or out of Switcher, is loaded into memory each time you start it up. Some programs require a minimum of memory, as little as 128K, and others require four times that much, using nearly 512K. Version 1.2 of PageMaker (the version used in this book), for example, uses nearly 400K and, with Switcher, it is recommended you set aside 512K.

When you load programs into Switcher, they are installed in what are known as "partitions" and, in effect, each partition is the equivalent of a little Macintosh in itself. For nearly all programs the partition should never be less than 128K. In a Macintosh 512K, you can use a maximum of four 128K programs. On a Macintosh Plus you could load up to eight 128K programs.

Conserving Memory with Switcher

In order to conserve as much memory as possible you need to "configure" each program using the "Configure then Install..." command under the Switcher menu. This command brings up a mini-finder that allows you to select a program to configure. In this example we configure Microsoft Word (see Figure A-1). As you can see, we are able to set minimum and maximum memory partitions for the program at this point. If you are concerned about how much memory you can use and how many programs you want to use in Switcher, make sure you configure each program you plan to use with this command. If you click "Permanent," each configuration is saved to disk with the program and remains that way for future use until you change it.

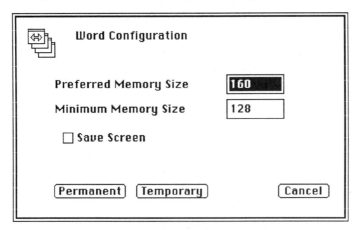

Figure A-1. Configure Dialog Box in Switcher.

The main thing you are concerned with here is the "save screen" option. You can save up to 22K of memory by turning this feature off. Often this is the difference between being able to install three programs in Switcher on a Macintosh 512K and four. You can, in fact, install four programs in four 128K partitions on a 512K Mac by turning save screen off. Likewise, on a Macintosh Plus, with save screen turned off, you can install PageMaker, MacDraw, Word, and MacPaint at the same time, each with fairly large memory partitions.

Given the memory constraints within which Switcher operates, you can see that Switcher has limited utility for desktop publishing with a Macintosh 512K. However, Switcher is quite powerful given the full megabyte of memory in the Macintosh Plus. Figure A-2 shows the minimum and optimum partition sizes for various programs in Switcher. Let's look at how you can use Switcher for desktop publishing with a Macintosh 512K or a Macintosh Plus.

	Minimum	Optimum
PageMaker	512K	512K
Microsoft Word	128K	160K or 256K
MacPaint	128K	178K
MacDraw	128K	196K
Excel	304K	512K
ThinkTank 512K	256K	512K

Figure A-2. Partition Sizes for Desktop Publishing Programs in Switcher.

Switcher on a Macintosh 512K

Since PageMaker requires a minimum memory partition of 512K, it is impossible to use PageMaker in Switcher on a 512K Mac. This somewhat limits the use of Switcher for desktop publishing on the smaller-memory Macintosh but you'll find it works well while you're developing copy and art. You can install Microsoft Word, MacDraw, and MacPaint all at the same time and switch between them as you go about preparing copy and art for use in a desktop-published publication.

When configuring programs for the 512K environment you should never set a partition for less than 128K. Even with 128K partitions, however, you may run into further constraints because the programs still need space to handle whatever graphics and text you're using them for. The more memory you can allocate, the better. You can refer to Figure A-2 for some ideal memory partitions for various programs.

In most cases, you're better off structuring your work in Switcher so you only have to use two programs at a time, giving each an ample memory partition. In this way, you could comfortably combine either Word and MacDraw, MacDraw and MacPaint, or Word and MacPaint. Although MacDraw benefits from the addition of memory in excess of 128K, of all these programs, it operates best within a minimum partition. Word tends to operate sluggishly in 128K. MacPaint regresses to its old 128K performance when in the smaller partition (that is, you cannot move an entire picture with the grabber hand and it tends to fault when you use the "Show Page" command).

You'll have to try out some sample configurations yourself. The configurations in Figure A-3 work fine on a 512K Mac.

	Partition Size	Save Screen
Microsoft Word	160K	OFF
MacPaint	178K	OFF
MacDraw	128K	OFF
Microsoft Word	160K	ON
MacDraw	196K	ON
Microsoft Word	160K	ON
MacPaint	178K	ON
Microsoft Word	256K	OFF
MacPaint	178K	OFF
Microsoft Word	256K	OFF
MacDraw	196K	OFF
Microsoft Word	256K	ON
MacDraw	128K	ON

Figure A-3. Sample Switcher Configurations for the Macintosh 512K.

Switcher on a Macintosh Plus

With a full megabyte (1024K) of memory at your disposal on a Macintosh Plus, using Switcher is no problem. You can do most of your desktop publishing in Switcher on a Macintosh Plus without ever returning to the Macintosh desktop except when you need to drag documents to the trash or create new folders. Most of the development for this book was done using Switcher on a Macintosh Plus. The only thing to note is that you should turn the RAM cache off in the Control Panel before starting Switcher on a Mac Plus. The configurations we've tested are shown in Figure A-4.

	Partition Size	Save Screen
PageMaker	512K	ON
Microsoft Word	256K	ON
MacPaint	178K	OFF
PageMaker	512K	ON
Microsoft Word	256K	ON
MacDraw	196K	OFF
PageMaker	512K	ON
Microsoft Word	160K	ON
MacPaint	178K	ON
PageMaker	512K	ON
Microsoft Word	160K	ON
MacDraw	196K	ON
PageMaker	512K	OFF
Microsoft Word	160K	OFF
MacPaint	178K	OFF
MacDraw	196K	OFF

Figure A-4. Sample Switcher Configurations for the Macintosh Plus.

Appendix B:
MacDraw and PICT Images

Whenever you save a MacDraw document the first time, you have the option of saving it in either the MacDraw format or the PICT format. As mentioned in earlier chapters (and as Aldus discusses in the PageMaker manual), in order to place a MacDraw document directly into PageMaker it must be saved in the PICT format. This is because the much more complex MacDraw format is protected as a proprietary property of Apple. This has some inherent problems for which there is a solution.

The Problem

PICT-formatted drawings do not contain all the information necessary to completely reconstruct the original image. They contain enough information to export the drawing to PageMaker but, unfortunately, not enough to recreate an exact duplicate of the original drawing in MacDraw if it is re-opened at a later date. Let's see how this can affect your work.

We create a drawing in MacDraw, save it in the PICT format, go to PageMaker, place the drawing in our publication and, on closer examination of the MacDraw object, decide we want to make some change to it and place it over again. Returning to MacDraw we open the original PICT-formatted document and, to our dismay, the picture isn't at all as we'd left it. A close inspection reveals that many of the lines and other objects in the drawing are shifted slightly in both vertical and horizontal directions. What was once positioned at one x,y location is now shifted to another nearby x,y location. This is part and parcel of the primitive PICT format that is good for one placement in PageMaker and no good for successive modifications and placements. This situation can occur frequently and now we'll learn how to work around it.

The Solution

Essentially, you want to keep two versions of every MacDraw document: one in the original MacDraw format to use with MacDraw, and another in the PICT format to use with PageMaker. The method for doing this is simple and doesn't take much time.

When you complete your drawing in MacDraw save it the first time in the MacDraw format and use that document whenever you want to make changes to the drawing. Next, copy everything in the image —[Command] [A] to select all and [Command] [C] to copy—and open a new MacDraw document. Paste your copied image into the new window and save the second MacDraw image in the PICT format. You use this version with PageMaker. You can save the first one as "drawing name/ DRAW" and the second one as "drawing name/PICT" so you know for sure which is which when you want to make changes later. This gives you the basic set of files.

Why not simply use the "Save as..." command with the first drawing? Why go to the trouble of opening an entirely new document? Experience has shown that the skewing of objects can sometimes occur in the act of saving the document the first time (that is, using "Save as..."). So to play it safe you open a new document for your PICT version and copy the objects there (the odd effect almost never occurs with copying).

Now, whenever you want to make a change to your drawing in the future return to the original MacDraw-formatted document, make your changes there, and then copy all of the objects. Before you quit MacDraw, open the old PICT document, select all the objects in the image, press [Backspace] to get rid of the old and press [Command] [V] to paste in the new. Press [Command] [S] to save and you're all set. Your changes will carry over to PageMaker when you need them.

Follow this procedure anytime you use a PageMaker drawing from MacDraw and you'll always be able to successfully make changes to it and use it again. If your drawing is relatively simple, involving only a few objects, you may not encounter the problem. But if you use complex MacDraw images, you are likely to encounter the problem and this is the only satisfactory method we've found to work around it.

Appendix C:
Disk Management

Proper organization will go a long way towards conserving time and energy, not to mention grief, in using your desktop publishing system. How you go about managing disk resources depends on what kind of equipment you're using and how much disk space you have. We have made some assumptions based on the equipment recommended in Chapter One.

Disk Management with a Macintosh 512K and 400K External Drive

In order to maximize disk space with a Macintosh 512K and 400K external drive, you should build separate sets of program disks and document disks. You also want to keep disk swapping down to a minimum. Understand that each set of two disks must have a System file on one of them. You must also have the program you're using on one of the disks and enough space remaining for your document. It's a tight fit on a 512K Mac with a 400K internal disk drive and only a 400K external drive but it can be done.

Build the smallest possible System file you can. Using Font/DA Mover (a utility available at your Apple dealer or from Macintosh User Groups) remove as many unnecessary fonts and desk accessories as you can. Make sure you store whatever you remove on backup disks. You must leave at least one desk accessory in the System file under the Apple menu otherwise the System will not work. The smallest functional System file for desktop publishing uses only the Chooser and Scrapbook accessories.

Remove any unnecessary program icons from the System Folder. If you are not using the Note Pad, remove the Note Pad icon. The next time you select the Note Pad desk accessory, the Macintosh will create a new icon to store your notes. If you don't plan to use an Imagewriter, you can save the Imagewriter driver onto another disk and remove it from the working set.

A common situation occurs when you want to take a PageMaker document to a nearby LaserWriter service bureau and print a document. To do this you need the System File, the Finder, LaserWriter, Laser Prep, Aldus Prep, PageMaker, and space for your documents. But wait! That adds up to more than 400K. Here is the solution. You can use three disks and only swap once. The System can be pared down to under 115K by removing all desk accessories except Chooser and Scrapbook, which you will probably use. You only need two of the LaserWriter fonts since you should not use any more than two different typefaces per document. You only need Chicago 12 and Monaco 9 and 12 to operate the Mac and not have your copy look funny. This makes for a very small System file. The Finder takes up another 47K and the LaserWriter, 36K.

You now should have a disk with less than 200K on it and nearly 200K left over. You should reserve approximately 40K for the clipboard. Put PageMaker (269K) on the external drive disk and you still have 130K. You can put your documents on the remaining space in either the internal or external drive disk.

But where do Aldus Prep and Laser Prep go? Put them on yet a third disk. When you get ready to print from PageMaker, it will ask you for the disk with Aldus Prep on it; it will prepare the LaserWriter, eject the disk and ask for your document disk back and never request the Aldus Prep disk again.

One further warning: you should reserve space on one of the disks equal to the size of the document you are printing because PageMaker keeps a running copy of the document on disk separate from the saved document.

You should prepare similar program and document disks for MacDraw, Word, and MacPaint. Economizing on disk space allows your programs to run more quickly and avoids constant disk swapping.

Disk Management with a Macintosh Plus and 800K External Drive

With a Macintosh Plus and 800K external drive, you will also want to conserve on disk space and can take note of what has already been mentioned. The Macintosh Plus owner can easily have both the program and system files on the same disk with some free space left over for extra fonts or desk accessories. You will still want to follow the same disk organization, though, and keep a separate set of program disks and a set of document storage disks.

Disk Management with a Macintosh 512K or Macintosh Plus and a Hard Disk Drive

If you can afford it, a hard disk is a sound desktop publishing investment. You will have ample space for both software and document storage. Hard disks access documents and programs more quickly than the floppy drives and will save you time as well as storage space. You don't have to be as meticulous about organizing your hard disk for proper management of disk space. However, if you don't have a LaserWriter and plan to print documents at some other location, you'd be well advised to prepare disks in the manner described in the above sections.

Glossary of Terms

Actual size
A view of a portion of the page in PageMaker that shows text and graphics in the publication window at the same size they will appear when printed on the LaserWriter.

Apple menu
The menu on the far left of the menu bar. Its title is an apple symbol ().

AppleTalk Personal Network
Apple's local area network (LAN) system. It involves connecting together Macintoshes, LaserWriters, disk drives, and file servers by way of AppleTalk cables and connectors.

Art or artwork
Any illustration, photograph, or element on a printed page (not including body type, heads, subheads, and by-lines).

Art direction
The design goals and objectives developed for a printed piece that provide guidance to a desktop publisher, photographer, or designer in making decisions regarding selection of art, photography, placement of text, and page composition.

Basis weight/basic weight
The weight of a single sheet of paper based on the weight of one ream (500 sheets) of uncut paper. A "20-pound bond paper" means that 500 sheets measuring 17" by 22" weighs twenty pounds.

Bindery
An independent company or a department in a print shop, whose sole business is finishing and binding printed works.

Bit map
A graphic image formed by a matrix of dots with a specific number of dots per inch. In the Macintosh environment this is 72 dots per inch. The graphic images created in MacPaint are bit-map images.

Bleed
Any part of an image that extends beyond the top, bottom, or outside edge of a page.

Blueline/blueprint
A proof made directly from a press negative onto photosensitive paper to show how the printed piece will look when actually printed with ink. This is the last chance you have to make any corrections to the work before giving your okay to have it printed.

Board
A stiff-backed cardboard with a smooth surface used to prepare camera-ready art or mechanicals.

Body type
The actual type used in setting the bulk of the text (not including heads and subheads). Type larger than 9 points and smaller than 12 points is commonly used for body type.

Bold/boldface
Type with a heavy, black appearance that is thicker than the rest of the text type with which it appears.

Bond paper
Paper characterized by light weight and suitability as a writing paper. It is commonly used for business correspondence and documents.

Book paper
Paper that encompasses the weights and grades commonly used for the text of printed pieces. It is heavier than bond paper but lighter than cover paper, sometimes referred to as "text" if it has a textured finish.

Border
A continuous decorative design or rule positioned around text or art on a page.

Box/box rule
A heavy rule or border that boxes in on all four sides an item of type or other graphic image.

Button
The place in a dialog box where you click to designate, confirm, or cancel an action.

By-line
The name of the author that appears above an article (i.e., by Lynn Maya).

Camera-ready art/camera-ready mechanicals
Material that is ready to be photographed by the printer for reproduction. This material can come direct from the LaserWriter, Allied Linotronic printers, or can be pasted onto boards along with other graphic or photographic elements.

Case binding
Binding method that attaches a hard cover to the inside pages by the endpapers and not directly at the spine. The way most hard cover books are bound.

Character
Any single letter, number, symbol, or punctuation mark you type at the keyboard of your Macintosh; also anything that can be set in type.

Choose
To pick a command from a menu by dragging. Usually you do this after you've selected some text or a graphic image in the program window to perform a menu-based action on.

Chooser
A desk accessory that permits you to choose any AppleTalk-based printer on which to print your document. Chooser also lets you specify whether you want to use the printer port or the modem port to make the connection between your Macintosh and printer. It must be installed in your System File in order to use the LaserWriter (replaces older desk accessory called "Choose Printer").

Circle tool
A tool in MacPaint, MacDraw, and PageMaker used to draw circles and ovals.

Click
To position the pointer on top of something in the program window, then press and release the mouse button in a single motion.

Clipboard
The holding place for temporarily storing the text, graphics, or group selection you last cut or copied.

Coated paper
A general term for papers whose surface has been chemically coated to produce a specific finish (such as high-gloss enamel) after the body paper is made.

Column
A section of a page divided vertically, containing text or graphics. It is measured by the horizontal width. Also a regular feature in a publication that repeats in successive issues (usually by the same author).

Column guides
In PageMaker, the nonprinting dotted vertical lines that mark the left and right edges of the columns you create with the "Column guides..." command. Column guides act as boundaries for flowing text onto the page.

Comb binding
Binding in which a row of slots is punched along the binding edge of a publication and a series of flat, curled, plastic teeth on a solid backbone is inserted to hold them together.

Command
A word or phrase, usually in a menu, describing a task for a program to perform. Also, a combination of the Command key and a character key that accomplishes the same action.

Command key
A key that, when held down while another key is pressed or a mouse action is performed, causes a command to take effect. This equates to a control key on other computers.

Comp/comprehensive
A detailed, full-sized mock-up showing how a printed piece will look, including text, graphics, and other elements. Used to see the full design before type is set and final art is pasted down and as a guide for pasteup. When assembled electronically in a desktop publishing environment, is much closer to the final product than conventional typesetting and pasteup methods.

Connection box
A small white box at one end of an AppleTalk connector. Cables plug into the box, allowing network signals to flow through the box.

Continuous tone
A photograph or other art having different values from black to white (greys) reproduced using a halftone screen and high-contrast film.

Copy
Any text you wish to use in a publication; usually the manuscript before it is typeset.

Copy camera
Another term for a process camera.

Copy command
To place something on the clipboard by selecting it and choosing "Copy" from the Edit menu.

Copyediting
Finalizing of copy prior to layout so that facts, grammar, spelling, and punctuation meet with your publication's standards. Also involves making sure the writing style is consistent and copy is complete, appropriate, and understandable.

Cover paper
Paper that is characterized by its weight and durability (heavier than book or bond papers), often used for the covers of documents.

Crop
To eliminate portions of a photograph or illustration to make it a desired size or to eliminate unwanted details. In PageMaker, you can crop the edges of MacDraw and MacPaint images.

Cropping tool
A tool in PageMaker used to trim graphics by dragging a handle towards the center from the top, bottom, right, left, or corners of the image.

Crossbar
The shape of the pointer in MacPaint, MacDraw, and PageMaker when you have selected any of the tools for drawing lines, rectangles, or ovals.

Cut
To remove something from a document by selecting it and choosing "Cut" from the Edit menu. What you cut is placed on the clipboard.

Debossing
Impressing an image on the front of a sheet of paper so that the design appears recessed.

Desk accessory
Mini-programs that are available from the menu regardless of which application you're using. Examples are the Calculator, Alarm Clock, Scrapbook, and MockWrite.

Desktop
The Macintosh's working environment—the menu bar, the grey area on the screen, and the folder and program icons associated with the Finder—from which you launch programs and to which you return when you quit.

Device
Any piece of equipment that can be attached to AppleTalk—a Macintosh, a Macintosh Plus, a LaserWriter, a LaserWriter Plus, a file server, or other peripheral.

Diagonal lines tool
A tool in MacPaint, MacDraw, and PageMaker used to draw straight lines in any direction.

Dialog box
A box containing a message requesting more information. Dialog boxes accompany any menu choice followed by an ellipsis (...). Sometimes the message is a warning that you've asked your Macintosh to do something it

can't do or that you're about to erase some of your information. In these cases the message is often accompanied by a beep.

Digitize
To convert a visual image into a form that can be stored on disk and electronically reconstructed in one of the Macintosh drawing programs (most often MacPaint).

Discretionary hyphen
A hyphen that you type with Microsoft Word or PageMaker to identify an optional place where the program can divide a word to better fit the text within the page margins or column width. Typed as [Command] [-], the hyphen does not appear on the screen unless the application actually uses it to break a line.

Disk or diskette
The magnetic medium on which the Macintosh stores information. The Macintosh Plus can use 800K, double-sided, 3.5-inch disks. Earlier versions of the Macintosh 512K use 400K, single-sided, 3.5-inch disks. All Macintoshes can be connected to hard disk drives.

Disk drive
The mechanism that holds the disk, retrieves information from it, and saves information on it. A hard disk has the disk permanently encased. A 3.5-inch disk drive requires that you insert a 3.5-inch disk.

Display type
Type, usually 14 point or larger and often in boldface and of a distinctive design—used for headings, in advertisements, or in smaller-size text to attract attention.

Document
Whatever you create with Macintosh programs—information you enter, modify, view, or save. This can be text, graphic images, or both. Desktop publishing has MacDraw, PageMaker, Word, and MacPaint documents, among others.

Double-click
To position the pointer on top of something, and then press and release the mouse button twice in rapid succession without moving the mouse.

Drag
To position the pointer on top of something, press and hold the mouse button, move the mouse and release the mouse button. When you release the mouse button, you either confirm a choice or move an object to a new location.

Drop shadow
A shaded area behind an image designed to bring the topmost image forward.

Dummy
The prototype of a publication, either sketched by hand or mocked up using PageMaker or MacDraw.

Editorial content
The range and scope of topics covered in a publication, most often determined by the publication's editor or, in the case of desktop publishing, the person planning the publication.

Element
Anything positioned on the page during layout, such as text, photographs, illustrations, line art, rules, or boxes.

Ellipsis
A sequence of three dots (...) indicating that part of a phrase or sentence has been omitted. On the Macintosh keyboard, true ellipses are typed with the [Option] [;].

On the Macintosh, an ellipsis following the name of a command in a pull-down menu indicates a dialog box will follow your choice.

Em
In typesetting and printing, a unit of measurement equal to the space occupied by letter M in a given font.

Em dash
A dash used in punctuating text that measures the length of one em. An em dash can be typed with the Macintosh keyboard by pressing [Command] [Shift] [Hyphen].

Embossing
Impressing an image on the back of a sheet of paper so that the design appears raised on the front.

Facing pages
The two pages that face each other when a publication is open and laid flat. Facing pages consist of an even-numbered page on the left and an odd-numbered page on the right. In PageMaker, you can view facing pages by making a choice from the Page menu.

Finder
An application that's always available on the Macintosh desktop. Although you may not be aware of its actions, you use it to manage documents and programs, and to get information to and from disks.

Fluorescent ink
Ink that has bright, intense color, often used with posters.

Flow
To place text in a page layout by clicking the mouse button at the location you wish the text to appear. If you flow text between column guides, PageMaker breaks the lines to fit between the guides. Otherwise, PageMaker uses the line breaks from the word-processed document.

Flush
To line up text or graphics so that all elements are even vertically with no indentation; for example, "flush left" means that all lines of type and all art line up on the left.

Folder
A holder of documents, programs, or other folders on the desktop. Folders allow you to organize information in any way you want.

Font
A complete collection of letters, figures, punctuation, and special characters with a consistent appearance, such as Helvetica or Palatino. With the Macintosh, font often refers to the "screen font" displayed in the program window (as opposed to the "typeface" that is printed on the LaserWriter).

Font file
A file containing screen fonts, which can be installed or removed from the disk's System file.

Font/DA Mover
An application available on the LaserWriter and LaserWriter Plus font disk that allows you to install or remove fonts and desk accessories from a disk's System file.

Format
Anything relating to the outward appearance, such as the typeface, arrangement, makeup, and binding of a publication.

When working with Macintosh word processing languages, format also refers to the way characters and text appear on the page. With Microsoft Word, you can format the position and appearance of characters as well as the alignment and spacing of lines and paragraphs.

Galley
A copy of typeset text made for the purpose of proofreading and checking accuracy. In the days of hot type, the term referred to a long, shallow, metal tray used by type compositors to hold type after it had been set by hand.

Glossary
A special document in Microsoft Word where text can be stored and later retrieved by name. To expand the glossary entry in a document, type the glossary name and hold down the [Command] key while pressing [Backspace].

Grabber hand
A PageMaker technique for moving around on the pasteboard. Hold down the [Option] key, then the mouse button. A hand icon appears, indicating that you can drag the publication window with the mouse. Also used in MacPaint for the same purpose, but chosen from the palette of tools on the left side of the screen.

Graphic artist or graphic designer
An artist or designer specializing in design and execution for publications. If you intend to consult one for desktop publishing, make sure the one you choose is familiar with how PageMaker functions and how it handles electronic pasteup.

Graphic design
Design based on two-dimensional print processes, such as illustration, typography, photography, and printing methods.

Gravure printing
A printing process in which the image to be printed is etched into the plate, which doubles as the impression cylinder.

Greeking
Simulated composition used in comps to show actual placement and size of type; this nonsense text is usually in Latin, despite the name.

Grid
In MacDraw and MacPaint this is an invisible drawing and moving aid. When the grid is turned on, all objects drawn or moved are constrained to the grid spacing, initially set to one-eighth inch intervals (user-adjustable in MacDraw).

Group
In MacDraw, to combine two or more objects so that they act as one object. You can manipulate grouped objects just as you do individual objects.

Guide
In PageMaker, one of three types of nonprinting dotted lines: marginal guides, horizontal and vertical ruler guides, and column guides. These act as visual aids or—when the "Snap to guides" feature is turned on —physical aids for aligning text and graphics. Column guides also limit the line length as you flow text.

Gutter
The inside margins on facing pages of a document; that is, the left side of odd pages and the right side of even pages. These margins are usually set wider than the outside margins to allow extra space for binding. Also commonly used to refer to the space between two columns of type or art.

Hairline
A very thin line rule; often the smallest rule that can physically appear on a printed page.

Halftone

A process in which a black-and-white photograph is rephotographed through a screen so that the gradations of light and dark in the original photograph are reproduced as a series of tiny dots that print as a continuous tone.

Handle

In MacDraw and PageMaker, eight small rectangles that surround a selected shape or object. In PageMaker specifically, text handles appear at the top and bottom of text blocks and are represented with an empty handle at the beginning, a + sign if there's more text to follow and a # sign to indicate the end.

Hardware

Anything about the Macintosh or connected devices that you can see or touch.

Head/heading/headline

The title introducing an article, chapter, or major subdivision of a publication. Usually set in various sizes of display type to distinguish between heading and text, and between main and subsidiary headings or subheads.

Hot type

Type set by a hot-metal process, as opposed to cold type set by a photographic or xerographic process.

Hyphenation

The use of a hyphen (-) to divide a word between syllables.

I-beam

A pointer in all Macintosh programs used to establish the location on the page where you want to start typing or editing text.

Icon

A graphic representation of an object, a concept, or a message. In the graphics-rich Macintosh operating environment, icons are used to represent programs, documents, folders, and provide many visual cues to guide your use of the computer.

Illustration

A drawing, diagram, or chart used in a publication to explain or supplement the text. Often used as a term to distinguish a drawn image from one that is photographed.

Imposition

The arrangement of pages of a publication for printing in one impression so that, when trimmed, finished and bound, they will appear in the proper page sequence.

Italic

Type that leans to the right; a sloping, slanted variation of a typeface: *italic* type.

Justify

To vertically align type and adjust sentence length so the text appears flush left and flush right within the same column.

Laser Prep

Laser Prep prepares the LaserWriter to work with the Macintosh the first time you print after the LaserWriter has been switched on. Thereafter, Laser Prep isn't used unless the LaserWriter is turned off and on again.

Layout

The arrangement of text and graphics on the page.

Leading/line spacing

The vertical spacing between lines of type expressed in points. In the days of hot type this was a thin strip of metal used to space out lines of type; pronounced "ledding."

Letterpress printing

Printing method whereby the image to be inked is raised above the printing plate.

Ligature

Two or more type characters that are connected and print as a single character. On the Macintosh keyboard, the lowercase letters "f" and "i," and "f" and "l" are joined into ligatures as "fi" ([Option] [Shift] [5]) and "fl" ([Option] [Shift] [6]).

Line art

Art with no shades of grey; diagrams, pictograms, and art that consists primarily of black lines often rendered with pen and ink.

Lithography

Printing process whereby the area containing images to be transferred is coated with a greaselike substance that attracts ink on the press.

Lock

In MacDraw, to anchor a selected object in place by choosing "Lock" from the Arrange menu. You can't move, remove, or resize a locked object.

Logo/logotype

A word or several letters cast as one unit. Also, the product or company name set in a distinctive design and used as a trademark.

Margins

The blank areas that border the printed-type page. The area from the edge of the page to the edge of the text (not including indents). In PageMaker and Microsoft Word, you use the "Page Setup..." command to set margins on the left, right, top, and bottom of the page.

Master page

In PageMaker, this is a page, opened by clicking the L or R page icon in the lower left of the publication window, where you put all the text, graphics, and guides you want repeated on every left-hand or right-hand page in the publication. PageMaker uses the master page as a template throughout a publication, so you only have to create repetitive information once. If your publication is double-sided, you have separate master pages for the left-hand and right-hand pages.

Measurement system

In PageMaker and Microsoft Word, the units you choose with the "Preferences" command from the Edit menu. The options include inches, millimeters, or picas and points. The units you choose appear on the rulers and in all dialog boxes that require measurements.

Mechanical

Another term for camera-ready art.

Memory

The place in the Macintosh main unit that stores information while you're working with it. The Macintosh Plus includes 1 megabyte (1024K) of memory you can use for your work, and 128K of ROM (read-only memory) that stores certain system information permanently. The Macintosh 512K includes one-half megabyte (512K) of memory, and, in older Macintoshes, 64K of ROM; newer Macintosh 512K models include 128K of ROM.

Menu

A list of commands that appears when you point to and press the menu title in the menu bar. Dragging through the menu and releasing the mouse button while a command is highlighted chooses that command.

Mouse

The small device you roll around on a flat surface next to your Macintosh. When you move the mouse, the pointer on the screen moves correspondingly.

Mouse button

The button on the top of the mouse. In general, pressing the mouse button initiates an action on whatever is under the pointer, and releasing the button confirms the action.

Network

A group of devices linked together that communicate by using the appropriate software (in the case of the Macintosh, this would be AppleTalk).

Non repro blue

A light turquoise-blue pen or pencil that does not reproduce photographically.

Object

The basic drawing unit of MacDraw. An object can be a geometric shape or text.

Offset lithography/offset printing

Printing process whereby the image is transferred or offset from a plate to a blanket, then printed onto paper. Also known as photo-offset lithography.

Opacity
The property of paper that prevents the printed image on one side from showing through on the other.

Outline
A typeface in which the letters are formed of outlines rather than solid strokes, accessed from the Type menu in PageMaker and the Character menu in Microsoft Word.

Page
One side of a sheet of paper in a publication.

Page composition
The arrangement of type and art elements on a page.

Page icon
In PageMaker, one of the icons in the bottom-left corner of the publication window identifying each master page and every regular page in the publication.

Page orientation
The way in which a document is printed, either vertically or horizontally on the page. PageMaker, Microsoft Word, and MacDraw permit you to print pages upright or sideways, depending on the orientation you choose in the "Page Setup..." dialog box.

Pagination
A publication's numbered pages in their proper sequence. Also, the act of numbering the pages.

Pantone® Matching System (PMS)
A standard commercial system of precise formulas using base colors to get a wide range of opaque color choices. Often referred to as simply "PMS colors."

Paragraph mark
In Microsoft Word, a character that marks the end of a paragraph—¶. This character is normally invisible. To insert a paragraph mark, you press the [Return] key. Use the "Show ¶" command from the Edit menu or press [Command] [Y] to make paragraph marks visible.

Paste
To put a copy of the contents of the clipboard—whatever was last cut or copied—at the insertion point.

Pasteup
The process of physically pasting down typeset galleys and final art with wax or glue. With desktop publishing, you do this electronically.

Pasteup artist
An individual who specializes in creating page layouts and pasteup for publications.

Pasteboard
In PageMaker, the area surrounding that page that you are working on (completely visible in the mini-page view). You can set text and graphics on the pasteboard while you work on the page. When you move to another page, whatever is on the pasteboard remains there.

Perpendicular tool
In MacDraw and PageMaker, a tool used to draw a straight line at any 45-degree angle.

Pica
Twelve points, an absolute unit of measure approximately 1/6 of an inch; a basic unit of typographic measure.

PICT
The option you must select in MacDraw's "Save" dialog box to save graphics in the "picture-format." Used most often to export drawings for use in PageMaker with the "Place..." command.

Place
In PageMaker, the command you use to read a text or graphics document directly from the disk where it is stored, then position it on the page.

Plate (printing)
A metal, plastic, rubber, or paper sheet on which the image to be printed is exposed, ready for the press.

Point

An absolute unit of measure, 1/12 of one pica, approximately 1/72 of an inch; a basic unit of typographic measure. One point also equals one pixel on the Macintosh screen.

Point size

The height of a font measured in points.

Pointer

A small shape on the screen, most often an arrow pointing up and to the left, that follows the movement of the mouse.

PostScript

Adobe's page-description language used by the LaserWriter and other high-resolution printers and typesetters.

Press run

The total number of copies produced in one printing of a publication.

Printer

A supplier who takes actual type or press plates and produces finished printed copies; may also perform other services such as folding and binding.

Printing resource

A program (sometimes called a driver) that translates the file you're printing into the language the printer understands—PostScript for the LaserWriter. A printing resource file is represented by an icon named after the printer. You cannot use a printer attached to the Macintosh unless the correct printing resource is installed in your System Folder.

Process camera

The type of camera used to produce a press negative of art. Also called a copy camera or graphic-arts camera.

Publication

What you produce with desktop publishing or any other professional publishing method. The collection of pages you create from documents prepared with Macintosh software, as well as text and graphics you create with PageMaker.

Quotes, quote marks
The use of inverted commas or apostrophes before and after a word or
phrase to indicate that it is a quotation. On the Macintosh keyboard these
characters (" ") are typed with the [Option] [left bracket] and [Option] [Shift]
[left bracket].

Ragged right
Text set with an unjustified right-hand margin.

RAM
Random access memory, the part of the Macintosh memory that stores
information temporarily while you're working on it. RAM can contain
both application programs and your own information. Information in
RAM is temporary, gone forever if you switch the power off. An exception
to this is a small amount of memory used to save settings, such as the clock
and Speaker Volume, that's powered by battery when your Macintosh is
switched off.

Reduce
In PageMaker, to make graphics smaller by dragging a handle. Holding
down the [Shift] key maintains the original proportions as the graphic gets
smaller.

Reduce or enlarge option
An option in the "Page Setup..." dialog box (or the "Print" command in
PageMaker) that lets you reduce or enlarge the text and graphics on a page
just as many copiers do.

Reverse
Copy is said to be "reversed" when the colors are reversed, as when the
white is printed as black and the black as white.

ROM
Read-only memory, the part of memory that contains information the
Macintosh uses (along with system files) throughout the system, including
the information it needs to get itself started. Information in ROM is
permanent; it doesn't vanish when you switch the power off. The
Macintosh Plus and new versions of the Macintosh 512K (with 800K
internal disk drives) contains 128K of ROM. Older Macintosh 512K models
(with 400K internal drives) contain 64K of ROM.

Rounded-corner tool
A tool in MacPaint, MacDraw, and PageMaker used to draw squares and rectangles with rounded corners.

Ruler
In MacDraw and PageMaker, the horizontal and vertical measurement lines that can be displayed on the top edge and left edge of the document window. In Microsoft Word, the ruler appears only at the top of page.

Ruler guides
In PageMaker, horizontal and vertical dotted lines on the page that are nonprinting extensions of the ruler. You can drag ruler guides from the inside edge of both rulers and position them anywhere on the page. To remove a ruler guide, drag it off the page.

Rules
Typographical term for any line that appears on the page; usually decorative and used to enclose or set off material in columns.

Sans serif
Certain typeface designs, such as Helvetica, without an ending stroke or serif on the arms, tails, and stems of characters.

Save
To store a permanent copy of a document on disk with the "Save" or "Save as..." command.

Scrapbook
A desk accessory where you can store text or graphics you use frequently. You can copy text and graphics from the scrapbook to the clipboard, then paste them into the current document.

Screen fonts
Fonts used to display text on the Macintosh screen that are the screen display equivalent of LaserWriter typefaces. Screen fonts for the typeface you wish to print in must be installed on the System file using the Font/DA Mover.

Scroll
To move a document or directory in its window so that you can see a different part of it.

SCSI
Small Computer System Interface—an industry standard interface that provides high-speed access to peripheral devices. The Macintosh Plus includes an SCSI port.

Select
To designate where the next action will take place. To select, you click or drag across the text or graphic.

Serif
The small terminal stroke at the end of the main stroke of a letter.

Snap-to guides
A PageMaker feature that, when turned on, causes column, ruler, and margin guides to exert a "magnetic" pull on the pointer, text, or a graphic that comes close to the guides. This feature is useful for accurately aligning text and graphics, as well as for drawing on the guides.

Software
Programs, or instructions for the Macintosh to carry out.

Specification/spec
How you describe the components, characteristics, and procedures of a particular job, product or activity to a specific vendor (such as a printer or designer).

Subhead
A heading that is subordinate to the main topic heading.

Symmetry
An object or image that, cut in half by an imaginary dividing line, appears the same on either side of the line.

System file
A file the Macintosh uses to start itself up or to provide system-wide information such as fonts and desk accessories. You can install or remove fonts and desk accessories in the System file using the Font/DA Mover.

Text
All characters that make up your document.

Text block
In PageMaker, the text identified by two handles when selected with the pointer tool. If the bottom handle contains a +, the text block contains more text than you can see on the page—you must click the + with the pointer tool to get a text icon, then continue placing the remaining text as another text block. A # handle indicates there is no further text in the block.

Text-only document
Text created or transmitted with another application or someone else's computer, then saved without any type specifications or other formatting.

Text tool
A tool in all Macintosh programs corresponding to the I-beam pointer; used to position the point at which to create text or select text to be edited.

Trim marks
Marks on a printed sheet to indicate where paper stock is to be trimmed or cut to required size.

Type/typeface
A specific style of printed character that is either set by hand, photo-composed, or set on the LaserWriter using desktop publishing software. Typefaces are usually copyrighted and licensed for use by the purchaser of typesetting equipment. Times, Helvetica, Palatino, and Avant Garde are the names of specific typefaces.

Typesetting
Methods of assembling type for printing—by hand, machine, photographic, or xerographic techniques.

Typography
The art, general design, and appearance of typeset material.

View
In PageMaker, the size of the pasteboard and page as they appear in the publication window. The smallest view shows a complete page; the largest view shows text and graphics at twice the size they will print. Intermediate views show actual size, 50-percent size and 70-percent size. You can also adjust your view of the page in MacDraw.

Widow
The last line of a paragraph in typeset copy that appears at the top of a column. Avoiding widows is one of the problems of page makeup, whether automatic or manual.

Window
The area that displays information on your Macintosh screen. You view documents through a window. You can open or close a window, move it around, and sometimes change its size, edit its contents, and scroll through it.

Word wraparound
A feature in all Macintosh text-processing programs (including MacDraw). As you reach the right margin of paragraph text, the last whole word you've typed is moved to the beginning of the next line.

Product
Manufacturers

Software

ClickArt
T/Maker Graphics
2115 Landings Drive
Mountain View, CA 94043

MacDraw (1.9)
MacPaint (1.5)
MacWrite (4.5)
Switcher (4.9)
Apple Computer, Inc.
20525 Mariani Avenue
Cupertino, CA 95014
(408) 996-1010

The MacMemories Series
ImageWorld, Inc.
P.O. Box 10415
Eugene, OR 97440
(503) 485-0395

MacSpell+
Creighton Development, Inc.
16 Hughes, Suite C-106
Irvine, CA 92718
(714) 472-0488

Mac The Knife
Miles Computing, Inc.
7741 Alabama Avenue, Suite 2
Canoga Park, CA 91304
(818) 884-2781

Microsoft Word (1.05)
Microsoft Excel (1.0)
Microsoft Corporation
10700 Northup Way
Box 97200
Bellevue, WA 98009
(206) 882-8080

MockWrite (4.2a), included in MockPackage
CE Software
801-73rd Street
Des Moines, IA 50312
(515) 224-1995

PageMaker (1.2)
Aldus Corporation
411 First Avenue South, Suite 200
Seattle, Wa 98104
(206) 622-5500

PostScript
Adobe Systems Inc.
1870 Embarcadero Road
Palo Alto, CA 94303
(415) 852-0271

Hardware

Dataproducts LZR-2665 Laser Printer
Dataproducts, Inc.
6250 Canoga Avenue
Woodland Hills, California 91365-0746
(818) 887-8000

Linotronic Series 100 and Series 300 Imagesetters
Allied-Linotype Company
425 Oser Avenue
Hauppauge, New York 11788
(516) 434-2000

Macintosh 512K, Macintosh Plus
LaserWriter, LaserWriter Plus
Hard Disk 20
Apple Computer, Inc.
20525 Mariani Avenue
Cupertino, CA 95014
(408) 996-1010

MacVision
Koala Technologies/PTI Industries
269 Mt. Hermon Road
Scotts Valley, CA 95066
(408) 438-0946

OmniLaser 2108 and 2115 Laser Printers
Texas Instruments, Inc.
Data Systems Group
P.O. Box 809063, H-860
Dallas, Texas 75080-4063

QMS-PS 800 Laser Printer
QMS
P.O. Box 81250
Mobile, Alabama 36689
(205) 633-4300

ThunderScan
Thunderware Inc.
21 Orinda Way
Orinda, CA 94563
(415) 254-6581

Recommended Reading

Books

Book Design—Systematic Aspects, Stanley Rice, R.R. Bowler Company, New York, 1978.

Book Design—Text Format Models, Stanley Rice, R.R. Bowler Company, New York, 1978.

The Copy-To-Press Handbook, Judy E. Pickens, John Wiley and Sons, New York, 1985.

Editing For Print, Geoffrey Rogers, Writer's Digest Books, Cincinnati, Ohio, 1985.

The Elements of Style, William Strunk Jr., and E.B. White, 2nd.ed., Macmillan Publishing Co., Inc., New York, 1972.

Eye and Brain: the psychology of seeing, R.L. Gregory, 2nd ed. World University Library, New York, 1966.

The Graphic Designer's Handbook, Alastair Campbell, Running Press, Philadelphia, 1983.

Hart's Rules For Compositors and Readers, 39th ed., Oxford University Press, Oxford, New York, 1983.

The Intelligent Eye, R.L. Gregory, McGraw-Hill Book Company, New York, 1970.

Notes On Graphic Design and Visual Communication, Gregg Berryman, William Kaufmann, Inc., Los Altos, California, 1984.

Pocket Pal®, 13th ed., International Paper Company, New York, 1983.

A Primer Of Visual Literacy, Donis A. Dondis, MIT Press, Cambridge, Massachusetts, 1973.

The Print Production Handbook, David Bann, North Light, Cincinnati, 1985.

Words Into Type, Prentice-Hall, Inc., Englewood Cliffs, New Jersey, 1974.

Magazines

Communication Arts, 410 Sherman Avenue, P.O. Box 10300, Palo Alto, CA 94303. Published bimonthly.

How—Ideas and Technique in Graphic Design, 6400 Goldsboro Road, Bethesda, MD 20817. Published bimonthly.

MacUser, 25 West 39th Street, New York, NY 10018. Published monthly.

MacWorld, 555 De Haro Street, San Francisco, CA 94107. Published monthly.

Print, 6400 Goldsboro Road, Bethesda, MD 20817. Published bimonthly.

Publish!, 555 De Haro Street, San Francisco, CA 94107. Published bimonthly.

Personal Publishing, P.O. Box 390, Itasca, IL 60143, Published monthly.

Index

typewriters, 3
typographic measurement, 110, 116,
   118, 179

U

underline, 173
universities, 14
unwanted page elements, 61
unworkable solutions, 69–70
user interface, 17–19, 29

V

video camera, 144, 147
visual elements, 172
visual interest, 170–171, 227

W

widow, 173
word processing, 90
word processor, 18, 26, 33–35
Wordstar, 99
writing, 22
WYSIWYG, 20

A Note About How this Book Was Produced

The pages of this book were composed and typeset using PageMaker and Microsoft Word. The title page, copyright page, and subsequent pages preceding page one were composed and laid out by the author in PageMaker. The opening page for each chapter was designed, composed and executed by the book designer, Jana Janus. Chapter text thereafter was typeset with Microsoft Word. Each chapter was painstakingly paginated in Word, leaving space for figures to be pasted in later.

Once these pages were proofed and corrections made, the title page and first page of each chapter were printed on the Linotronic 300 imagesetter. Subsequent pages for each chapter and all digital images were printed on a LaserWriter Plus. These masters were given to pasteup artists who cut and waxed the pages onto pasteup boards in the traditional manner. The assembled boards were proofed, minor corrections made and then shipped to New American Library in New York for printing, binding and distribution.

The text type is 11 point Palatino set on 12 point leading. The display type is also Palatino, set in various point sizes. The author's photo was half-tone screened and pasted in.

All Macintosh graphics were created by the author and the author served as desktop publishing consultant to the production staff.

Icons appearing on the title page and first page of each chapter were executed on the Macintosh by Barbara Chan based on designs created by Kim Straitiff and Barbara Chan.

Line art by Kim Straitiff.

Book design and typography by
Jana Janus
of H.S. Dakin Company.

COMPUTER GUIDES FROM PLUME

☐ **THE NEW AMERICAN COMPUTER DICTIONARY by Kent Porter.** The acclaimed reference on the language of computer, revised and updated to reflect the rapidly changing computer scene, with 2,400 entries. A Comprehensive A-Z reference source, it covers every term one needs to know to buy and use a computer.   (256534—$8.95)*

☐ **ALMOST FREE COMPUTER STUFF FOR KIDS by Linda Gail Christie and Gary Bullard.** Hundreds of companies across the country offer a tremendous array of products for computer fun and educational challenge at startlingly low prices—or even no cost—if you know where to write. This book tells you all the things you can get and provides the send-away-for coupons you need to enjoy special discounts on everything from software to T-shirts.   (255619—$9.95)*

☐ **THE COMPUTER FREELANCER'S HANDBOOK: Moonlighting with Your Home Computer by Ardy Friedberg.** This practical guide will show you how you can use your personal computer for extra income. Step-by-step advice, a wealth of real-life success stories, and inspiring ideas offer all the information you'll need for choosing the right home-based business, figuring prices, attracting customers, and growing as much and as fast as you want.   (255627—$10.95)*

☐ **DATABASE PRIMER: AN EASY-TO-UNDERSTAND GUIDE TO DATABASE MANAGEMENT SYSTEMS by Rose Deakin.** The future of information control is in database management systems—tools that help you organize and manipulate information or data. This essential guide tells you how a database works, what it can do for you, and what you should know when you go to buy one.
(254922—$9.95)†

☐ **BEGINNING WITH BASIC: AN INTRODUCTION TO COMPUTER PROGRAMMING by Kent Porter.** Now, at last, the new computer owner has a book that speaks in down-to-earth everyday language to explain clearly—and step-by-step—how to master BASIC, Beginner's All-Purpose Symbolic Instructional Code. And how to use it to program your computer to do exactly what you want it to do.   (254914—$10.95)*

*Prices higher in Canada.
†Not available in Canada.

To order use coupon on next page.

Related titles from PLUME

BUSINESS SENSE

(0452)

☐ **THE ENTREPRENEURIAL WORKBOOK by Charlotte Taylor.** Here is a step-by-step guide to starting and operating your own small business that will tell you how to develop a long-range business plan, how to make key start-up decisions, where to go for financing, and more. Plus a model for planning your marketing strategy, and other solutions to typical business problems.

(256607—$9.95)

☐ **HOW TO MAKE YOUR HOME-BASED BUSINESS GROW: GETTING BIGGER PROFITS FROM YOUR PRODUCTS by Valerie Bohigian.** A step-by-step guide that will take you from the first rung of home-business success to the top of the ladder. Make your dreams of making money at home into a rewarding reality with this inside, experience-wise advice that will save you vast amounts of time, effort, and expense.

(256208—$8.95)

☐ **HOW TO PROMOTE YOUR OWN BUSINESS by Gary Blake and Robert W. Bly.** A practical primer to the ins and outs of advertising and publicity, complete with actual case histories, illustrations, charts, letters and press releases. This is the only promotional guide you'll ever need to make your business a solid success.

(254566—$10.95)

☐ **THE COMPLETE GUIDE TO BUYING AND SELLING A BUSINESS by Arnold S. Goldstein.** Filled with fascinating case histories and the author's own experience as a top business acquisition consultant, this valuable guide is designed to help to maximize your profits and minimize your risks when buying or selling a business. Includes quizzes, check lists, legal form samples, and a glossary of key terms.

(256224—$9.95)

Prices slightly higher in Canada.
To order use coupon on next page.